Environmental Regulation and Market Power

Environmental Regulation and Market Power

Competition, Time Consistency and International Trade

Edited by

Emmanuel Petrakis

Associate Professor of Economics, Department of Economics, University of Crete, Greece

Eftichios S. Sartzetakis

Assistant Professor of Economics, Business School, University College of the Cariboo, Canada

Anastasios Xepapadeas

Professor of Economics and Dean, Faculty of Social Sciences, University of Crete, Greece

Edward Elgar
Cheltenham, UK • Northampton, MA, USA

333.7
E 61

Published by
Edward Elgar Publishing Limited
Glensanda House
Montpellier Parade
Cheltenham
Glos GL50 1UA
UK

Edward Elgar Publishing, Inc.
136 West Street
Suite 202
Northampton
Massachusetts 01060
USA

A catalogue record for this book
is available from the British Library

Library of Congress Cataloguing in Publication Data

Environmental regulation and market power : competition, time
   consistency and international trade / edited by Emmanuel Petrakis,
   Eftichios S. Sartzetakis, Anastasios Xepapadeas.
      Includes bibliographical references and index.
      1. Environmental impact charges. 2. Environmental policy.
   3. Competition.   4. International trade.   I. Petrakis, Emmanuel,
   1956–   . II. Sartzetakis, Eftichios Sofokles, 1962– .
   III. Xepapadeas, Anastasios.
   HJ5316.E5795 2000
   333.7—dc21   99–15587
                                                                    CIP

ISBN 1 85898 889 6

Printed and bound in Great Britain by Bookcraft (Bath) Ltd.

Contents

Figures

Tables

Contributors

Allen Blackman, Fellow, Resources for the Future, Washington, DC, USA

James Boyd, Fellow, Resources for the Future, Washington, DC, USA

Carlo Carraro, University of Venice, Italy

Udo Ebert, University of Oldenburg, Germany

Robert W. Godby, University of Wyoming, USA

Peter W. Kennedy, University of Victoria, Canada

Alan Krupnick, Senior Fellow, Resources for the Future, Washington, DC, USA

Andreas Lange, University of Heidelberg, Germany

Benoit Laplante, World Bank

Ngo Van Long, McGill University, Canada

Janice Mazurek, United States Environmental Protection Agency, Washington, DC, USA

Donald G. McFetridge, Carleton University, Canada

Stuart Mestelman, McMaster University, Canada

Massimo Motta, Universitat Pompeu Frabra, Spain and European University Institute, Italy

R. Andrew Muller, McMaster University, Canada

Emmanuel Petrakis, University of Crete, Greece

Till Requate, University of Heidelberg, Germany

Eftichios S. Sartzetakis, University College of the Cariboo, Canada

Antoine Soubeyran, Université de la Méditerranée, France

Jacques-François Thisse, CORE, Catholic University of Louvain, Belgium, and CERAS, Paris, France

Alistair Ulph, University of Southampton, UK

Anastasios Xepapadeas, University of Crete, Greece

Introduction

This book presents the state-of-the-art developments regarding interactions between environmental regulation and market structure. Environmental policies based on economic incentives receive continuously increasing attention at the policy level. Evidence of the serious consideration that these policies command includes the recent studies by the European Environmental Agency on environmental taxes and the studies by the National Round Table on the Environment and Economy in Canada and the continued discussion both at the federal and the provincial level on the use of tradable emission permits. Emission taxes, tradable emission permits and voluntary compliance policies are becoming the instruments of choice in controlling environmental problems at the national and international level. Implementation of these policy instruments within imperfectly competitive environments is considered to be one of the main barriers to achieve the maximum potential efficiency gains. Careful design of environmental policies in second-best environments is thus a very important factor for their success. The aim of this book is to contribute to this discussion by offering both up-to-date reviews of the literature and cutting-edge research contributions.

The book examines the impact that imperfectly competitive markets have on the implementation of market-based environmental policies within different frameworks. The first five contributions to this volume employ static frameworks to explore the potential negative impacts that emission taxes, emission permits and tailored regulation could have on competitiveness under various market structures. The subsequent three contributions examine, within a dynamic framework, the effects that time inconsistency in the implementation of emission taxes and emission permits could have on environmental innovation. Utilizing open economy frameworks, the last four contributions analyse the impact of market imperfections on the structure of environmental policies across countries.

The authors agree that market imperfections could impact negatively on social welfare. However, they identify key characteristics of market-based policies that could be modified in such ways as to overcome most of the implementation barriers. The authors argue for increased awareness of problems associated with strategic behaviour when designing and implementing market-based policies. The appropriate policy modifications that ameliorate problems associated with strategic behaviour will allow market-based policies to achieve the maximum of their advantages over direct control policies.

The first five chapters deal with issues regarding the design of second-best environmental policies in the face of market distortions and the effects that market-based environmental policies could have on competition and welfare. In a seminal work, Buchanan (1969) was first to point to the impact that imperfect market structures have on optimal pollution taxation. Within a homogeneous monopoly framework he shows that although a pollution tax reduces the environmental externality it also increases the product market distortion. As a result regulators face a tradeoff between any environmental protection and total output, and thus the second-best pollution tax must be less than marginal environmental damages (see Barnett 1980 and Misiolek 1980). Similar results have been derived in the case of homogeneous product oligopolies with a fixed number of firms (see Levin 1985; Ebert 1992; and Requate 1993 for the derivation of second-best pollution taxes within Cournot and Bertrand oligopoly frameworks). When the market structure is endogenous, pollution taxation has been shown to have additional effects. Within a homogeneous Cournot oligopoly framework with free entry, Katsoulacos and Xepapadeas (1995) and Requate (1997) show that second-best pollution tax should be set above marginal damage if the market distortion results in excess production. Pollution taxation could have a dramatic effect on market structure in the case of a vertical product differentiation framework by inducing the entry of a large number of single-product firms in the market, as shown in Cremer and Thisse (1999) and Constantatos and Sartzetakis (1999). The first chapter of the volume completes the examination of second-best taxation under imperfectly competitive market structures. The subsequent two chapters review the theoretical and the experimental literature on the effects that market power has on the efficiency of emission permits trading. The next two chapters examine minimum environmental standards and tailored regulations respectively and their effects on market structure and welfare.

Lange and Requate (Chapter 1) examine second-best pollution taxation within the following three horizontal differentiation frameworks: a price-setting duopoly with differentiated products and two models of monopolistic competition, the Dixit–Stiglitz model and Salop's circular city. Consistent with the case of quantity setting with a fixed number of firms, price-setting behaviour leads to a second-best pollution tax that is below marginal social damage. This result is independent of whether the commodities are complements or substitutes but it could reverse if firms have extreme differences in technology. The results in both cases of monopolistic competition examined are also consistent with intuition. Within a Dixit–Stiglitz framework that does not lead to excess entry, second-best taxation is below marginal damage, while within the circular city framework that allows for excess entry the reverse might be true. Lange and Requate complete the examination of second-best taxation under imperfectly competitive market structures by confirming the main results in the literature.

Imperfectly competitive market structures have been identified as a potential problem in the case of emission permits trading as well. Sartzetakis and McFetridge (Chapter 3) review the literature on the problems that might arise from the implementation of tradable permits programmes in the presence of small numbers in both the product and the permits market. The chapter cautions regulators that pooling polluters from different non-competitive industries in a single permits market (with the intent of increasing competition in the permits market) might aggravate product market distortions. It is shown that the trading of emission permits among firms in an oligopolistic industry might result in welfare-decreasing redistribution of production even if oligopolists behave as price-takers in the permits market. If there are no restrictions on firms' behaviour in the permits market, both cooperative and non-cooperative strategies can be observed. Depending on the firmness of the anti-trust policy, firms could either condition their permits trading on the product market outcome and arrive at collusive outcomes or use permits trading to manipulate their aggregate costs. In both cases, permits trading provides a venue for credibly dividing the profits resulting from cooperation. In the case that one of the firms has power in the permits market, this firm could either manipulate the permits price to minimize its permits cost or it could attempt to use its leadership in the permits market to improve its position in the product market.

Godby, Mestelman and Muller (Chapter 4) review the experimental literature regarding the effects that market power could have on the efficiency of permits trading. The chapter first presents an introduction to laboratory methods with emphasis on the treatment of market power. A brief review of the theoretical literature on permits price manipulation follows. The main part of the chapter discusses the significance of trading institutions on the emergence of market power. The studies reviewed indicate that there is strong laboratory evidence that market power could result in permits price manipulation. In terms of the trading institutions, it is shown that double auction is not as effective as previously thought in limiting the exercise of market power.

Motta and Thisse (Chapter 2) study the impact of a minimum environmental standard (MES) on market structure and welfare. If consumers are concerned about the environmental damage caused by the consumption of particular goods, but differ in their degree of environmental consciousness, firms have an incentive to differentiate their products in terms of environmental quality. In a framework where producing a less-polluting good involves a higher R&D cost, a minimum quality standard is shown to be always welfare improving. In a closed economy, the optimal MES leads both firms to increase the environmental quality of their products, and thus reduce their emissions of pollutants. When economies are open to international trade, the domestic firms which had to meet higher environmental standards under autarky earn higher profits than their foreign competitors. The MES in the domestic country leads, through international trade, to an upgrade of the environmental qualities of all the (home and foreign) firms' products. Moreover, the imports in the 'green' country are restrained, and as a result its welfare increases.

Boyd, Mazurek, Krupnick and Blackman (Chapter 5) examine the effect that 'tailored' regulation can have on the market structure. Tailored regulation is a one-to-one agreement between a firm and the regulator that allows the firm higher flexibility in compliance, which in turn agrees to increase its environmental performance. Flexibility in compliance can take the form of aggregate emission standards or facilitation of speedy changes in the production process. The chapter identifies the effects that tailored regulation has on market structure as one of the regulation's challenges. It argues that tailored regulations are more likely to favour market leaders since those firms are the ones most likely to have access to this type of regulation. Thus, the potential welfare benefits should be weighed against possible anti-competitive consequences. The benefits and costs of tailored regulation are discussed using the particular example of the Intel-XL Air Permit programme.

The next three chapters deal with the design of time-consistent environmental policies in the presence of market distortions. The issue of time consistency of environmental policies and its impact on welfare has been recently recognized in environmental economics. If the regulator is unable to precommit to a specific policy measure, an *ex ante* efficiency improving policy may, in fact, be welfare reducing *ex post*. The regulator is then called to design carefully time-consistent policies that will contribute to an increase in overall efficiency. Biglaiser *et al.* (1995) show that, if polluting firms are price-takers in the product market and the damage function is linear, an emissions tax is time consistent and leads to efficient adoption of clean technologies. However, technology adoption is distorted under emissions trading because the regulator is unable to precommit to a specific supply of permits programme. Laffont and Tirole (1996a, b) also consider technological change under emissions trading, focusing however on the time-consistency problems arising from a non-unitary cost of public funds. They show that incentives for innovation are weakened if the regulator cannot commit to distort future permit prices for the purpose of raising revenue.

Kennedy and Laplante (Chapter 6) reconsider adoption of clean technologies from firms that are price-takers in the product market, but under a more general specification of the damage function. If the damage is linear then efficiency requires either universal adoption of the new technology, or universal retention of the old technology, depending on the cost of adoption. Both the emission tax and the permit supply policy are time consistent and lead to the efficient adoption pattern. However, if damage is convex in aggregate emissions, efficiency may require partial adoption of the new technology and then *ex ante* efficient policies are time inconsistent. Moreover, optimal *ex post* policies (or equivalently, policy ratcheting) often induce suboptimal adoption patterns. If there are relatively few firms, then tax ratcheting leads to excessive adoption of the new technology, while permit supply ratcheting involves too little adoption.

Petrakis and Xepapadeas (Chapter 7) investigate the effect of non-credibility of government policies on environmental innovation and welfare in an industry where firms have market power. They compare two scenarios: in the first the government precommits to an emission tax and then a monopolist selects its abatement effort and output. In the second, which emerges whenever the government's policy is non-credible, the monopolist selects its abatement effort first, the government then sets its emission tax, and finally the monopolist chooses its output. In this case, the monopolist strategically selects its abatement effort in order to influence the emission tax that the government will set. It is shown that the optimal time-consistent emission tax is lower than the optimal emission tax when the government is able to precommit; also that, if the government is unable to commit to a specific emission tax, the monopolist's abatement effort is higher than under government precommitment. Finally, welfare is always lower when the government cannot credibly commit to an emission tax.

Petrakis (Chapter 8) examines time-consistent (pre-emptive) adoption patterns of green technologies in a differentiated duopoly where firms compete in quantities, or prices, in the product market, and compares those patterns with the adoption patterns when the firms are able to precommit to a specific adoption date. The green technology is available at date zero, and its purchasing and implementation costs decrease over

xvi   *Environmental regulation and market power*

time. A firm faced with an emission tax has the incentive to adopt the green technology which reduces its per unit of output emissions in order to gain market share from its rival. It is shown that the last adoption occurs at the same date in both the pre-emptive and the precommitment equilibrium, while the first adoption is always earlier in the pre-emptive equilibrium, independently of the type of market competition; further, that the last adoption is always earlier under quantity competition than under price competition. Also, in a precommitment equilibrium the first adoption under price competition is earlier than under quantity competition but only if the goods are close enough substitutes. However, in a pre-emptive equilibrium the first adoption under price competition is always earlier than under quantity competition.

The last four chapters of this volume deal with the interaction between environmental regulation and market power in an open economy framework. The attention that has recently been given to the exploration of environmental policy issues under market structures other than perfect competition or monopoly has led to situations where environmental policy had to be designed in the context of multiple distortions. These distortions are the result of market power and the important feature of the policy design problem is that, in general, the regulator does not have enough instruments to correct for all distortions. The regulator possesses instruments to correct for the environmental distortion but not for the distortions due to market power. This lack of instruments leads to more complex environmental policy schemes, since instruments have to be adjusted so that they will account, to some extent, for the market-power distortions and to multiple types of responses from the firms given their specific characteristics. Perhaps more importantly, this type of analysis reveals the need to combine environmental policy with other micro-economic policies, such as industrial or trade policy, in order to obtain efficient policy schemes. In this context, these chapters analyse the design of environmental policy in open economies when multiple distortions are present and the environmental regulator has in principle at his/her disposal only environmental policy instruments.

Chapter 9, by Van Long and Soubeyran, builds upon earlier results regarding Pigouvian taxation when, in addition to market failure due to environmental damage, more market failures in particular in the form of market power are present. By considering heterogeneous firms, in contrast to the most common assumption of firm homogeneity, the chapter analyses the structure of optimal environmental taxation in a two-country model with four different sources of market failure: environmental damage; non-equalization of domestic marginal costs; 'rent' earning by foreign firms; and low domestic output. Van Long and Soubeyran show that firm-specific emission taxes at the non-cooperative Nash equilibrium between the two governments tend to be smaller than the average for the larger firms. They also show that, under partial trade liberalization, domestic emission taxes will be significanly reduced and domestic emissions will increase, if the weight associated with consumer surplus is relatively high.

Carraro and Soubeyran (Chapter 10) consider simultaneously firms' decisions to: (a) invest in R&D in order to develop environment-friendly technologies; (b) use the clean technology developed by other firms by buying a licence; and (c) relocate. The authors show that with identical firms the introduction of environmental taxation induces different responses. Some firms will invest in R&D in order to develop the environmentally friendly technologies, some will buy the technology instead of developing it and some will relocate to a foreign country. The sizes of the three groups depend on the government's industrial policy. Thus R&D subsidies, or stimulation of R&D efforts, cooperation and spillovers within coalition members, two industrial policy instruments examined in the chapter, can be used to alter the size of the groups of firms that invest in R&D, buy licences to use new technologies, or relocate.

Ebert (Chapter 11) analyses policy issues when the number of instruments is less than the number of distortions, a case which often arises when environmental externalities and market imperfections are present and only environmental policy instruments are available. In particular the chapter examines the environmental policy issues in an open economy with imperfectly competitive markets and production and consumption externalities, when the policy instrument available to governments is a relative emission standard that restricts the level of emissions per unit of commodity produced or consumed. It is shown that when no tariffs or subsidies are available governments have incentives to strategically distort the relative standard away from the first- or the second-best optimum in order to obtain welfare gains. The general result is that governments prefer to weaken the relative standard compared to the closed economy case.

Chapter 12 by Ulph analyses the subsidiarity principle with respect to environmental policy, an issue associated with the Maastricht Treaty. In particular, the role of a supranational authority in influencing national policies regarding domestic environmental problems in order to prevent 'environmental dumping' is analysed. Assuming that the supranational authority cannot implement cooperative policies that can improve over non-cooperative solutions because of asymmetric information or influences of interests groups, two policy approaches to prevent environmental dumping are discussed. These are the harmonization of environmental regulations and the use of minimum standards for environmental regulation. It is shown that, depending on the degree of differences in key characteristics (such as

Environmental regulation and market power

damage costs) among countries and the environmental policy instruments used by national governments, neither harmonization of environmental regulations nor the use of minimum standards for environmental regulation can make countries better off as compared to the case where they act non-cooperatively.

REFERENCES

Barnett, A.H. (1980), 'The Pigouvian tax rule under monopoly', *American Economic Review*, **70**, 1037–41.
Biglaiser, G., J. Horowitz and J. Quiggin (1995), 'Dynamic pollution regulation', *Journal of Regulatory Economics*, **8**, 33–44.
Buchanan, J.M. (1969), 'External diseconomies, corrective taxes and market structure', *American Economic Review*, **59**, 174–7.
Constantatos, C., and E.S. Sartzetakis (1999), 'On commodity taxation in vertically differentiated markets', *International Journal of Industrial Organization*, forthcoming.
Cremer, H. and J.-F. Thisse (1995), 'On the taxation of polluting products in a differentiated industry', *European Economic Review*, **43**, 575–94.
Ebert, U. (1992), 'On the effect of effluent fees under oligopoly: comparative static analysis', Institute of Economics, University of Oldenburg, mimeo.
Katsoulacos, Y. and A. Xepapadeas (1995), 'Environmental policy under oligopoly with endogenous market structure', *Scandinavian Journal of Economics*, **97**, 411–20.
Laffont, J.J. and J. Tirole (1996a), 'Pollution permits and compliance strategies', *Journal of Public Economics*, **62**, 85–125.
Laffont, J.J. and J. Tirole (1996b), 'Pollution permits and environmental innovation', *Journal of Public Economics*, **62**, 127–40.
Levin, D. (1985), 'Taxation within Cournot oligopoly', *Journal of Public Economics*, **27**, 281–90.
Misiolek, S.W. (1980), 'Effluent taxation in monopoly markets', *Journal of Environmental Economics and Management*, **7**, 103–7.
Requate, T. (1993), 'Pollution control under imperfect competition: asymmetric Bertrand duopoly with linear technologies, *Journal of Institutional and Theoretical Economics*, **149**, 415–42.
Requate, T. (1997), 'Green taxes in oligopoly if the number of firms is endogennous', *Finanzarchiv*, **54**, 261–80.

1. Emission taxes for price-setting firms: differentiated commodities and monopolistic competition

Andreas Lange and Till Requate

1.1 INTRODUCTION

In this chapter we investigate second-best taxation of emissions if firms supply differentiated commodities. On the one hand, we consider a differentiated price-setting duopoly; on the other hand, we study what is probably the most realistic form of market structure, namely monopolistic competition.

It is an empirical fact that a considerable proportion of industries contributing to the deterioration of the natural environment do not belong to the species of perfect competitors. Hence, the Pigouvian tax rule requiring the charge of an emission fee equal to marginal social damage cannot be applied to internalize externalities resulting from pollution. This was pointed out by Buchanan (1969) almost 30 years ago. However, whereas Buchanan generally rejects charging emission taxes if polluting firms engage in imperfect competition, several researchers during the last two decades have investigated the rule according to which a benevolent regulator should set an emission tax if polluting firms have market power and if there is no other regulatory device to mitigate distortions resulting from monopoly or oligopoly power.

Barnett (1980) was the first to find a second-best optimal rule in order to tax a polluting monopolist. Requate (1993a) considers the regulation of several local monopolists contributing to global pollution. Levin (1985), Requate (1993b) and Simpson (1995) consider asymmetric Cournot duo- and oligopolies, whereas Ebert (1992) focuses on symmetric oligopolies. Requate (1993c) considers an asymmetric Bertrand duopoly where firms produce homogeneous commodity. All these papers conclude that the second-best optimal Pigouvian tax should be set below marginal social damage. The reason for this is that monopolistic or oligopolistic firms impose two market imperfections on the society: they

1

hold down output and they generate pollution. However, by reducing output they voluntarily produce less, and thus they pollute less than a competitive industry. Hence, it is not necessary to charge an emission tax equal to the full marginal social damage. Only in exceptional cases, for example if the firms are extremely asymmetric, will the second-best optimal tax possibly exceed marginal social damage.

More recently, both Katsoulacos and Xepapadeas (1995) and Requate (1997) conclude that the typical result for imperfect competition, requiring to set the second-best optimal emission tax below marginal social damage, does not hold if the number of firms is endogenous. Whereas the second-best tax may sometimes even exceed marginal social damage in order to mitigate excess entry of firms, Requate (1997) demonstrates that the Pigouvian tax rule (tax equal to marginal damage) is a good rule of thumb if market demand is approximately linear and if no abatement technologies exist, as in the case for CO_2.

Up to now little attention has been paid to polluting firms which engage in price competition and offer differentiated commodities, although this is probably the most realistic and hence the most relevant market structure. In this chapter we close this gap by studying three prototype models of imperfect price competition. The first is a price-setting duopoly with differentiated commodities, that is, the number of firms is exogenous. In the other two models, the number of firms is determined endogenously by a free entry condition. The first of those two models is the Dixit–Stiglitz–Spence model; the second is a modified version of the circular city.

With respect to the duopoly model we find that accepted wisdom to the effect that the second-best optimal tax should be set below marginal damage is not corrupted under imperfect price competition unless firms are extremely different. This holds true irrespective of whether the commodities are substitutes or complements. Only if the firms are extremely different with respect to their technology and their market demand functions will the second-best optimal tax possibly exceed marginal social damage.

For the Dixit–Stiglitz–Spence model we also find that the second-best optimal tax is always lower than marginal damage. In other words, in a Dixit–Stiglitz type of model there is no need to mitigate excess entry by means of Pigouvian taxes. Moreover, we find that the more competition we have, the closer to marginal social damage the second-best optimal tax should be set. These results hold true under rather general conditions. On the one hand, the result is quite intuitive and is in line with what we know about regulation of monopolistic firms. On the other, it is not obvious in the light of Katsoulacos and Xepapadeas (1995) and Requate (1997), who have demonstrated that in a Cournot model with free entry the Pigouvian tax may exceed social marginal damage in order to mitigate excess entry.

We arrive at different results for the model of the circular city, which we slightly modify by relaxing the usual assumptions of unit demand, assuming instead downward-sloping demand. Here, the second-best optimal tax may fall short of or may exceed marginal social damage. This is the case because we know (see Salop 1979) that there is always excess entry in that model, Note, moreover, that in Salop's model the commodities offered by the *n* firms are physically identical after purchase. They only differ by the different transportation costs faced by the consumers. Thus, the model of the circular city is much more similar to the Cournot model with free entry than to the Dixit–Stiglitz–Spence type of model.

The chapter is organized as follows: section 1.2 deals with the price-setting duopoly model with differentiated commodities, section 1.3 investigates the Dixit–Stiglitz–Spence model and section 1.4 the circular city. The final section concludes.

1.2 PRICE-SETTING DUOPOLY WITH DIFFERENTIATED COMMODITIES

In this section we focus on the strategic effects among price-setting firms in a duopoly with differentiated commodities.

1.2.1 Consumers

Here and in most of the chapter we pursue partial analysis. Hence the utility of a representative consumer is given by a separate quasi-linear utility function:

$$u = U(q_1, q_2) + q_0 - S(e_1, e_2), \tag{1.1}$$

where commodity 0 is a numeraire with price normalized to one. The subutility function U is quasi-concave and monotonically increasing. Further assumptions are imposed on the Marshallian demand functions for the two commodities 1 and 2. We denote the firms' emissions by e_1 and e_2, as defined below. $S(e_1, e_2)$ denotes the disutility (or damage) caused by the pollution of the two firms. The utility-maximizing consumer clearly sets:

$$U_i := \frac{\partial U(q_1, q_2)}{\partial q_i} = p_i, \tag{1.2}$$

where p_i is the price of commodity i. Let $D^i(p_1, p_2)$ be the demand for commodity i as the solution of (1.2). The two commodities are substitutes (complements) if:

$$D_j^i := \frac{\partial D^i}{\partial p_j} > 0 \quad (<0). \tag{1.3}$$

Further we assume that:

$$D_i^i := \frac{\partial D^i}{\partial p_i} < 0,$$

and that $p_i \cdot D^i$ is concave.

1.2.2 The Firms

The firms produce with constant marginal costs $c_i \geq 0$, and generate pollution which is proportional to output, that is, $e_i = d_i q_i$, where q_i and e_i are output and emissions, respectively, of firm i.

If the firms have to pay an additional tax τ_i (which may be uniform as a special case), the firms' profit is given by:

$$\pi^i(p_1, p_2) = (p_i - c_i - d_i \tau_i) D^i(p_1, p_2). \tag{1.4}$$

Since $p_i D^i$ is assumed to be concave in p_i, we also obtain $\pi_{ii}^i = \partial^2 \pi^i / \partial (p_i)^2 < 0$ for $p_i \geq c_i$ which holds in equilibrium.[1]

Furthermore, we assume that the absolute value of the cross-price elasticity of D^i is bounded by 1, that is:

$$\left| \frac{D_{ji}^i}{D_j^i} p_i \right| < 1 \tag{1.5}$$

which implies:

$$\text{sign}(\pi_{ij}^i) = \text{sign}(D_j^i), \quad i = 1, 2; j = 3 - i.$$

Finally we assume:

$$|\pi_{ij}^i| < |\pi_{ii}^i|$$

for $i = 1, 2; j = 3 - i$, which implies that:

$$\Delta := \pi^1_{11} \pi^2_{22} - \pi^1_{12} \pi^2_{21} > 0 . \qquad (1.6)$$

Equation (2.6) is the well-known stability condition for Nash equilibrium.

The Nash equilibrium of the simultaneous price-setting game is then determined by:

$$D^i(p_1, p_2) + (p_i - c_i - d_i\tau_i)D^i_i(p_1, p_2) = 0 \quad \text{for } i = 1, 2. \qquad (1.7)$$

1.2.3 Differentiated Taxes: Comparative Statics

First we consider the case of *differentiated* taxes. Differentiating the two equilibrium conditions (1.7) with respect to τ_1 yields:

$$\pi^1_{11} \frac{\partial p_1}{\partial \tau_1} + \pi^1_{12} \frac{\partial p_2}{\partial \tau_1} = d_1 D^1_1 \qquad (1.8)$$

$$\pi^2_{12} \frac{\partial p_1}{\partial \tau_1} + \pi^2_{22} \frac{\partial p_2}{\partial \tau_1} = 0 \qquad (1.9)$$

Solving for $\dfrac{\partial p_1}{\partial \tau_1}$ and $\dfrac{\partial p_2}{\partial \tau_1}$ we obtain:

$$\frac{\partial p_1}{\partial \tau_1} = \frac{d_1 D^1_1 \pi^2_{22}}{\Delta} > 0 \qquad (1.10)$$

$$\frac{\partial p_2}{\partial \tau_1} = \frac{-d_1 D^1_1 \pi^2_{12}}{\Delta} > 0 \qquad (1.11)$$

if the commodities are substitutes. If commodity 2 is a complement of commodity 1, we get $\partial p_2 / \partial \tau_1 < 0$. Analogously, by differentiating with respect to τ_2 we obtain:

$$\frac{\partial p_2}{\partial \tau_2} = \frac{d_2 D^2_2 \pi^1_{11}}{\Delta} > 0 \qquad (1.12)$$

$$\frac{\partial p_1}{\partial \tau_2} = \frac{-d_1 D^2_2 \pi^1_{12}}{\Delta} > 0 \qquad (1.13)$$

if the commodites are substitutes. If commodity 1 is a complement of commodity 2, we obtain $\partial p_1/\partial \tau_2 < 0$.

1.2.4 Second-best Differentiated Taxes

We now investigate which pair of second-best differentiated taxes the regulator should choose to take into account the strategic behaviour of price-setting firms. The problem is to maximize welfare as a function of the tax rates, given the behaviour of the consumer and the firms:

$$W(\tau_1, \tau_2) = U(D^1, D^2) - c_1 D^1 - c_2 D^2 - S(d_1 D^1, d_2 D^2) ,$$

where the D^is can be interpreted as (reduced) functions of the τ_js. Differentiating with respect to τ_i yields:

$$[U_1 - c_1 - d_1 S_1]\frac{dD^1}{d\tau_i} + [U_2 - c_2 - d_2 S_2]\frac{dD^2}{d\tau_i} = 0 \quad \text{for } i = 1, 2.$$

Since $U_i = p_i$ by (1.2) and $p_i - c_i = d_i\tau_i - D_i/D^i$ by (1.7), we obtain:

$$\left[d_1(\tau_1 - S_1) - \frac{D^1}{D_1^1}\right]\frac{dD^1}{d\tau_i} + \left[d_2(\tau_2 - S_2) - \frac{D^2}{D_2^2}\right]\frac{dD^2}{d\tau_i} = 0 \quad \text{for } i = 1, 2.$$

We see immediately that the pair (τ_1, τ_2) of second-best taxes has to satisfy:

$$\tau_i = S_i + \frac{D^i}{d_i D_i^i} = S_i - \frac{p_i}{d_i\eta_i} \tag{1.14}$$

if:

$$\begin{vmatrix} \dfrac{dD^1}{d\tau_1} & \dfrac{dD^2}{d\tau_1} \\ \dfrac{dD^1}{d\tau_2} & \dfrac{dD^2}{d\tau_2} \end{vmatrix} \neq 0 \tag{1.15}$$

where $\eta_i = -D_i^i/D_i p_i$ denotes demand elasticity. In appendix A we show that (1.15) is indeed satisfied.

Formula (1.14) gives us the same structure for the second-best optimal tax rates as in the pure monopoly case (see Barnett 1980). Of course, the two rules for τ_1 and τ_2 given by (1.14) are not independent of each other. But if both marginal damage and demand elasticity are known or can be determined empirically, rule (1.14) is easy to handle if taxes can be differentiated, in particular if the two firms offering different commodities emit different pollutants.

1.2.3   Uniform Tax

We now consider a uniform tax $\tau_i = \tau$. Differentiating (1.7) with respect to τ and writing $p'_i = \partial p_i / \partial \tau$, we obtain:

$$\pi^1_{11} p'_1 + \pi^1_{12} p'_2 = d_1 D^1_1 \tag{1.16}$$

$$\pi^2_{12} p'_1 + \pi^2_{22} p'_2 = d_2 D^2_2. \tag{1.17}$$

Solving for p'_i yields:

$$p'_1 = \frac{d_1 D^1_1 \pi^2_{22} - d_2 D^2_2 \pi^2_{12}}{\Delta}$$

$$p'_2 = \frac{d_2 D^2_2 \pi^1_{11} - d_1 D^1_1 \pi^1_{12}}{\Delta}.$$

We see that if the commodities are substitutes, that is, $\pi^i_{12} > 0$, both prices are increasing if the tax rate goes up. If the commodities are complements and the firms are sufficiently different, one of the prices may go down.

   In order to determine the formula for the second-best tax rate we differentiate welfare:

$$W(\tau) = U(D^1, D^2) - c_1 D^1 - c_2 D^2 - S(d_1 D^1, d_2 D^2)$$

with respect to τ. This yields:

$$[U_1 - c_1 - d_1 S_1] \frac{dD^1}{d\tau} + [U_2 - c_2 - d_2 S_2] \frac{dD^2}{d\tau} = 0 .$$

Again using U_i and p_i and $p_i - c_i = d_i \tau - D_i / D^i_i$, we obtain:

$$\left[d_1 (\tau - S_1) - \frac{D^1}{D^1_1} \right] \frac{dD^1}{d\tau} + \left[d_2 (\tau - S_2) - \frac{D^2}{D^2_2} \right] \frac{dD^2}{d\tau} = 0 .$$

Solving for τ yields:

$$\tau = \frac{d_1 S_1 \dfrac{dD^1}{d\tau} + d_2 S_2 \dfrac{dD^2}{d\tau} + \dfrac{D^1}{D_1^1}\dfrac{dD^1}{d\tau} + \dfrac{D^2}{D_2^2}\dfrac{dD^2}{d\tau}}{d_1 \dfrac{dD^1}{d\tau} + d_2 \dfrac{dD^2}{d\tau}}. \tag{1.18}$$

If the pollutant is uniform, that is, if $S(e_1, e_2) = \tilde{S}(e_1 + e_2)$ implying $S_1 = S_2 = \tilde{S}'$, we obtain:

$$\tau = \tilde{S}' + \frac{\dfrac{D^1}{D_1^1}\dfrac{dD^1}{d\tau} + \dfrac{D^2}{D_2^2}\dfrac{dD^2}{d\tau}}{d_1 \dfrac{dD^1}{d\tau} + d_2 \dfrac{dD^2}{d\tau}}. \tag{1.19}$$

Note that if firms are similar, that is, if $D^1 \approx D^2$ and $D_1^1 \approx D_2^2$ as well as $d_1 \approx d_2$, the second term on the right-hand side of (1.19) is approximately equal to:

$$\frac{D^1}{d_1 D_1^1} \approx \frac{D^2}{d_2 D_2^2} < 0.$$

This is independent of whether the two commodites are complements or are substitutes.

If firms are extremely different, however, the second term on the right-hand side of (1.19) accounting for the strategic intersection between the firms may be positive, resulting in a second-best optimal tax which *exceeds* the marginal damage. Here is an example:

Example 1
Choose:

$$D^1(p_1, p_2) = (1 - 1.3p_1 + 0.8p_2),$$
$$D^2(p_1, p_2) = (1 - 0.8p_2 + 0.8p_1),$$
$$S(E) = \frac{E^2}{2},$$

further, $c_1 = 0$, $c_2 = 0.5$, $d_1 = 1.0$, $d_2 = 0$, that is, firm 1 has the lower private unit cost but at the same time is the worse polluter. These functions induce a second-best optimal tax of $t^* = 1.2$, where the marginal damage amounts to S'(E) = 0.366 while the strategic term is equal to 0.834. Under this tax, firm 1 produces $D^1 = 0.366$ units, whereas firm 2 produces 0.834 units.

The reason for the high tax in this example is firm 1's extreme advantage with respect to the private cost. In order to offset this advantage of firm 1, the regulator has to set a tax which is higher than marginal damage.

1.3 THE DIXIT–STIGLITZ MODEL

We now turn to the famous Dixit–Stiglitz model as *the* prototype model of monopolistic competition. Again we assume that pollution is caused by production.

1.3.1 The Basics of the Model

The representative consumer draws utility from $n + 1$ commodities, a compound commodity I which is supplied in n different varieties, and a numeraire commodity 0. The consumer also suffers from the aggregate level of pollution $E = \sum_{i=1}^{n} e_i$, where e_i is the amount of pollution generated by firm i. The damage from pollution, measured in units of the numeraire commodity, is denoted by S(E). Thus we can write the utility as:

$$u = U\left(q_0 - S(E), \left(\sum_i q_i^\rho\right)^{1/\rho}\right),$$

where:

$$q_0 = I - \sum_{i=1}^{n} p_i q_i + \tau E$$

is the consumption of the numeraire commodity, that is, gross income minus expenditures for the commodities $i = 1, \ldots, n$, plus tax revenues which are redistributed lump-sum to the consumer. The price for the commodity i is denoted by p_i, the price from commodity 0 is normalized to 1.

We assume that the numeraire commodity 0 and the compound commodity I are normal goods. This implies:

$$G := \frac{U_{11} U_2 - U_{12} U_1}{(U_1)^2} < 0 \text{ and}$$

$$H := \frac{U_{22}U_1 - U_{12}U_2}{(U_1)^2} < 0.$$

Utility maximization leads to the following relationship:

$$U_1 \cdot p_i = U_2 \cdot \left(\sum_{j=1}^{n} q_j^{\rho} \right)^{\frac{1}{\rho}-1} q_i^{\rho-1} \quad \text{for } i = 1, \ldots, n.$$

If n is large, a change of price p_i and thus a change in demand for commodity i has little effect on $\sum_{j=1}^{n} q_j^{\rho}$ and hence little effect on U_1 and U_2.[2] Hence the demand for commodity i can be approximated by:

$$q_i(p_i) \approx k \cdot p_i^{\frac{1}{\rho-1}}$$

where k is a constant.

The firms produce at constant marginal cost, $c > 0$. As throughout the chapter, pollution is assumed to be proportional to output. Without loss of generality we can therefore identify pollution with output. If the government charges a tax τ on pollution, the firms' profit – if they decide to enter the market – is given by:

$$\Pi_i = (p_i - c - \tau)q_i(p_i) - F$$
$$\approx (p_i - c - \tau)k \cdot p_i^{\frac{1}{\rho-1}} - F.$$

Profit maximization leads to the monopoly price:

$$p_i = \frac{(c + \tau)}{\rho}.$$

Zero profit through free entry implies $q_i = F/s(c+\tau)$, where $s = 1/\rho - 1$. Thus a symmetric equilibrium, with price p, a firm's output q, and the number of firms n as endogenous variables, is represented by the following equations:

$$p = \frac{(c + \tau)}{\rho}, \tag{1.20}$$

$$q = \frac{F}{s(c + \tau)}, \tag{1.21}$$

$$\frac{U_2(A, B)}{U_1(A, B)} = n^{-s} \frac{(c + \tau)}{\rho}, \tag{1.22}$$

where:

$$
\begin{aligned}
A &= I - npq + n\tau q - S(nq) \\
&= I - n(F + cq) - S(nq) \\
&= I - n\left(F + c\,\frac{F}{s(c + \tau)}\right) - S\left(n\,\frac{F}{s(c + \tau)}\right), \\
B &= n^{1/\rho} q.
\end{aligned}
$$

1.3.2   The Effect of Increasing the Tax Rate

We now execute the comparative statics of the equilibrium, given by (1.20)–(1.22), with respect to a change of the tax rate. First, we differentiate the expressions A and B. Writing for short $A' := dA/d\tau$, $n' := dn/d\tau$ and so on, we get:

$$
A' = -n'F - (c + S')\left[n'\,\frac{F}{s(c + \tau)} - n\,\frac{F}{s(c + \tau)^2}\right] \tag{1.23}
$$

$$
B' = \frac{1}{\rho}\,n^s n'\,\frac{F}{s(c + \tau)} - n^{1/\rho}\,\frac{F}{s(c + \tau)^2}. \tag{1.24}
$$

Differentiating (1.22) with respect to the tax rate τ, we obtain:

$$
-\frac{U_{11}U_2 - U_{12}U_1}{(U_1)^2}\,A' + \frac{U_{22}U_1 - U_{12}U_2}{(U_1)^2}\,B' = \frac{1}{\rho}\,n^{-s} - \frac{c + \tau}{\rho}\,s n^{-1/\rho} n'.
$$

Solving for n' yields after some manipulations:

$$
n' = \frac{n}{s(c + \tau)}\,K, \tag{1.25}
$$

where:

$$
K := \frac{1 + K_1 + K_2}{1 + K_1/(1 - \rho)} \tag{1.26}
$$

and:

$$
K_1 = \frac{n^{1/\rho}\,F\,\rho}{s(c + \tau)}\left[H\,\frac{n^s}{(c + \tau)} + G\left(1 - \rho\,\frac{\tau - S'}{(c + \tau)}\right)\right], \tag{1.27}
$$

$$K_2 = G \; \frac{n^{1/\rho} F \rho}{s(c + \tau)} \; (\rho - 1) \; \frac{\tau - S'}{(c + \tau)} . \tag{1.28}$$

Note that since $G < 0$ and $\rho < 1$, we have $K_2 < 0$ if and only if $\tau < S'$. On the other hand, $S' > 0$ implies $\tau - S'/(c + \tau) < 1 < 1/\rho$, which by definition of K_1 leads to $K_1 < 0$. The sign of n', however, is ambiguous. It may even occur that an increase in the tax rate τ leads to a higher total emission level, that is, $(nq)' > 0$. The reason is that the newly entering firms may offset the decrease of the firm-specific emission level.[3]

1.3.3   The Second-best Optimal Tax Rate

However, although such perverse cases may exist, it is possible to make a general statement about the second-best optimal tax rate:

> **Proposition 1** If in the Dixit–Stiglitz model pollution is proportional to output and the emission tax is the government's only regulatory device, the second-best emission tax rate is smaller than marginal social damage.

The proof is given in appendix B. Note that it is not possible – at least we are not able – to obtain an expression of the kind: 'tax rate is equal to marginal social damage plus a (negative) term' accounting for imperfect competitive behaviour, as we have done in section 1.2 and which is typical in the results on second-best taxation of pollutants under imperfect competition. Rather, we shall show that $c + \tau/c + S'$ is smaller than 1, implying $\tau < S'$.

We see that, in contrast to the Cournot model (see Katsoulacos and Xepapadeas 1995 and Requate 1997), the Dixit–Stiglitz model does not lead to excess entry in a way that requires the regulator to set a tax above marginal social damage.[4]

Whereas this result is rather general,[5] the comparative statics with respect to the tax rate does not deliver unique results. Hence, we further simplify the utility function by assuming:

$$U(q_0 - S(E), q_1) = q_0 - S(E) + V(q_1),$$

where $q_1 = n^{1/\rho} q$ and q is the quantity consumed of each of the differentiated commodities from the I sector.

In analogy to (1.25)–(1.28), differentiating the equilibrium conditions with respect to τ yields:

$$n' = \frac{n}{(c+\tau)s} \cdot \frac{\frac{1}{\rho}n^{-s} + V''n^{1/\rho}\frac{F}{s(c+\tau)^2}}{\frac{1}{\rho}n^{-s} + V''n^{1/\rho}\frac{F}{s(c+\tau)^2(1-\rho)}}$$

$$= \frac{n}{(c+\tau)s} \cdot \frac{1-\eta}{1 - \frac{\eta}{(1-\rho)}},$$

where $\eta = -V''(q_1)q_1/V'(q_1)$ denotes the elasticity of marginal utility. We see immediately that:

$$n' < (>)\, 0 \Leftrightarrow \frac{1-\eta}{1 - \frac{\eta}{(1-\rho)}} < (>)\, 0.$$

This implies that:

$$n' < 0 \text{ iff } 0 < 1 - \eta < \rho$$

and:

$$n' > 0 \text{ iff } 1 - \eta < 0 \text{ or } 1 - \eta > \rho.$$

Note, however, that if we assume that demand for each particular product decreases as the number of firms, that is, product diversity, increases (the price being fixed), it follows that $1 - \eta - \rho < 0$.[6] This result is derived in appendix C. If we further assume that $\eta = 1$,[7] we obtain $n' < 0$. Both assumptions together also guarantee a finite number of products (= firms) in the first-best solution, given an arbitrary social damage function. Hence $n' < 0$ is more likely to hold, although $n' > 0$ cannot be excluded.[8]

Let us assume that we have the 'natural' case $1 - \eta - \rho < 0$ at lease for ρ close to one.[9] Then we are able to show the following proposition:

Proposition 2 Assume that $1 - \eta - \rho < 0$ for ρ close to one. Then, the more competition there is, that is, the better substitutes the goods are (the closer ρ is to one), the closer the second-best tax rate is to marginal social damage. In the limit, when the commodities become perfect substitutes, the second-best tax rate coincides with marginal social damage.

The proof is given in appendix D.

The results obtained in this section confirm generally accepted wisdom on second-best taxation on monopoly, that is, that the second-best optimal tax falls short of marginal social damage but converges to it as competition gets tighter. This is not, however, trivial since, as we know from Cournot models, free entry could cause excess entry. In the next section we shall see, however, that the conclusion of Proposition 1 does not necessarily hold in general.

1.4 THE CIRCULAR CITY

In this section we investigate another prototype model of monopolistic competition, the circular city.

1.4.1 The Model

In the standard model as outlined in Salop (1979) it is assumed that each consumer has unit demand, that is, total output is fixed. This is not very interesting if we are concerned with environmental problems. Hence we assume that each consumer has elastic demand for the consumption good supplied by *n* firms also located on the circle. The consumers are located uniformly on the circle, density is unitary around this circle with perimeter 1.

Again pursuing partial analysis, for a consumer with distance *x* to the nearest firm, utility is given by:

$$u_x = U(q) - pq - tx \, ,$$

where *q* is the quantity of the commodity consumed, *p* is the price, and *tx* are the consumer's total transportation costs. Let $q(p)$ denote the consumer's Marshallian demand and $V(p) := U(q(p)) - pq(p)$ the consumer's gross indirect utility function, that is, the utility disregarding the transportation costs.[10] We assume that $2(q')^2 - qq'' > 0$.[11]

As in the last section, the firms are identical and produce constant marginal costs $c \geq 0$ and pollute proportional to output. Again we can identity pollution with output. Given that the firms are located at equal distances around the circle[12] and all potential competitors offer at price *p*, the demand for firm *i*'s good is given by:

$$D^i(p_i, p) = q(p_i) \left[\frac{V(p_i) - V(p)}{t} + \frac{1}{n} \right] ,$$

where the second term is the share of consumers buying at firm *i*. If the firms are subject to an emission tax, which in this case can also be charged on output, a firm's profit is determined by:

$$\pi^i(p_i, p) = [p_i - c - \tau]\, D^i(p_i, p)$$

$$= [p_i - c - \tau]\, q(p_i) \left[\frac{V(p_i) - V(p)}{t} + \frac{1}{n} \right].$$

Profit maximization leads to:

$$\frac{\partial \pi^i}{\partial p_i} = D^i(p_i, p) + [p_i - c - \tau]\, q'\,(p_i) \left[\frac{V(p_i) - V(p)}{t} + \frac{1}{n} \right]$$

$$= [p_i - c - \tau]\, q(p_i) \frac{V'(p_i)}{t} = 0 . \tag{1.29}$$

The second-order condition is:

$$\frac{\partial^2 \pi^i}{\partial p_i^2} = 2q'(p_i) \left[\frac{V(p_i) - V(p)}{t} + \frac{1}{n} \right]$$

$$-2\frac{q(p)^2}{t} + (p_i - c - \tau) \left[q''(p_i) \left[\frac{V(p_i) - V(p)}{t} + \frac{1}{n} \right] - 3\frac{qq'}{t} \right]$$

$$\leq 0 . \tag{1.30}$$

Using Roy's identity, that is $V'(p_i) = -q(p_i)$, and the symmetry of equilibrium we can write: $p = p_i$ and $q = q(p)$. We also write $q' := q'(p)$. Thus, the first-order Nash equilibrium condition (1.29) becomes:

$$q + (p - c - \tau) \left[q' - q^2 \frac{n}{t} \right] = 0 . \tag{1.31}$$

The zero profit condition yields:

$$(p - c - \tau) \frac{q}{n} = F . \tag{1.32}$$

The second-order condition (1.30) becomes:

$$0 \geq 2q' - 2q^2 \frac{n}{t} + (p - c - \tau) \left[q'' - 3qq' \frac{n}{t} \right] . \tag{1.33}$$

Note that the second-order condition (1.33) is satisfied under our assumption $2(q')^2 - qq'' > 0$ and condition (1.31), as we show in appendix E.

1.4.2   The Effect of Increasing the Tax Rate

Differentiating (1.31) and (1.32) with respect to the tax rate τ, we obtain:

$$q'p' + (p' - 1)\left(q' - q^2\frac{n}{t}\right) + (p - c - \tau)\left[q''p' - 2qq'p'\frac{n}{t} - q^2\frac{n'}{t}\right] = 0 \quad (1.34)$$

$$(p' - 1)\, q + (p - c - \tau)\left[q'p' - q\,\frac{n'}{n}\right] = 0 . \qquad (1.35)$$

Multiplying (1.35) by q''_t and subtracting this equation from (1.34) leads to:

$$0 = q'p' + (p' - 1)\left(q' - 2q^2\frac{n}{t}\right) + (p - c - \tau)\left(q'' - 3qq'\,\frac{n}{t}\right)p'.$$

Solving for p' yields:

$$p' = \frac{q' - 2q^{2n}_t}{2q' - 2q^{2n}_t + (p - c - \tau)\,(q'' - 3qq''^{n}_t)} \qquad (1.36)$$

The numerator is clearly negative and the denominator is negative by the second-order condition (1.33). Thus $p' > 0$, which was to be expected.

Solving (1.35) for n' and using the zero profit condition (1.32), we obtain:

$$n' = \frac{(p' - 1)n}{p - c - \tau} + \frac{q'p'n}{q}$$

$$= \frac{1}{F}\,(p'(q + q'(p - c - \tau)) - q)$$

Substituting (1.36) for p', using (1.31) and rearranging terms, we obtain:

$$n' = \frac{(p - c - \tau)(2(q')^2 - qq'')}{F[2q' - 2q^{2n}_t + (p - c - \tau)(q'' - 3qq''^{n}_t)]} .$$

The denominator is again negative by the second-order condition. Moreover, we assumed $2(q')^2 - qq'' > 0$, hence $n' < 0$.

1.4.3 The Second-best Optimal Tax Rate

We now turn to the regulator's problem. If we again assume that the tax is the only instrument available to the regulator, she or he maximizes welfare defined as follows:

$$W(\tau) := U(q(p)) - 2nt \int_0^{\frac{1}{2n}} s\,ds - cq(p) - nF - S(q(p)), \qquad (1.37)$$

where p and n, determined by (1.31) and (1.32), are functions of the tax rate. Note that the second term on the right-hand side of (1.37) accounts for the consumers' transportation costs. It is easy to calculate that this term is equal to $t/4n$.

Differentiating (1.37) with respect to the tax rate τ yields:

$$W'(\tau) = [p - c - S']q'p' + n'\left(\frac{t}{4n^2} - F\right) = 0, \qquad (1.38)$$

where $p' = \partial p/\partial \tau$ and $n' = \partial n/\partial \tau$. By contrast, q' denotes the exogenously given derivative of the consumer's Marshallian demand.

Solving (1.31) for $(p - c)$, substituting into (1.38) and solving for τ yields:

$$\tau = S' + \frac{q}{q' - q_t^{2n}} - \frac{n'}{p'q'}\left(\frac{t}{4n^2} - F\right). \qquad (1.39)$$

Since we have not made use of the zero profit condition in this section so far, we immediately obtain the following result:

Proposition 3 If the number of firms is fixed or if a regulator has direct control over it, for example by a licence scheme, the second-best rate is given by:

$$\tau = S' + \frac{q}{q' - q_t^{2n}} \qquad (1.40)$$

and thus falls short of marginal damage.

The proof is clear since in that case $\partial n/\partial \tau = 0$.

Let us now go back to the case where the regulator has no direct control over n. Since the second term of (1.39) is clearly negative and $n' < 0$,

$p' > 0$, the second-best tax rate falls short of marginal damage if $F < t/4n^2$. Using (1.32) by solving for n, we obtain:

$$\frac{t}{4n^2} - F = F\frac{tF - 4(p - c - \tau)^2q^2}{4(p - c - \tau)^2q^2}.$$

Using (1.31) and (1.32) to substitute tF and rearranging terms, we get:

$$\frac{t}{4n^2} - F = F\frac{-(3q + 4(p - c - \tau)q')}{q + (p - c - \tau)q'},$$

where the denominator is positive by (1.31). This means $t/4n^2 - F > 0$ if and only if

$$3q + 4(p - c - \tau)q' < 0. \tag{1.41}$$

However, the left-hand side of (1.41) may be greater or smaller than zero.

Example 2
Let $q(p) = (2 - p^4)^{1/4}$, $c = 0.25$, $F = 1/16$, $S(q) = q^2/12$, and $t = 8$. Then for $\tau = 0.25$ we obtain $p = 1$, $q = 1$, $q'(p) = -1$, $q''(p) = -6$ and $W'(0.25) = 0$. However, $S'(q) = q/6$, thus $S'(1) = 1/6 < 1/4 < \tau$. Thus, in this example the second-best tax *exceeds* marginal damage.

Example 3
Choose $q(p) = 10 - p$, $S(q) = q^2/2$, $c = 0.1$, $F = 0.5$, and $t = 100$. Then we obtain $p = 3.5$ and $n = 13$. The second-best optimal tax is now 2.4, whereas the marginal damage is equal to 3.25. So in this case the second-best optimal tax *falls short* of marginal damage.

Inspecting (1.38) once again, we see that $W'(\tau) = 0$ requires:

$$[p - c - S'(q)]q'p' = n'\left[F - \frac{t}{4n^2}\right].$$

Now in the *first-best case* we would clearly have:

$$p = c + S'(q).$$

But this implies that the socially optimal number of firms is given by:

$$n = \frac{1}{2}\sqrt{\frac{t}{F}},$$

that is, the first-best number of firms depends only on the consumers' transportation costs and the firms' fixed cost, which is quite intuitive.

Summarizing, we see in the model of the circular city that the excess entry problem can be so severe that the second-best optimal tax may exceed marginal damage. This will certainly be no different if we introduce abatement technologies and if the complementarity between emissions and output is sufficiently strong.

1.5 CONCLUSIONS

In this chapter we have investigated second-best taxation of polluting firms engaging in imperfect price competition. We study three models: a price-setting duopoly with differentiated commodities and two models of monopolistic competition, the Dixit–Stiglitz model and Salop's circular city. We find that in the duopoly model, where the number of firms is exogenous, the usual result of second-best optimal taxes falling short of marginal damage continues to hold. It does not even matter whether the commodities offered by the two firms are complements or substitutes. Only if firms are very different will the second-best optimal tax possibly exceed marginal social damage. With respect to the Dixit–Stiglitz model, we find that the second-best optimal tax always falls short of marginal damage. This result is satisfying since it does not contradict our knowledge about second-best taxation of a monopolist; after all, pure monopolies rarely exist. Every monopolist competes with other firms in some way. On the other hand, the result is not trivial, since from Cournot competition with free entry we know that the second-best optimal emission tax may exceed marginal damage in order to mitigate excess entry. However, if we consider a model with physically identical commodities, only differing with respect to their location to the consumers, that is, the circular city, excess entry may be a serious problem, as is well known. And indeed we show by example that the second-best tax may indeed exceed marginal damage.

In all these models we have assumed that pollution is proportional to output and that no further abatement technology exists. Introducing abatement technologies, which would result in a cost function which depends not only on output but also on the emission level, makes the analysis very complicated. With respect to the models of monopolistic competition in particular, we have not been able to derive very general results. It is not clear whether the existence of an abatement technology with lead to a lower or higher tax in comparison to the case where no abatement technology exists. On the one hand, the regulator has direct control over emissions without directly affecting output. This might prompt him or her to set the tax higher in the presence of abatement technology than in its absence. On the other hand, if the regulator wants to use the tax to influence other market distortions such as too little production, the tax must be set lower in the case of abatement technologies than in their absence because the regulator can only influence output indirectly. However, our conjecture is that the direction of our results will not be affected. Since in the circular city the second-best optimal tax may exceed or fall short of social marginal damage, it is easy to construct examples with abatement technologies where both cases can occur as well. In the Dixit–Stiglitz model, it is unlikely that the second-best optimal tax will exceed social marginal damage because we know that the excess entry problem is very weak in that model in general. In the price-setting duopoly we also believe that the second-best optimal tax will fall short of social marginal damage in the presence of abatement technologies if the firms are not too different.

The results in this chapter confirm our knowledge derived from simpler models, that is, monopoly and Cournot oligopolies. This means that in most cases imperfect competition works in favour of the environment. Hence the regulator can set taxes lower than in the case of perfect competition. Only if excess entry is a severe problem, as is the case for the circular city, and if there is no other regulatory device, can an emission tax be used to mitigate excess entry by fixing it higher than marginal social damage. In this chapter we have not covered cases of vertical product differentiation. This must be left for further research.

APPENDIX A

Let us now show that under the assumptions we made (1.15) is satisfied. To guarantee that demand is implicitly given by (1.2) as a function of prices, it is necessary that $U_{11}U_{22} - (U_{12})^2 \neq 0$.[13] Differentiating (1.2) with respect to p_1 and p_2, respectively, yields:

$$U_{11}D_1^1 + U_{12}D_1^2 = 1 \quad U_{21}D_1^1 + U_{22}D_1^2 = 0$$

$$U_{11}D_2^1 + U_{12}D_2^2 = 0 \quad U_{21}D_2^1 + U_{22}D_2^2 = 1 .$$

Solving D_i^j yields:

$$D_1^1 = \frac{U_{22}}{U_{11}U_{22} - (U_{12})^2} \qquad D_2^2 = \frac{U_{11}}{U_{11}U_{22} - (U_{12})^2}$$

$$D_2^1 = D_1^2 = -\frac{U_{12}}{U_{11}U_{22} - (U_{12})^2},$$

and thus:

$$D_1^1 D_2^2 - D_1^2 D_2^1 = 1 .$$

Now note that in (1.15):

$$\frac{dD^j}{d\tau_i} = D_1^j \frac{\partial p_1}{\partial \tau_i} + D_2^j \frac{\partial p_2}{\partial \tau_i} \quad (i, j = 1, 2).$$

Therefore, we obtain:

$$\begin{vmatrix} \dfrac{dD^1}{d\tau_1} & \dfrac{dD^2}{d\tau_1} \\ \dfrac{dD^1}{d\tau_2} & \dfrac{dD^2}{d\tau_2} \end{vmatrix} = \frac{\partial p_1}{\partial \tau_1} \frac{\partial p_1}{\partial \tau_2} [D_1^1 D_1^2 - D_1^1 D_1^2] + \frac{\partial p_1}{\partial \tau_1} \frac{\partial p_2}{\partial \tau_2} [D_1^1 D_2^2 - D_2^1 D_1^2]$$

$$+ \frac{\partial p_2}{\partial \tau_1} \frac{\partial p_2}{\partial \tau_2} [D_2^1 D_2^2 - D_2^1 D_2^2] + \frac{\partial p_2}{\partial \tau_1} \frac{\partial p_1}{\partial \tau_2} [D_2^1 D_1^2 - D_1^1 D_2^2]$$

$$= \underbrace{[D_1^1 D_2^2 - D_2^1 D_1^2]}_{= 1} \left[\frac{\partial p_1}{\partial \tau_1} \frac{\partial p_2}{\partial \tau_2} - \frac{\partial p_1}{\partial \tau_2} \frac{\partial p_2}{\partial \tau_1} \right]$$

$$= \left[\frac{d_1 d_2 D_1^1 D_2^2 \pi_{11}^1 \pi_{22}^2}{\Delta^2} - \frac{d_1 d_2 D_1^1 D_2^2 \pi_{12}^2 \pi_{21}^1}{\Delta^2} \right]$$

$$= \frac{d_1 d_2 D_1^1 D_2^2}{\Delta^2} \underbrace{[\pi_{11}^1 \pi_{22}^2 - \pi_{12}^2 \pi_{21}^1]}_{= \Delta}$$

$$= \frac{d_1 d_2 D_1^1 D_2^2}{\Delta}$$

$$\neq 0 .$$

APPENDIX B

In this appendix we outline the proof of Proposition 1. We define:

$$W(\tau) = U(A(\tau), B(\tau)).$$

Differentiating yields:

$$W'(\tau) = U_1 \cdot A' + U_2 \cdot B' = 0$$

or

$$A' + \frac{U_2}{U_1} B' = 0 .$$

Using (1.22) we obtain:

$$A' + n^{-s} \frac{c + \tau}{\rho} B' = 0 .$$

Using (1.23) and (1.24) we derive:

$$0 = -n'F - (c + S') \left[n' \frac{F}{s(c + \tau)} - n \frac{F}{s(c + \tau)^2} \right] + \frac{Fn'}{\rho^2 s} - \frac{nF}{\rho s(c + \tau)}.$$

Using (1.25) and after some rearranging, we get the following first-order condition for the second-best tax:

$$\frac{c + \tau}{c + S'} = 1 - J, \tag{1A.1}$$

where

$$J = \frac{(1 - \rho)(K - \rho s)}{K(1 - \rho + \rho^2) - \rho s}, \tag{1A.2}$$

and K is defined by (1.26).
  Now observe that

$$K - \rho s = \frac{K_2 + \rho}{1 + \dfrac{K_1}{1-\rho}}$$

and

$$K(1 - \rho + \rho^2) - \rho s = \frac{\rho(\rho - K_1(1 - \rho)) + K_2(1 - \rho + \rho^2)}{1 + \dfrac{K_1}{1-\rho}}.$$

Inserting this into (1A.1) we obtain:

$$J = \frac{(1 - \rho)(K_2 + \rho)}{\rho(\rho - K_1(1 - \rho)) + K_2(1 - \rho + \rho^2)}. \qquad (1A.3)$$

Now assume $\tau > S'(E)$ for the second-best tax rate τ. By definition of K_2 (see equation (1.28)), this implies $K_2 > 0$. Since $K_1 < 0$, we obtain $-K_1(1 - \rho) > 0$. Since, moreover, $1 - \rho + \rho^2 > 0$, we get $J > 0$. But then (1A.1) implies $\tau < S'(E)$, a contradiction. Hence we get $\tau < S'(E)$. QED

APPENDIX C

In this section we show that $1 - \rho - \eta < 0$ is necessary to obtain decreasing demand for each commodity if the number of products increases.

Consumer's demand q as a function of the price p and the number of offering firms n satisfies the following relationship:

$$V'(n^{1/\rho}q) = n^{-s}p.$$

Differentiating with respect to n (the price level being fixed) gives:

$$V''(n^{1/\rho}q)\frac{1}{\rho}n^s q + V''(n^{1/\rho}q)n^{1/\rho}\frac{\partial q}{\partial n} + sn^{-1/\rho}p = 0.$$

Solving for $\partial q/\partial n$ yields:

$$\frac{\partial q}{\partial n} = -\frac{sn^{-1/\rho}p + V''(n^{1/\rho}q)\frac{1}{\rho}n^s q}{V''(n^{1/\rho}q)n^{1/\rho}} \qquad (1A.4)$$

$$= -\frac{1}{V''(n^{1/\rho}q)n^{1/\rho}}\left[sn^{-1/\rho}p + \frac{V''(n^{1/\rho}q)n^{1/\rho}q}{V'(n^{1/\rho}q)}\frac{p}{\rho n^{1/\rho}}\right] \qquad (1A.5)$$

$$= -\frac{p}{V''(n^{1/\rho}q)n^{2/\rho}}\left[\frac{1}{\rho} - 1 - \frac{\eta}{\rho}\right] \qquad (1A.6)$$

$$= -\ \underbrace{\frac{p}{V''(n^{1/\rho}q)n^{2/\rho}\rho}}_{>\,0}\ [1 - \rho - \eta]\,. \qquad (1A.7)$$

Hence, the assumption $1 - \rho - \eta < 0$ is necessary to ensure that the demand for each individual good decreases in the number of firms.

APPENDIX D

In this appendix we give the proof of Proposition 2. In (1A.1) (see appendix B) we defined $(c + \tau)/(c + S') =: 1 - J$ for given ρ, where J was given by:

$$J = \frac{(1 - \rho)(K_2 + \rho)}{\rho(\rho - K_1(1 - \rho)) + K_2(1 - \rho + \rho^2)}$$

as in (1A.3). In the special case of separable utility functions, this degenerates to:

$$J(\rho) = \frac{(1 - \rho)}{\rho + \eta(1 - \rho)}\,. \qquad (1A.8)$$

Since $(c + \tau)/(c + S') > 0$, it immediately follows $J \le 1$. In the proposition we assumed that $1 - \eta - \rho < 0$ for ρ close to 1. Hence, we obtain:

$$\eta(1 - \rho) > (1 - \rho)^2.$$

Thus, it follows that:

$$J(\rho) = \frac{1 - \rho}{\rho + \eta(1 - \rho)} \le \frac{1 - \rho}{\rho + (1 - \rho)^2} \le \frac{1 - \rho}{1 - \rho + \rho^2}\,.$$

This term goes to zero as $\rho \to 1$. Hence, $J \to 0$, implying $(c + \tau)/(c + S') \to 1$, that is, the better substitutes the goods are (ρ approaches 1), the closer the second-best tax rate is to marginal social damage. Tax rate and marginal social damage coincide in the limit. QED

APPENDIX E

In this section we shown that the second-order condition (1.33) is implied by our assumption $2(q')^2 - qq'' > 0$ and the first-order condition (1.31):

$$2q' - 2q^2 \frac{n}{t} + (p - c - \tau) \left[q'' - 3qq' \frac{n}{t} \right]$$

$$< 2q' - 2q^2 \frac{n}{t} + (p - c - \tau) \frac{2(q')^2}{q} - (p - c - \tau)3qq' \frac{n}{t}$$

$$= 2q' - 2q^2 \frac{n}{t} + \frac{2q'}{q} \underbrace{(p - c - \tau)(q' - q^2 \frac{n}{t}) - (p - c - \tau)qq' \frac{n}{t}}_{1.31 = -q}$$

$$= -q \frac{n}{t} (2q + (p - c - \tau)qq')$$

(1.31)

$$< 0.$$

Hence, (1.33) is satisfied.

NOTES

1. To see this, observe that $\pi_{ii}^i = 2D_i^i + (p_i - c_i)D_{ii}^i$. This is smaller zero for $D_{ii}^i \leq 0$ since in equilibrium $p_i \geq c_i$ and since $D_i^i < 0$ by assumption. If $D_{ii}^i \geq 0$, we rewrite $\pi_{ii}^i = [2D_i^i + p_i D_{ii}^i] - c_i D_{ii}^i$. This is also smaller zero since the term in brackets is non-positive by concavity.
2. See Tirole (1988: 298–9).
3. If, for example, $\rho = 1/2$ and the utility is given by $U(q_0, q_1) = q_0 + 4/3q_1^{3/4}$, total output can be derived to be $nq = 4F^{3/2}(c + \tau)^{1/2}$. Thus, total emissions are increasing in τ!
4. A complete analysis of excess entry at this stage is not possible. In general there are several conflicting forces that lead to a deviation of the number of firms from the social optimal level. Spence (1976) analyses the problem of excess entry in a standard model of monopolistic competition, that is, without social damage caused by production. Even in this context the question of excess entry cannot be answered in general but only for some special cases. In addition, in our model the impact of an increase in the tax rate on the number of firms is ambiguous. Hence we are not able to compare the number of firms with the social optimal level.
5. The utility function chosen by us does not have the *most* general form. Assuming $u = U(q_0, q_1, E)$, however, requires very complicated conditions with respect to normality.
6. Dixit and Stiglitz (1977: 298) refer to the same assumption in their original model as to the 'natural' case.
7. This assumption corresponds to a price elasticity of demand for the compound commodity that is greater than 1. Assume for a moment than the n firms collude and jointly maximize their profits. Then $\eta < 1$ is a necessary condition in order to guarantee the existence of a joint profit maximum.
8. Note, moreover, that an infinite number of firms or a corner solution where the consumers only consume commodities from the I sector but nothing from the numeraire commodity is neither compatible with partial analysis nor compatible with neoclassical preferences on the 0 and the I sector.

9. For this it suffices to assume that the elasticity of marginal utility is bounded away from 0, that is, $\eta > \varepsilon > 0$ for some ε.
10. Note that since demand is independent of the consumer's distance x to the firm, we obtain identical gross indirect utility functions for each consumer.
11. This corresponds to the usual assumption of concave revenues in the Cournot case, since $0 < 2(q')^2 - qq'' = 2/(p')^2 - q\,(-p''/(p')^3)$ implies $2p' + p''q < 0$.
12. This assumption again follows the Salop (1979) model. Economides (1989) shows that there exists such a symmetric equilibrium in location and prices if the firms can decide about entering the market and their location sequentially. However, his result holds for quadratic transportation costs only.
13. Since we assumed a quasi-concave subutility function, this implies $U_{11}U_{22} - (U_{12})^2 > 0$.

REFERENCES

Barnett, A.H. (1980), 'The Pigouvian tax rule under monopoly', *American Economic Review*, **70**, 1037–41.

Buchanan, J.M. (1969), 'External diseconomies, corrective taxes, and market structures', *American Economic Review*, **59**, 174–7.

Dixit, A.K. and J.E. Stiglitz (1997), 'Monopolistic competition and optimum product diversity', *American Economic Review*, **67**, 297–309.

Ebert, U. (1992), 'Pigouvian taxes and market structure: the case of oligopoly and different abatement technologies', *Finanzarchiv*, **49**, 154–66.

Economides, N. (1989), 'Symmetric equilibrium existence and optimality in differentiated product markets', *Journal of Economic Theory*, **47**, 178–94.

Katsoulacos, Y. and A.P. Xepapadeas (1985), 'Pigouvian taxes under oligopoly', *Scandinavian Journal of Economics*, **97**, 411–20.

Lee, D.R. (1975), 'Efficiency of pollution taxation and market structure', *Journal of Environmental Economics and Management*, **2**, 69–72.

Levin, D. (1985), 'Taxation within Cournot oligopoly', *Journal of Public Economics*, **27**, 281–90.

Requate, T. (1993a), 'Equivalence of effluent taxes and tradeable permits for environmental regulation of several local monopolies', *Economics Letters*, **42**, 91–5.

Requate, T. (1993b), 'Pollution control in a Cournot duopoly via taxes or permits', *Journal of Economics*, **58**, 255–91.

Requate, T. (1993c), 'Pollution control under imperfect competition: asymmetric Bertrand duopoly with linear technologies', *Journal of Institutional and Theoretical Economics*, **149**, 415–42.

Requate, T. (1997), 'Green taxes in oligopoly if the number of firms is endogenous', *Finanzarchiv*, **54**, 261–80.

Salop, S.C. (1979), 'Monopolistic competition with outside goods', *Bell Journal of Economics*, **10**, 141–56.

Simpson, R.D. (1995), 'Optimal pollution taxes in a Cournot duopoly', *Environmental and Resource Economics*, **6**, 359–69.

Spence, M. (1976), 'Product selection, fixed costs and monopolistic competition,' *Review of Economic Studies*, **43**, 217–35.

Tirole, J. (1988), *The Theory of Industrial Organization*, Cambridge, Mass.: MIT Press.

2. Minimum quality standard as an environmental policy: domestic and international effects

Massimo Motta and Jacques-François Thisse

2.1 INTRODUCTION

It is enough to look at newspapers and magazines to understand the role of environmental issues in modern industrialized societies. Problems such as the greenhouse effect, the disposal of toxic wastes and the pollution created by oil spills are just a few of the many examples we can think of. Given the importance of these issues, it seems to us that economists should try to apply their analytical tools to address them. The objective of this chapter is not so ambitious. More precisely, we want to study the impact of a *minimum environmental standard* on market structure and welfare. The goal of this policy is to protect the environment by imposing restrictions on the emission of pollutants generated when consuming the goods in question. Such standards have been imposed, both at the national and international levels, to regulate air and water pollution. For example, the European Community has set rules for fuel emissions of diesel engines. Recently, Germany has approved a law specifying that manufacturers must ensure by 1 July 1995 that 80 per cent of all packaging is collected and that 80 per cent of this amount is recycled (*The Financial Times*, 27 January 1993).

Our starting observation is that consumers seem to be more and more concerned about the environmental damage caused by the consumption of particular goods. However, even if all consumers tend to prefer environment-friendly goods, they differ in their degree of consciousness towards environment protection. A typical example is given by cars which do not have catalytic converters. Everybody probably agrees that this is going to harm the environment, but not every consumer would accept paying the same premium for equipping his or her car with a catalytic converter.

There is certainly an externality involved in the consumption decisions, but what matters from an individual consumer's perspective is the environmental quality of the product personally bought. This quality attribute which is, for instance, an inverse measure of pollutant emissions, contributes to the consumer's utility very much like any other attribute does. The empirical significance of this phenomenon is illustrated by the increasing number of environmental labelling programmes by means of which producers attempt to signal (possibly unobservable) dimensions of environmental friendliness. In this perspective, the oldest such programme is the German 'Blue Angel', awarded to 3 600 products between 1978 and 1993; more recent programmes include the 'Green Seal' (USA), and the 'White Swan' (Nordic Council) (see Kuhre 1997 for a detailed presentation of these programmes). As a result, consumers in several OECD countries seem to be willing to pay slightly more in order to have cleaner products (OECD 1991; Dufour 1992), thus justifying our approach in terms of vertical differentiation.

Once it is recognized that some consumers are willing to pay more than others to consume less-polluting goods, it follows that firms have a strategic incentive to differentiate their products in terms of environmental characteristics; in other words, firms supply less-polluting and more-polluting goods in response to the difference in consumers' attitudes. The resulting market structure is then akin to that encountered in vertical product differentiation: consumers agree on the ranking of goods but differ in their willingness to pay for any given product (see, for example, Mussa and Rosen 1978 and Gabszewicz and Thisse 1979). Specifically, we consider a vertically differentiated duopoly in which producing a less-polluting good involves a higher R&D cost. In a closed economy, it is shown that choosing the minimum environmental standard in such a way that both firms earn positive profits is always welfare-improving. Furthermore, at the resulting product equilibrium, both firms reduce their emission of pollutants. These results are somewhat comparable to those obtained by Ronnen (1991) in a model formally similar to ours, the main difference being that we derive explicitly the equilibrium qualities chosen by the firms.

It has also been argued by a growing number of politicians and businessmen that stiff 'green' standards can boost competitiveness in the international market place and/or be used as an instrument to protect domestic markets (*The Economist*, 5 December 1992). For example, Germany would dominate the European market for catalytic converters because it was quick to introduce high standards for car exhausts. This important problem is tackled in the second part of this chapter, using the same model as above. More precisely, we suppose that the governments of two countries may unilaterally impose the minimum environmental standard which is optimal at autarky. Two cases are considered when economies are open to international trade. In the first one, firms are assumed to offer the same good as in the autarky equilibrium and can revise their prices only (short-run analysis). In the second case, firms compete in both prices and environmental qualities (long-run analysis); it is assumed that by producing a good with a lower pollution level a firm incurs investments in R&D which depend only upon the improvement in the environmental characteristics of the good relative to the autarky level.

Suppose that one country chooses to regulate pollution while the other country does not. In the short run, environmental qualities are fixed so that the industry of the 'green' country is automatically protected against the importation of foreign polluting goods – which are also the cheapest ones. Since their market is less competitive and since their environmental qualities are higher on average than those produced abroad, the domestic firms earn more profit than foreign competitors. This turns out to be sufficient to make social welfare in the green country larger than in the other country.

In the long run, both domestic and foreign firms can adjust their environmental qualities when economies are open to international trade. Because they had to meet higher standards at autarky, domestic firms have a dominant position in the trade equilibrium. In particular, it is not profitable for the more-polluting foreign firm to increase its environment quality enough in order to sell in the green country. Imports are therefore restrained, as in the short-run case but for a different reason. However, at the trade equilibrium all firms choose to produce goods generating less pollutants. This means that the environmental policy adopted by the green country affects the strategies of the foreign firms through international competition.

The remainder of the chapter is organized as follows. The model is presented and the effects of a minimum environmental standard in a closed economy are discussed in section 2.2. The short-run impact of international trade is studied in section 2.3, while a similar analysis for the long-run case is conducted in section 2.4. Some remarks conclude the chapter in section 2.5.

2.2 THE MODEL: THE CASE OF A CLOSED ECONOMY

To analyse competition in an economy in which consumers have a preference for environment-friendly goods, we consider a standard model of vertical product differentiation. The demand side consists of a continuum of consumers indexed by θ which is uniformly distributed over $[0, \bar{\theta}]$ with density one. The surplus of consumer θ who buys one unit of product e at price p is given by $\theta e - p$ (the surplus is zero if the consumer does not buy the differentiated product).[1] In this framework, e stands for the 'environmental quality' of the product; it is expressed by a characteristic which is an inverse measure of the damage that the product consumption causes to the environment. For example, e could be represented by an index negatively related to the level of fuel emissions generated by a car. In this case, the higher is e the lower is the level of air pollution. Except for the environmental characteristics, products are considered as functionally identical.

Consumers agree on the ranking of products in terms of their environmental quality. The higher is the environmental friendliness of a good, the higher is the corresponding consumer surplus at a given price. Hence, given two products e_i and e_j with $e_i > e_j$, if $p_i = p_j$ product j has no customers. However, consumers differ in their degree of consciousness for environment protection: some of them are willing to pay more than others when buying goods that generate less pollutants. This 'environmental awareness' is described by the parameter θ: the higher is θ, the higher is the willingness to pay to reduce environmental damages.

There are two firms in the industry. They are identical in that each firm offers a single product and faces the same cost of developing the technology that enables it to provide a good of quality: $e \geq 0$. This cost is given by $F(e) = e^2/2$ and is assumed to be independent of the number of units produced. In other words, producing a more environment-friendly good involves higher expenses in R&D. For simplicity, the common marginal production cost is supposed to be invariant with respect to quality and quantity. Therefore, we do not consider the case where less-polluting goods are produced through the use of less-polluting raw materials or intermediate goods.[2] Without loss of generality, we take this cost to be zero.

Competition between firms is modelled as a two-stage game. In the first stage, firms decide simultaneously on the environmental qualities $e_1 \geq 0$ and $e_2 \geq 0$ to be produced and incur the fixed costs $e_1^2/2$ and $e_2^2/2$. In the second stage, firms simultaneously choose prices $p_1 \geq 0$ and $p_2 \geq 0$ at which they are willing to supply their products. The solution concept used is subgame perfect Nash equilibrium. As usual, the game is solved by backward induction.

We want to compare two different situations: (a) firms choose their qualities with no restrictions whatsoever; and (b) firms choose their qualities when they have to respect some minimum environmental standard (MES) imposed by the government. They correspond to the unregulated and regulated cases. In both cases, the analysis of the price stage is the same since the products e_1 and e_2 are given *a priori*.

Denote by $e_1 > e_2$ the two environmental qualities available on the market. The consumer indifferent between buying either quality is $\theta_{12} = (p_1 - p_2)/(e_1 - e_2)$ with $p_1 > p_2$; the consumer indifferent between buying the differentiated product and not buying at all is $\theta_2 = p_2/e_2$ (this consumer's surplus is zero). All consumers θ for whom $\bar{\theta} \geq \theta \geq \theta_{12}$ will buy product 1 (the consumers more sensitive to environment protection patronize the less-polluting good); those for whom $\theta_{12} \geq \theta \geq \theta_2$ will buy product 2 (the consumers less sensitive to environment protection consume the more-polluting good); and those for whom $\theta_2 \geq \theta \geq 0$ will not buy (because environmental differentiation leads firms to charge prices which might be too high to make consumption desirable). Consequently, firm 1's demand is $D_1 = \bar{\theta} - \theta_{12}$ while firm 2's demand is $D_2 = \theta_{12} - \theta_2$. Note that, unlike many spatial models of product differentiation, the market is not covered here since some consumers choose not to buy the differentiated product.

In the second stage of the game, firms choose their prices for given qualities (e_1, e_2). The equilibrium prices are then obtained by applying the first-order conditions to the profit functions $\pi_1 = p_1 D_1$ and $\pi_2 = p_2 D_2$:[3]

$$p_1^*(e_1, e_2) = 2\bar{\theta}e_1(e_1 - e_2)/(4e_1 - e_2) \tag{2.1}$$

$$p_2^*(e_1, e_2) = \bar{\theta}e_2(e_1 - e_2)/(4e_1 - e_2) \tag{2.2}$$

As expected, $p_1^* > p_2^*$: the less-polluting good is sold at a higher price. The corresponding profits are:

$$\Pi_1^*(e_1, e_2) = 4(e_1 - e_2)\,[\bar{\theta}e_1/(4e_1 - e_2)]^2 \tag{2.3}$$

$$\Pi_2^*(e_1, e_2) = e_1 e_2\,[\bar{\theta}/(4e_1 - e_2)]^2 \tag{2.4}$$

Clearly, the less-polluting firm earns more than the more-polluting firm. When $e_1 = e_2$, both profits are equal to zero because the two products are homogeneous. Functions (2.3) and (2.4) are therefore continuous at $e_1 = e_2$ even though demand functions are not defined in this case.

2.2.1 Quality Competition When There Is No Minimum Standard

Firms choose their qualities in order to maximize their profits:

$$\pi_i(e_i, e_j) = \Pi_i(e_i, e_j) - e_i^2/2, \qquad i, j = 1, 2 \text{ and } i \neq j \tag{2.5}$$

where $\Pi_i(e_i, e_j) = \Pi_1$ if $e_i > e_j$, while $\Pi_i(e_i, e_j) = \Pi_2$ if $e_j > e_i$. Assume without loss of generality that $e_1 > e_2$. Applying the first-order conditions to (2.5) yields:

$$\partial\pi_1/\partial e_1 = 4\bar{\theta}^2\, e_1(4e_1^2 - 3e_1e_2 + 2e_2^2)/(4e_1 - e_2)^3 - e_1 = 0 \qquad (2.6)$$

$$\partial\pi_2/\partial e_2 = \bar{\theta}^2\, e_1^2(4e_1 - 7e_2)/(4e_1 - e_2)^3 - e_2 = 0 \qquad (2.7)$$

Bringing e_1 and e_2 on the right-hand side of (2.6) and (2.7) respectively, dividing the corresponding expressions and rearranging terms, we obtain:

$$8e_2^3 - 12e_2^2e_1 + 23e_2e_1^2 - 4e_1^3 = 0 \qquad (2.8)$$

Setting $e_1 = \lambda e_2$ (with $\lambda > 1$ since $e_1 > e_2$) and substituting into (2.8) gives after simplifications:

$$4\lambda^3 - 23\lambda^2 + 12\lambda - 8 = 0$$

The only root of this equation greater than 1 is $\lambda = 5.2512$.[4] After substitution, we obtain:

$$e_1^* = e_H = 0.2533\bar{\theta}^2 \qquad (2.9)$$

$$e_2^* = e_L = 0.0482\bar{\theta}^2 \qquad (2.10)$$

These expressions represent the candidate equilibrium qualities. It is readily verified that $\partial^2\pi_i/\partial e_i^2 < 0$ for $i = 1, 2$ so that e_i^* maximizes $\pi_i(e_i, e_j^*)$ given that $e_1 > e_2$. Finally, Motta (1993) has shown that no firm has an incentive to leapfrog its rival, that is it is not profitable for firm 1 (firm 2) to choose a quality lower (higher) than $e_2^*(e_1^*)$. The corresponding equilibrium prices are:

$$p_1^* = 0.1077\bar{\theta}^2 \qquad (2.11)$$

$$p_2^* = 0.0102\bar{\theta}^2 \qquad (2.12)$$

and the quantities sold are:

$$D_1^* = 0.5246\bar{\theta}^2 \qquad (2.13)$$

$$D_2^* = 0.2638\bar{\theta}^2 \qquad (2.14)$$

which means that approximately 78 per cent of the consumers buy the product.

To sum up: when there is no MES there exists a unique quality equilibrium (up to a permutation of firms) given by e_H and e_L.

2.2.2   Quality Competition When There Is a Minimum Standard

Suppose now that the government imposes a minimum environmental standard $\underline{e} > 0$. This means that no firm can choose a product specification that generates a pollution level higher than a given threshold corresponding to $\underline{e}$. For the regulation to be effective, it must be that $\underline{e} > e_L$, where e_L is given by (2.10) – otherwise the constraint on quality does not bind and we fall back on the previous case. Hence, at equilibrium, the low-quality firm chooses to produce $\underline{e}$. Indeed, if it were profitable for this firm to offer a less-polluting good, there would exist two equilibria in the unregulated case, which contradicts the result above. The high-quality firm must therefore choose a product specification for (2.6) to be satisfied when $e_2 = \underline{e}$. In order to get an explicit solution, we set without loss of generality $\underline{e} = k\overline{\theta}^2$ with $k > 0$. It can then be verified that (2.6) has a unique solution given by:

$$e^s = \overline{\theta}^2 \{(1 + 3k)/12 + (1 - 3k) [3.2^{5/3} (f(k))^{1/3}] + [(f(k))^{1/3}/3.2^{7/3}]\}$$
$$\equiv \overline{\theta}^2 g(k)$$

where $f(k) \equiv 2 - 9k + 162k^2 + 3^{3/2} k (23 - 104k + 972k^2)^{1/2}$. Accordingly, if an equilibrium exists in the regulated case, it is given by $e_1^{**} = e^s$ and $e_2^{**} = \underline{e}$. As shown by Figure 2.1, when $\underline{e}$ raises, firm 1 increases its quality in order to relax price competition.[5]

For $(e^s, \underline{e})$ to be an equilibrium, it must be that both firms earn non-negative profits at these qualities. Using (2.5):

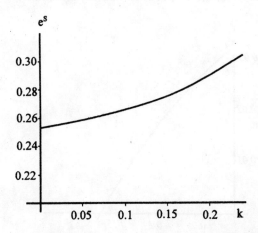

Figure 2.1   *The high-quality e^s as a function of* k *in the regulated case (for $\overline{\theta} = 1$)*

$$\pi_1^s = \bar{\theta}^4 \{g(k) [g(k) - k]/[4g(k) - k]^2 - 1/2\} \qquad (2.15)$$

$$\pi_1^s = \bar{\theta}^4 \{g(k) [g(k) - k]/[4g(k) - k]^2 - k^2/2\} \qquad (2.16)$$

It follows from these expressions that the sign of π_1^s and of π_2^s depends on k but not on $\bar{\theta}$. It can be shown that π_1^s is always decreasing and intersects the k axis at $k = 0.165$ (see Figure 2.2 for an illustration). As for the function π_2^s, it first increases, reaches a maximum at $k = 0.005$, and decreases afterward (this is illustrated in Figure 2.3). Imposing an MES gives rise to a credible commitment by firm 2 on its quality choice, which cannot be lower than $\underline{e}$ (see also Ronnen 1991). This obliges firm 1 to increase its own quality. Higher profits for the former firm are due to the higher quality produced at the regulated equilibrium, while lower profits for the latter follow from larger R&D costs. Of course, beyond some level, firm 2's costs increase enough to result in lower profits. Furthermore, the value of the k for which π_2^s equals zero is $\bar{k} = 0.0962$. Hence, if the government chooses an MES such that k exceeds $\bar{k}$, at most one firm is effective in the market. In other words, by selecting too high a minimum standard, the government may prevent the existence of a duopoly because price competition becomes too fierce for the two firms to be able to cover their R&D costs. For this reason, it is assumed from now on that $\underline{e}$ is such that $k \leq \bar{k}$.[6]

Thus, when there is an MES such that $k \leq \bar{k}$, a quality equilibrium exists. At this equilibrium, both firms reduce their emission of pollutants. Furthermore, the less-polluting firm is always worse off, but the more-polluting firm is better off when $\underline{e}$ is sufficiently close to e_1.[7]

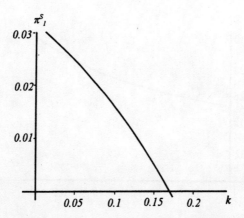

Figure 2.2   Profits of the high-quality firm as a function of k *(for* $\bar{\theta} = 1$*)*

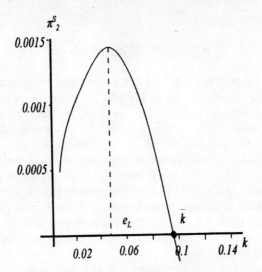

Figure 2.3   Profits of the low-quality firm as a function of k *(for* $\bar{\theta} = 1$*)*

The corresponding equilibrium prices are:

$$P_1^{**}(e^s, \underline{e}) = 2\bar{\theta}^3 g(k) [g(k) - k]/[4g(k) - k]$$

$$P_2^{**}(e^s, \underline{e}) = \bar{\theta}^3 k [g(k) - k]/[4g(k) - k]$$

Using these prices, the total consumer surplus can be determined as

$$CS = \theta^4 \{g(k) [(4g(k) - k)^2 - 4(g(k) - k) (4g(k) - k)$$

$$+ [4g(k) - k] [2g(k) - k]^2 + k[g(k) - k]^2\}/\{2[4g(k) - k]^2\} \quad (2.17)$$

Figure 2.4 shows that CS always increases with $\underline{e}$.

Welfare is defined as $W = CS + \pi_1^s + \pi_2^s$ which, by (2.15)–(2.17), can be written as $W = \bar{\theta}^4 G(k)$. The function $G(k)$ is depicted in Figure 2.5 which shows that G is strictly concave with a maximum at $k = 0.17$. However, it should be kept in mind that this function is defined in the duopoly case only, that is, for $k \le \bar{k}$. A government which would have the appropriate information should therefore set an MES for which $k = \bar{k}$. This would guarantee the highest possible welfare when firms are free to choose their prices and environmental qualities. The corresponding qualities are:

$$e^{**} = 0.2641\bar{\theta}^2, \ e_2^{**} = 0.0962\bar{\theta}^2$$

while prices are:

$$p_1^{**} = 0.09230\bar{\theta}^3, p_2^{**} = 0.01680\bar{\theta}^3$$

Thus, at the optimal regulation, both environmental qualities are higher and both prices are lower (see (2.11)–(2.12)). Prices decrease because the quality gap narrows $(e_1^{**} - e_2^* < e_1^* - e_2^*)$; this is due to the high R&D costs associated with improvements in environmental qualities. Furthermore, $D_1^{**} = 0.5501\bar{\theta}$ and $D_2^{**} = 0.2750\bar{\theta}$ so that more than 82 per cent of the market is now served. Comparing the quantities D_1^{**} and D_2^{**} to (2.13) and (2.14), it follows immediately that all the consumers who buy the less-polluting good in the unregulated case still buy this good when the market is optimally regulated; some consumers purchasing the more-polluting good now choose the less-polluting one; finally, the total mass of consumers operating on the market is larger because qualities are higher and prices lower.

It is also worth comparing welfare in the unregulated and regulated cases for intermediate values of k. In the unregulated case, welfare is equal to $0.06910\bar{\theta}^4$ (see Motta 1993: table 1). Let $\underline{k}$ be such that $\underline{e} = e_1$, that is, $\underline{k}$ is the largest value of k for which the minimum standard does not bind the firms' choice. Since G is increasing on $[\underline{k}, \bar{k}]$, regulating the industry by imposing an MES increases welfare, provided $\underline{e}$ is chosen for k to be in the interval $[\underline{k}, \bar{k}]$. In other words, when $\underline{e}$ is binding but not too large, it is still true that consumers benefit from more environment-friendly goods and lower prices, and that the gain made by consumers dominates the loss made by firms.

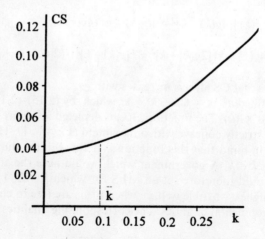

Figure 2.4   Consumer surplus as a function of k *(for* $\bar{\theta} = 1$*)*

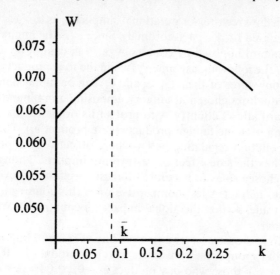

Figure 2.5   Welfare as a function of k *(for* $\bar{\theta} = 1$*)*

2.3   INTERNATIONAL TRADE: THE SHORT-RUN CASE

We now study the impact of foreign competition on market equilibrium and welfare when governments make independent choices on regulating pollution. In this section, it is supposed that firms' environmental qualities are chosen at autarky and cannot be changed when economies are open to international trade (short-run analysis).

Consider two countries A and B in which consumer preferences for environmental quality are uniformly distributed over the same interval $[0, \bar{\theta}]$. There are two firms in each country; each firm offers a single quality. Qualities are chosen in closed economies and the corresponding R&D costs are sunk. In country A, pollution is regulated through the imposition of an MES given by the socially optimal threshold when country A is closed. The qualities in this country are therefore $e_{1A}^* = 0.2641\bar{\theta}^2$ and $e_{2A}^* = 0.0962\bar{\theta}^2$. In country B, pollution is not regulated so that $e_{1B}^* = 0.2533\bar{\theta}^2$ and $e_{2B}^* = 0.0482\bar{\theta}^2$. Suppose now that both countries are open to international trade and that firms can react by adjusting prices only. More precisely, qualities cannot be changed and firms choose prices independently in the two markets (that is, there is market segmentation).

Since the two countries adopted different policies regarding pollution, the qualities supplied in each of them are different. Clearly, $e_{1A}^* > e_{1B}^* >$

$e_{2A}^* > e_{2B}^*$, which we rewrite, for notational simplicity, as $e_1 > e_2 > e_3 > e_4$; firms are re-indexed $i = 1 \ldots 4$ accordingly. Since e_3 is the minimum environmental standard imposed by country A, $e_4 < e_3$ cannot be sold in A. This generates the following asymmetry: while the four products compete in country B, only three of them (e_1, e_2 and e_3) can be supplied in country A. Given the qualities chosen at autarky, imposing a minimum environmental standard allows country A to protect its domestic market from the competition of some foreign products (here product e_4). Thus, in the short run, a pollution-regulating policy whose objective is to protect the environment has the side effect of restraining imports. Though e_3 has been initially chosen so as to maximize domestic welfare, the existence of an MES makes market A less competitive once this country is open to international trade, so that the global impact on country A's welfare is *a priori* ambiguous.

Consider first the case of country A. The corresponding market is divided into four groups: the consumers who buy product $1 - \bar{\theta} \geq \theta \geq \theta_{12} = (p_1 - p_2)/(e_1 - e_2)$, those who buy product $e_2 - \theta_{12} \geq \theta \geq \theta_{23} = (p_2 - p_3)/(e_2 - e_3)$, those who buy product $e_3 - \theta_{23} \geq \theta \geq \theta_3 = p_3/e_3$ and those who do not purchase the differentiated product. Firms' demands are then defined as follows: $D_1 = \bar{\theta} - \theta_{12}$, $D_2 = \theta_{12} - \theta_{23}$, and $D_3 = \theta_{23} - \theta_3$. Some simple, but tedious, calculations show that the equilibrium prices are:

$$p_{1A}^* = 0.007027\bar{\theta}^3, \qquad p_{2A}^* = 0.003308\bar{\theta}^3, \qquad p_{3A}^* = 0.000628\bar{\theta}^3$$

while the quantities sold are

$$D_{1A}^* = 0.65396\bar{\theta}, \qquad D_{2A}^* \ 0.32898\bar{\theta}, \qquad D_{3A}^* = 0.010153\bar{\theta}$$

so that more than 99 per cent of the market is served.

Thus, domestic products are sold at lower prices ($p_{1A}^* < p_1^{**}$ and $p_{3A}^* < p_{3A}^{**} < p_2^{**}$) when there is international trade (remember that the foreign product is supplied at an intermediate quality level). At this price equilibrium, almost all consumers choose to buy one of the three goods available. In particular, the consumers patronizing e_1, at autarky still buy this product ($D_{1A}^* > D_1^{**}$); those who buy e_3 at autarky purchase e_1 or the foreign product $e_2(D_{1A}^* > D_{2A}^{**} > D_1^{**} + D_2^{**} > D_{1A}^*)$; finally, all the consumers buying e_3 do not purchase at autarky. Note also that the domestic consumer surplus $CS_A = 0.125669\bar{\theta}^4$ increases under international trade because domestic prices decrease and because more consumers buy better products (that is, e_1 and e_2).

As for country B, the market is divided in five consumer groups since all the products are supplied. It can be shown that the equilibrium prices associated with $e_1 \ldots e_4$ are given by:

$$p_{1B}^* = 0.0070230\overline{\theta}^3, \qquad p_{2B}^* = 0.0033000\overline{\theta}^3,$$

$$p_{3B}^* = 0.0004260\overline{\theta}^3, \qquad p_{4B}^* = 0.0001070\overline{\theta}^3.$$

Hence introducing product e_4 leads to a more competitive market but prices do not drop in the same proportion: prices of e_1 and e_2 decrease slightly but the price of e_3 decreases more because e_4 is a closer rival and because $e_1 - e_2 < e_2 - e_3$. Each consumer is strictly better off because the surplus associated with e_1, e_2 and e_3 is higher and because the set of alternatives is larger. The domestic consumer surplus in country B is $CS_B = 0.125677\overline{\theta}^4$, which is larger than CS_A.

Total welfare in each country is defined as the sum of domestic consumer surplus and of the profits earned by the domestic firms on the domestic and foreign markets:

$$W_A = 0.134866\overline{\theta}^4$$

$$W_B = 0.127849\overline{\theta}^4.$$

Thus country A, in which an optimal environmental standard is imposed, achieves a higher welfare level. Though consumers are strictly better off in country B, country A's firms earn much higher profits ($\Pi_A = \Pi_{1A} + \Pi_{3A} + \Pi_{1B} + \Pi_{3B} = 0.009197\overline{\theta}^4$) than country B's firms ($\Pi_B = \Pi_{2A} + \Pi_{2B} + \Pi_{4B} = 0.002172\overline{\theta}^4$) because they offer less-polluting goods. In other words, regulating pollution is always socially desirable despite the resulting loss of competitiveness on the domestic market.

So far we have assumed that only one country has chosen to regulate pollution. If both countries impose the same optimal MES (which is plausible since countries are identical), all consumers buy product e_1 and profits are zero because this product is supplied by two firms. Then $\overline{W}_A = \overline{W}_B = 0.132\overline{\theta}^4$. On the other hand, if no country regulates pollution, profits are still zero but consumers now buy product e_2. It is readily verified that $\overline{W}_A = \overline{W}_B = 0.1266\overline{\theta}^4$, which is lower than $\overline{W}$ because $e_2 < e_1$. Consequently, we have the payoff matrix:

A \ B	No MES		MES	
No MES	$0.1266\overline{\theta}^4$,	$0.1300\overline{\theta}^4$	$0.1300\overline{\theta}^4$,	$0.13480\overline{\theta}^4$
MES	$0.1348\overline{\theta}^4$,	$0.1300\overline{\theta}^4$	$0.132\overline{\theta}^4$,	$0.132\overline{\theta}^4$

Thus welfare in both countries is always higher when they both decide to regulate pollution optimally. Since no country has an incentive to deviate unilaterally, (MES, MES) is a Nash equilibrium of the game between governments. Furthermore, even if one country does not regulate pollution, it is always optimal for the other to do so, which implies that (MES, MES) is an equilibrium in dominant strategies. It should be kept in mind, however, that environmental policies are chosen in conditions of autarky. A full analysis would require the governments to anticipate the impact of regulation pollution when economies are open. This turns out to be very difficult to carry out; however, we believe that the partial results obtained above shed some light on this important topic.

2.4 INTERNATIONAL TRADE: THE LONG-RUN CASE

In the previous section, qualities were assumed to be given at their autarky levels. We now allow firms to adjust both qualities and prices in response to the opening of the national economies to trade (long-run analysis). In particular, when firm i has chosen to supply a quality e_i in a closed economy and chooses to offer a quality $\hat{e}_i > e_i$ in an open economy, it incurs a *fixed adjustment cost* equal to $(\hat{e}_i - e_i)^2/2$. Hence firms capitalize on previous R&D investments and bear costs that depend only upon the quality increments. Note that firms may want to produce lower-quality products when more products compete together in order to broaden the quality range and to relax price competition. However, because of environmental considerations, it seems natural to assume here that governments do not allow firms to produce more-polluting goods when there is international trade.

Though there is still market segmentation at the price stage (firms choose country-specific prices) national markets are now linked through the choice made by each firm to supply the *same* quality in the two countries. In other words, markets are tied (or integrated) at the quality stage. So our model combines segmented markets and tied markets at different stages of the game (see Venables 1990 for a similar assumption in a different, but related, context).

In this section, we consider the following three cases. First, no country regulates pollution through an optimal MES. Then, one country imposes an optimal MES while the other does not. Finally, both countries apply the same policy against pollution.

When no governments regulate pollution, the qualities chosen at autarky are $e_{1A}^* = e_{1B}^* = 0.2533\bar{\theta}^2$ and $e_{2A}^* = e_{2B}^* = 0.0482\bar{\theta}^2$ (see section 2.2). For any given quadruple $e_1 > e_2 > e_3 > e_4$, the equilibrium prices are the same in each country and are uniquely determined from the first-order conditions. Substituting these prices into the profit functions yields the payoffs used in the quality game. These payoffs are obtained by summing the profits earned on the domestic and foreign markets minus the cost of adjusting quality.

Given the assumption $e_4 \geq 0.0482\bar{\theta}^2$, it can be shown that $\hat{e}_1^* = 0.7795\bar{\theta}^2$, $\hat{e}_2^* = 0.3152\bar{\theta}^2$, $\hat{e}_3^* = 0.0670\bar{\theta}^2$ and $\hat{e}_4^* = 0.0482\bar{\theta}^2$,[8] which are sold respectively at prices $\hat{p}_1^* = 0.2546\bar{\theta}^3$, $\hat{p}_2^* = 0.0440\bar{\theta}^3$, $\hat{p}_3^* = 0.00190\bar{\theta}^3$ and $\hat{p}_4^* = 0.0007\bar{\theta}^3$. Hence all firms, except firm 4, improve their environmental qualities in order to soften price competition, which is otherwise exacerbated by the presence of more firms than under autarky. The corresponding equilibrium profits are:

$$\pi_1^* = 0.1408\bar{\theta}^4, \qquad \pi_2^* = 0.0231\bar{\theta}^4$$

$$\pi_3^* = 0.0002\bar{\theta}^4, \qquad \pi_4^* = 0.00007\bar{\theta}^4.$$

As in many models of international trade with product differentiation, it is not possible to determine which products are supplied by firms established in country A or B. For example, we do not know whether $\hat{e}_1^*$ is supplied by the high-quality firm set up in country A or by that set up in country B. *A priori*, the following combinations are possible in either country: $(\hat{e}_1^*, \hat{e}_3^*)$, $(\hat{e}_1^*, \hat{e}_4^*)$, $(\hat{e}_2^*, \hat{e}_3^*)$, $(\hat{e}_2^*, \hat{e}_4^*)$. In other words, each country offers one, and only one, of the top two qualities; moreover, $\hat{e}_1^*$ and $\hat{e}_2^*$ are supplied by the two firms producing the top quality at autarky. Consequently, profits earned by domestic firms change with the corresponding configuration.

Because prices are the same in either country, the consumer surplus is the same: $CS_A = CS_B = 0.18626\bar{\theta}^4$.

Social welfare depends on the goods produced by the domestic firms and cannot be the same in both countries. Four cases may arise:

$$W_A = CS_A + \pi_1^* + \pi_3^* = 0.32730\bar{\theta}^4$$

$$W_A = CS_A + \pi_1^* + \pi_4^* = 0.32720\bar{\theta}^4$$

$$W_A = CS_A + \pi_2^* + \pi_3^* = 0.20960\bar{\theta}^4$$

$$W_A = CS_A + \pi_2^* + \pi_4^* = 0.20940\bar{\theta}^4.$$

Compared to the short-run case (see section 2.3), we see that regardless of the emerging configuration of products, welfare is unambiguously higher in both countries when firms can adjust qualities. This result is basically driven by the increase in consumer surplus. This in turn is due to a broader supply of products – four instead of two – and to higher-quality levels than at the short-run equilibrium.[9]

Consider now the second case, that is, country A's government imposes an MES corresponding to the optimal threshold in a closed economy. Then we know that qualities chosen at autarky are such that $e_{1A}^{**} = 0.26041\bar{\theta}^2$ and $e_{2A}^{**} = 0.0962\bar{\theta}^2$ while $e_{1B}^{*} = 0.2533\bar{\theta}^2$ and $e_{2B}^{*} = 0.0482\bar{\theta}^2$. If the low-quality firm in country B wants to export, it must increase its quality in order to meet the MES imposed in country A. In this case, the resulting equilibrium configuration must be such that $\hat{e}_4^{*} = 0.0962\bar{\theta}^2$. Otherwise, there would be an equilibrium in which firm 4's quality would be higher. This would imply the existence of two equilibria when pollution is not regulated, which contradicts the uniqueness property established above.

Using the same approach as in the unregulated case, it can be shown that $\hat{e}_1^{*} = 0.7842\bar{\theta}^2$, $\hat{e}_2^{*} = 0.3237\bar{\theta}^2$ and $\hat{e}_3^{*} = 0.1176\bar{\theta}^2$ so that firms 1–3 increase their environmental quality. When profits are evaluated at these qualities, it appears that the profit of firm 4 is negative. In other words, the imposition of an optimal MES in country A makes it unprofitable for the low-quality firm in country B to adjust its quality in order to export. Thus, as in the short-run case, regulating pollution acts as a barrier to trade by reducing the number of products competing on the domestic market.

Hence only three goods can be supplied in country A: they are produced by the high- and low-quality firms established in A($\hat{e}_1^{*}$ and $\hat{e}_3^{*}$) and by the high-quality firm established in B. Put in a different way, it is now possible to identify which firm produces which product. Specifically, the products sold in countries A and B can be shown to have environmental qualities given by $\hat{e}_1^{*} = 0.7862\bar{\theta}^2$, $\hat{e}_2^{*} = 0.3203\bar{\theta}^2$ and $\hat{e}_3^{*} = 0.1091\bar{\theta}^2$. The fourth product, the quality of which is now $\hat{e}_4^{*} = 0.0489\bar{\theta}^2$, does not meet the MES imposed in country A and is sold in country B only. Compared to the autarky situation, we see that *all* firms offer less-polluting products. In particular, though the low-quality firm in country B does not sell in country A, it is profitable for this firm to increase its product's quality because its direct competitor, firm 3, has sufficiently increased its own quality.

The resulting profits are

$$\pi_1^{*} = 0.14010\bar{\theta}^4, \qquad \pi_2^{*} = 0.02160\bar{\theta}^4,$$

$$\pi_3^{*} = 0.00110\bar{\theta}^4, \qquad \pi_4^{*} = 0.000004\bar{\theta}^4.$$

Thus, the imposition of an MES in country A guarantees the corresponding top-quality firm at autarky to be the top-quality firm in the open economy. Furthermore, the low-quality firm in country A at autarky (firm 3) benefits from regulating pollution because the MES prevents the importation of country B's low-quality product in country A and, therefore, allows firm 3's domestic market to be protected.

The asymmetry in trade resulting from unilateral pollution control implies that consumer surplus differs between countries: $CS_A = 0.1904\bar{\theta}^4$ and $CS_B = 0.1911\bar{\theta}^4$. So, as in the short-run case, consumers are better off in the country which does not impose an optimal MES. Regarding total welfare in each country, it is readily verified that

$$W_A = CS_A + \pi_1^* + \pi_3^* = 0.3317\bar{\theta}^4$$

$$W_B = CS_B + \pi_2^* + \pi_4^* = 0.2128\bar{\theta}^4$$

so that the country enforcing an optimal environmental standard reaches a higher welfare level than the other. Again, this result is identical to that obtained in the short-run case.

It remains to deal with the situation in which the two countries adopt the optimal MES at autarky. This means that $e_{1A}^{**} = e_{1B}^{**} = 0.2641\bar{\theta}^2$ and $e_{2A}^{**} = e_{2B}^{**} = 0.0962\bar{\theta}^2$. After trade, the new equilibrium environmental qualities are $\hat{e}_1^* = 0.7860\bar{\theta}^2$, $\hat{e}_2^* = 0.3319\bar{\theta}^2$, $\hat{e}_3^* = 0.1178\bar{\theta}^2$ and $\hat{e}_4^* = 0.0962\bar{\theta}^2$. This configuration has one striking feature: the top quality is lower than under unilateral regulation while the other three qualities are higher. It appears difficult to understand the intuition behind this result.[10]

Since prices and qualities are the same in both countries, the consumer surplus is the same: $CS_A = CS_B = 0.1963\bar{\theta}^4$.

As in the unregulated case, products cannot be assigned to countries. Four configurations may arise, yielding the following welfare levels:

$$W_A = CS_A + \pi_1^* + \pi_3^* = 0.3296\bar{\theta}^4$$

$$W_A = CS_A + \pi_1^* + \pi_4^* = 0.3294\bar{\theta}^4$$

$$W_A = CS_A + \pi_2^* + \pi_3^* = 0.2167\bar{\theta}^4$$

$$W_A = CS_A + \pi_2^* + \pi_4^* = 0.2165\bar{\theta}^4.$$

For each possible configuration, welfare is always higher in the regulated case than in the unregulated case. Furthermore, whatever the configuration that arises, no country has an incentive to deregulate pollution unilaterally so that (MES, MES) is the only Nash equilibrium of the games between governments. This confirms the results obtained in the short-run case.

2.5 CONCLUDING REMARKS

Despite the highly stylized character of the model used in this chapter, our analysis sheds some light on an important topic and seems to confirm the idea that 'greener means richer'. When the economy is closed, imposing an MES turns out to be welfare-improving. When economies are open, the same property holds regardless of the environmental policy followed by the other country. Furthermore, when an MES is unilaterally imposed, domestic firms are better off both in the short- and long-run cases and imports are restrained. As a result, introducing a minimum environmental standard seems to be a sensible policy for a government.

However, this claim needs qualification. First, the welfare function should be generalized in order to include a term accounting for the social cost of pollution. To be sure, imposing an MES leads to the production of less-polluting goods, which tends to reduce the cost of pollution. But more consumers operate in the market when an MES is introduced so the total level of pollution could increase. Since the first effect has an impact on all the consumers while the second affects only a fraction of the population, it seems reasonable to expect the first effect to dominate the second one.

For simplicity, we have assumed two identical countries. If consumers in one country are more concerned about pollution than those in the other country, the MES chosen at autarky are no longer the same. In particular, this would imply import restraints in the country with a stiffer standard. Furthermore, negotiating a common MES when governments anticipate its impact on international trade seems to be a very difficult problem to study.

Finally, it would be worth studying what happens when a country decides to subsidize pollution-reducing investments. At autarky, it seems clear that a government would choose to cover part of the additional fixed costs incurred by firms to produce 'cleaner' goods. Indeed, the more-polluting firm would stay on the market for higher values of the MES. This topic is left for further research.

NOTES

1. In accordance with most of the literature on product differentiation, we assume that consumers buy at most one unit of the differentiated product.

2. See Crampes and Hollander (1995) for a study where an improvement in the environmental quality falls upon variable costs. Using this alternative assumption on the teechnology leads to similar results.
3. It is well known that there exists a unique price equilibrium for any price subgame; see, for example, Tirole (1988; ch.7).
4. Throughout this chapter, we give 'approximate' values that have been computed numerically.
5. Of course, we assume that firm 1 earns positive net profits; otherwise, it would exit the market.
6. When $k > \bar{k}$ at most one firm is active. It can be shown that firm 1 chooses a quality higher than the MES for $\bar{k} < k \leq 0.25$; when $k > 0.25$ firm 1's quality is given by the MES. In both cases, the quality supplied is lower than the quality chosen by the high-quality firm in duopoly (disregarding the non-negativity profit condition). Therefore, if firm 2 were to enter, the quality gap would be narrower and price competition would be fiercer. Firm 2's profits would still be negative so that firm 1 is a monopolist who does not fear entry. In other words, the MES acts as a non-strategic entry barrier.
7. This quality equilibrium is not always unique. For some values of the parameters where the duopoly equilibrium exists, there also exists another equilibrium, where firm 1 selects a quality e_m (with $\underline{e} < e_m < e_s$) and firm 2 would prefer not to enter, since by entering and producting a quality $\underline{e}$ it would make nagative profits. See Lutz (1996) for a characterization of this equilibrium.
8. We focus here and in the whole of the present section on only one of the possible equilibria, namely the equilibrium where the quality ranking of the firms is the same under autarky and international trade. There might exist other equilibria where this ranking is inverted. For instance, it is possible that the firms having the lowest quality before trade opens end up with the highest at the trade equilibrium and vice versa. This is the case of 'leapfrogging'. In a recent paper, written after the previous version of this chapter, Motta *et al.* (1997) show that this leapfrogging equilibrium does not always exist, and that it is always risk-dominated in the sense of Harsanyi and Selten (1988) by the equilibrium where the quality ranking under trade and under autarky is unchanged.
9. This confirms previous results obtained in international trade models with vertical product differentiation (see Motta 1992; Shaked and Sutton 1984).
10. The same result holds for other 'initial' qualities.

REFERENCES

Crampes, C. and A. Hollander (1995), 'Duopoly and quality standards', *European Economic Review*, **39**(1), 71–82.
Dufour, A. (1992), 'Les Français et l'environnement: de l'intention à l'action', *Economie et statistique*, **258/259**, 19–26.
Gabszewicz, J.J. and J.-F. Thisse (1979), 'Price competition, quality, and income disparities', *Journal of Economic Theory*, **20**, 340–59.
Harsanyi, J.C. and R. Selten (1988), *A General Theory of Equilibrium in Games*, Cambridge, Mass.: MIT Press.
Kuhre, W.L. (1997), *ISO 14020s Environmental Labelling-Marketing: Efficient and Accurate Environmental Marketing Procedures*, Upper Slade River, NJ: Prentice-Hall.
Lutz, S. (1996), 'Trade effects of minimum quality standards with and without deterred entry', CEPR D.P. 1384 (April), London: Centre for Economic Policy Research.

Motta, M. (1992), 'Sunk costs and trade liberalization', *Economic Journal*, **102**, 578–87.

Motta, M. (1993), 'Endogenous quality choice: price vs. quantity competition', *Journal of Industrial Economics*, **41**(2), 113–31.

Motta, M., J.-F. Thisse and A. Cabrales (1997), 'On the persistence of leadership or leapfrogging in international trade', *International Economic Review*, **38**(4), 809–24.

Mussa, M. and S. Rosen (1978), 'Monopoly and product quality', *Journal of Economic Theory*, **18**, 301–17.

OECD (1991), *L'etiquettage écologique des produits dans les pays de l'OCDE*, Paris: OECD.

Ronnen, V. (1991), 'Minimum quality standards, fixed costs, and competition', *Rand Journal of Economics*, **22**, 490–504.

Shaked, A. and J. Sutton (1984), 'Natural oligopolies and international trade', in H. Kierzkowski (ed.), *Monopolistic Competition and International Trade*, Oxford: Clarendon Press.

Tirole, J. (1988), *The Theory of Industrial Organization*, Cambridge Mass.: MIT Press.

Venables, A. (1990), 'International capacity choice and national market games', *Journal of International Economics*, **29**, 23–42.

3. Emissions permits trading and market structure

Eftichios S. Sartzetakis and Donald G. McFetridge

3.1 INTRODUCTION

When private actions fail to internalize environmental externalities, regulatory intervention is potentially beneficial. There are two broad forms of environmental regulation: centralized and decentralized. Decentralized regulation involves the use of emissions charges, abatement subsidies or tradable emissions permits, with individual sources of emissions being free to determine their respective optimal responses to a given charge, subsidy rate or emissions permit price.

In recent years, the concept of tradable emissions permits has attracted considerable interest among environmental policy makers. One of the attractions of a tradable permits regime is that, in its idealized 'frictionless' form, emissions permits trading allocates abatement effort among sources of emissions so as to minimize the aggregate cost of achieving a given reduction in emissions. This result is independent of the initial distribution of permits and does not require that regulators have any special knowledge of the characteristics of individual sources of emissions.

While limited, practical experience with emissions permits trading reveals that the efficiency gains actually realized are much less than promised by idealized permits markets.[1] A number of impediments to the operation of permits markets have been identified. These include small numbers, transaction costs,[2] cheating and monitoring costs,[3] costs of transition from pre-existing regulations,[4] and uncertainty that leads to the hoarding of permits.[5]

The most frequently challenged assumption of the idealized model is the assumption of large numbers competition. This chapter analyses the possible effects of small numbers competition in both the product and the permits markets on the operation of permits markets, and develops a taxonomy of the different cases presented in the literature. It identifies problems of implementing tradable emission permit regulations in second-best situations which arise because of small numbers. We assess the

importance of market power in reducing the efficiency of emissions trading policies in allocating abatement efforts, and the possible ways in which
permits trading might change the structure of the product market. We
believe that this presentation of the problems associated with market
imperfections is important in cautioning policy makers, as well as providing some suggestions for efficiency-enhancing modifications of proposed
emissions trading programmes.

The rest of the chapter is organized as follows. Section 3.2 considers
situations in which either inter- and intra-industry permits trading in
competitive permits markets aggravates existing product market distortions. Section 3.3 distinguishes three possible ways in which emissions
permits trading can be used to manipulate the product market structure
when firms are not price-takers in the permits market. We examine the
cases of collusive behaviour, as well as cooperative and non-cooperative
strategies for manipulating the dispersion of industry production costs.
Some conclusions are offered in section 3.4.

3.2   PRICE-TAKING BEHAVIOUR IN THE PERMITS MARKETS

It is well understood that emissions permits trading in competitive markets can achieve minimization of aggregate abatement costs. The result is
explained in the following subsection. The argument there makes no
assumption regarding the structure of the product markets involved.
Abatement cost minimization may not improve social welfare if the product markets involved are not competitive. Emissions permits trading, even
in the case of price-taking behaviour in the permits market, can aggravate
existing distortions in the product market. Thus, in the presence of product market distortions, the effect on welfare of emissions permits trading
is ambiguous. We examine such cases in the second part of this section.

3.2.1 Cost Minimization Property

Under a tradable emissions permits regime, the regulator's principal task
is to determine the allowable aggregate level of emissions of the pollutant
in question (the emissions ceiling). The regulator then issues permits,
each allowing the emission of a certain amount of the pollutant. After
the initial distribution of permits, trade of permits is allowed. Each
source is allowed to emit the amount of the pollutant stipulated in the
permits it has received from the regulator or has purchased from others
and is obliged to control (abate) the rest. If sources are price-takers in the

permits market, they will engage in abatement up to the point at which the marginal cost of abatement is equal to the price of permits. As a consequence, the respective marginal costs of abatement of all sources of emissions will be equal to the price of permits. This occurs regardless of the initial distribution of permits. Since permits are a valuable asset, however, the net worth of firms receiving them will increase.[6]

The equalization of the marginal cost of abatement across all sources of emissions implies that aggregate abatement costs are minimized.[7] When marginal abatement costs are equalized across sources of emissions, there is no reallocation of abatement effort that can further reduce the cost of achieving a given reduction in aggregate emissions.[8]

3.2.2 Competitive Permits Markets in the Presence of Product Market Distortions

The abatement cost minimizing property of emissions trading is crucially dependent on the assumption of a perfectly competitive permits market. The structure of many industries that might make use of emissions trading may not support competition in the permits market. A good example is the electricity generating industry which accounts for most of the sulphur dioxide (SO_2) emissions, an important source of acid rain. The electricity generating industry in most countries is characterized by small numbers and heavy regulation. High concentration ratios in electric power generation have been noted in the UK (see Owen *et al.* 1992) and in Canada (see Canada 1992).

When a small number of firms dominate the product market, their market power may carry over into permits markets. One solution is to extend the permits market to include other pollutants or to expand the boundaries of the markets internationally.[9] While expanding the boundaries of the permits market may increase the number of participants and thus the likelihood of price-taking behaviour, it may also aggravate existing product market distortions. In this case, the increase in the efficiency of the allocation of abatement effort may be offset by a reduction in the efficiency in the allocation of production effort.

Inter-industry emissions permits trading

Assume two industries producing goods X and Y. Each industry's emissions are increasing functions of output q_i and decreasing functions of abatement effort, A_i, $e_i = h_i (q_i, A_i)$, $i = X, Y$. The total cost of production is $c_i(q_i, A_i)$, which we assume to be convex in both its elements. Consumers derive utility $u(q_x, q_y)$ from the consumption of the two goods while suffering disutility $v(\Sigma e_i)$ from pollution. Policy makers impose a ceiling on emissions $\bar{E} \le \Sigma e_i$ and they issue an equal amount of permits.[10] Permits are distributed to industries, each receiving l_i, with $\bar{E} = \Sigma l_i$. Given the emissions ceiling, the constrained optimal allocation of resources is achieved through the maximization of social welfare:

$$\max_{q_X, q_Y} W(q_X, q_Y) = u(q_X, q_Y) - v(\bar{E}) - \sum c_i(q_i, A_i)$$

$$\text{subject to: } \bar{E} = \sum h_i(q_i, A_i).$$

Assuming that the second-order conditions are satisfied, the first-order conditions of the constrained maximization problem are:

$$\partial u/\partial q_X = \partial c_X/\partial q_X + \lambda \partial h_X/\partial q_X, \text{ and } \partial u/\partial q_Y = \partial c_Y/\partial q_Y + \lambda \partial h_Y/\partial q_Y, \quad (3.1)$$

$$-\partial c_X/\partial A_X - \lambda \partial h_X/\partial A_X = 0, \text{ and } -\partial c_Y/\partial A_Y - \lambda \partial h_Y/\partial A_Y = 0, \quad (3.2)$$

where λ is the shadow value of the constraint.

Each industry chooses output and abatement effort so as to maximize profits $\Pi_i = p_i q_i - ci(q_i, A_i) - P^e[h_i(q_i, A_i) - l_i]$, where $p_i = \partial u/\partial q_i$, are the product prices and P^e is the permits price. If firms in both industries are price-takers in the permits market, abatement cost minimization is achieved, and the first-order conditions in equation (3.2) are satisfied. If in addition both industries are competitive, the individually rational choice of q_X and q_Y yields the socially optimal allocation of resources, since the first-order conditions in equation (3.1) are also satisfied.

Assume instead that one of the industries, for example Y, is monopolistic. The first-order condition of the monopolist's profit maximization with respect to output is $p_Y + q_Y(\partial p_Y/\partial q_Y) = \partial c_Y/\partial q_Y + \lambda_Y(\partial h_Y/\partial q_Y)$, where λ_Y is the value of the monopolist's emission allowances which is equal to the permit price under permits trading. Subtracting the monopolist's first-order condition from that of the policy maker, we get $-\partial p_Y/\partial q_Y + (\lambda_Y - \lambda)(\partial h_Y/\partial q_Y) = 0$, which is not satisfied when permits markets are competitive, that is, $\lambda_Y = \lambda = P^e$, since $\partial p_Y/\partial q_Y < 0$. A distribution of non-tradable emission allowances that favours the monopolist (yields a shadow value for emission allowances $\lambda_Y < \lambda$) exists that increases social welfare relative to permits trading. The optimal difference between the shadow values of emissions in the two industries depends on the magnitude of the market distortion as well as the technological structure in the two industries. If information on costs and margins in the relevant product markets were readily available to policy makers, a command and control policy could be welfare-superior to permits trading.

A diagrammatical illustration of this result in the absence of abatement is provided by Hung and Sartzetakis (1997) and is replicated here as Figure 3.1. Quantities of goods X and Y are measured in the horizontal and vertical axes respectively. The contour $\bar{E}(q_X, q_Y)$ which depicts the aggregate emissions constraint is assumed strictly concave, while social welfare indifference curves, $W(q_X, q_Y)$ are assumed strictly convex. $W^*(q_X, q_Y)$ is the highest social welfare indifference level attainable under the emissions constraint and corresponds to a unique constrained maximum at the point $A(q_X^e, q_Y^e)$ defined by the solution of the first-order conditions in equation (3.1). At point T, which depicts the output allocation under permits trading, the slope of the social indifference curve is smaller than the slope of the aggregate emissions constraint. The monopolist produces less than the unregulated level of output, $q_Y^t < q_Y^m$. In the no-abatement case illustrated here, the optimal distribution of non-tradable emission allowances is such that $\lambda_Y = 0$, that is, the monopolist does not reduce emissions and produces q_Y^m. This result is independent of the initial allocation of emission permits.

The scenario sketched out above is an example of a second-best problem. Although participation of both industries in a competitive permits market minimizes the sum of their abatement costs, it aggravates the pre-

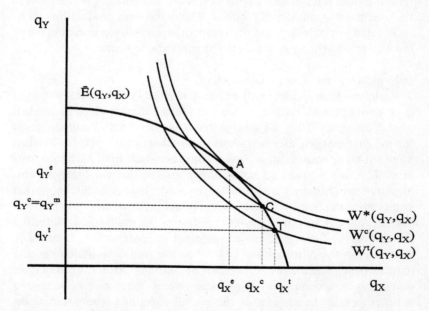

Figure 3.1   *Inefficiency of emissions permits trading within competitive permits markets*

existing product market monopoly problem. Prior to the introduction of the emissions ceiling with permits trading, there are two offsetting distortions: the product market monopoly and the environmental externality. Removal of only one distortion, the environmental externality, may make matters worse. If the product market monopoly cannot be removed, it may be preferable to impose a less stringent source-specific environmental standard on the monopoly industry. Permits trading would then be confined to the competitive industry which would be required to undertake a disproportionate share of the reduction in emissions. The determination of the optimal allocation of abatement effort between the two industries requires knowledge of the magnitude of the monopoly distortion as well as the respective abatement costs of the two industries.

In the simple case in which one industry is a monopoly and one is competitive, the information requirements of the policy maker are arguably quite modest and a source-specific standard-setting policy that allocates the burden of emissions reduction more heavily to the competitive industry is potentially more efficient than a permits trading policy. If one of the industries is oligopolistic while the other is competitive, however, the information requirements increase dramatically. In order to estimate the increase in the output distortion in the oligopolistic industry resulting from inter-industry permits trading, information on all firms in the oligopolistic industry is required. That is because production will be reallocated not only between the competitive and oligopolistic industries but also among the firms within the oligopolistic industry.

Intra-industry emissions permits trading
The analysis here focuses on the allocative effects of the introduction of competitive permits trading within an industry characterized by product market oligopoly. Thus, we assume that while firms act as oligopolists in the product market, they behave as price-takers in the permits market. The post-trade equilibrium has two characteristics: first, marginal costs of abatement are equalized across oligopolists so that the aggregate cost of emissions reduction is minimized; second, there is a shift in market shares from the firms that are more efficient in abatement to the firms that are less efficient in abatement relative to the pre-trade equilibrium. In essence, the firms that are less efficient in abatement become more aggressive in the output market as the acquisition of emission permits reduces their abatement cost per unit of output.[11] This shift in market shares may be accompanied by an increase or a decrease or no change in industry output. In some cases, the overall effect of permits trading on welfare is ambiguous.

To illustrate these points, we begin with the simple case of Cournot duopolists with constant and identical marginal production costs, c, and a linear market demand. Assume further that abatement cost is linear in output and also increases with abatement per unit of output (so that marginal cost is the sum of marginal production cost, c, and abatement cost per unit of output). Let firm 1 be more efficient in abatement than firm 2. Firm 2, which is less efficient in abatement, increases its market share at the expense of firm 1. This is illustrated in Figure 3.2. Points E_1 and E_2 in Figure 3.2 illustrate the pre- and post-trade Cournot equilibria, respectively. At E_1 firm 1 produces more than firm 2. With emissions trading, firm 1 increases its abatement activity, its marginal cost increases and its reaction function shifts in. Firm 2 reduces its abatement activity, its marginal cost decreases and its reaction function shifts out. Firm 1's output decreases while firm 2's increases. At point E_2, firm 1 produces the same output as firm 2 and their combined output is at least equal to the pre-trade level.[12] Under these assumptions, permits trading is unambiguously welfare-increasing. If industry output remains the same, welfare increases because industry-wide abatement costs decrease. If industry output increases, there is a further increase in welfare.

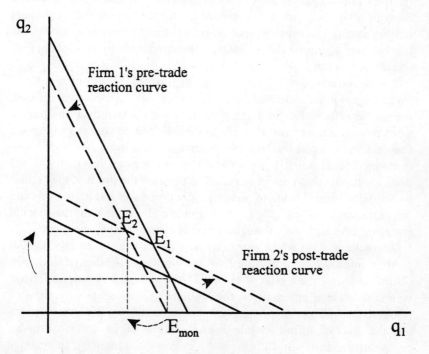

Figure 3.2 Permits trading effect on market shares

Sartzetakis (1997b) derives these results analytically in a framework that differs from the one described above only in assuming that abatement costs are quadratic in both abatement effort and output. With similar assumptions about production and abatement technology, Malueg (1990) has shown that permits trading could be welfare-decreasing. Malueg derives his results using a specification of permits trading that does not yield minimization of industry-wide abatement costs, while he assumes extreme differences in firms' abatement costs. While Malueg's result is a special case, it does point to an important effect of permits trading first noted in Borenstein (1988): namely, that permits trading leads to a redistribution of market shares which, under imperfect competition, could be welfare-decreasing.

The intuition underlying results of this nature is easier to understand in the context of the second-best problem. The Cournot model has the characteristic that efficient firms produce too little relative to inefficient firms, that is, the distribution of output does not minimize the industry-wide cost of production. Under source-specific emissions standards, firms that are less efficient in abatement engage in too much abatement relative to firms that are more efficient in abatement so that industry-wide costs of abatement are not minimized. Introducing emissions permits trading among Cournot oligopolists fixes the abatement allocation problem but may aggravate the output misallocation problem. Removing only one distortion can make things worse.

The introduction of permits trading aggravates the output misallocation problem if, for example, the firms that are less efficient in abatement are also less efficient in production. In this case, the introduction of emissions trading allows firms that are less efficient in production to expand their market share at the expense of firms that are more efficient in production. While industry abatement cost (at a given level of output) declines, production cost increases. The price of the product may either rise or fall. When it leads to higher production costs and higher product prices, permits trading may result in lower welfare than source-specific emissions standards even though it reduces aggregate abatement costs.

There are ways in which emissions permits trading can be modified so as to minimize the importance of inter-industry and intra-industry output redistribution effects. If one of the industries is monopolistic while the other is competitive, the regulator can allocate enough non-tradable permits to the monopoly industry so that it produces its unrestricted level of output, while allowing trade of permits within the competitive industry. In the case of an oligopolistic industry, the regulator could allocate non-tradable permits to the lower-cost producers in the industry. The extra permits decrease the abatement requirements of the more efficient firms and reduce the intra-industry output redistribution effect. Theoretically, these modifications would require only minimal information both in the case of the monopolistic and in the case of the oligopolistic industry.

3.3 MARKET POWER IN BOTH THE PRODUCT AND THE PERMITS MARKETS

We examined above the case in which oligopolists are price-takers in the permits market. We now turn to examine the behaviour of product market oligopolists when they are also the only firms participating in the permits market. In this case, both the product and the permits markets are imperfectly competitive. Permits market power can be used by one or more incumbent firms to decrease product market competition.[13] We examine three types of permits market manipulation by the oligopolists: first, assuming away anti-trust legislation, we consider the role of permits trading in facilitating merger agreements by securing merger profits against potential entry; second, assuming that agreements linking permits sales to production are not permitted, we consider cooperative cost manipulation strategies; third, we consider the role of permits trading in non-cooperative cost manipulation strategies. In all these cases, emissions trading does not achieve the objective of abatement cost minimization.

3.3.1 Collusive Behaviour

Returning to the Cournot duopoly examined above: suppose that before the introduction of permits trading, each firm is required to reduce emissions by a given amount, such that the resulting emissions are $\bar{E}$. Assume that the cost of abatement is an essential component of the total cost of production and the Cournot equilibrium is at point E_2 in Figure 3.2. Industry profits would be higher if the monopoly output were produced. This could be achieved by means of a merger which leaves firm 1 producing at point E_{mon} in Figure 3.2, and firm 2 producing nothing. The merged entity would, however, be vulnerable to the threat of entry.

Assume now that policy makers decide to achieve the emissions ceiling $\bar{E}$, by issuing an equal number of permits, which they allocate entirely to the incumbent firms, that is, $\bar{E} = l_1 + l_2$, where l_i, $i = 1, 2$ is firm 1's endowment of permits. If firm 2 were to sell all its permits to firm 1 and stop producing, the resulting monopoly would be secure against entry since potential entrants have no emissions permits. Assuming a

Cournot duopoly, Fehr (1993) and Requate (1992) have independently derived the conditions under which this strategy of monopolization is profitable. In another paper, Requate (1993) derives the conditions under which the sale of all the emissions permits of one Bertrand competitor to another is a profitable strategy for monopolizing the product market. This strategy is normally welfare-decreasing (the increase in profits is less than the decrease in consumer surplus). In some cases, however, the shift in production from a less to a more efficient firm reduces industry production costs and increases welfare.

Although illustrative of the potential influence of permits trading on product market structure, the discussion above neglects the role of anti-trust authorities. In the case of monopolization, the price of emission permits is contingent on the agreement of the seller of the permits to exit the product market. Anti-trust authorities could challenge such permits contracts, not only when they lead to monopolization, but in any case in which sales of permits are conditioned on a product market outcome.

3.3.2 Cooperative Cost Manipulation Strategies in the Permits Market

Even when trades of permits are not conditional on production decisions, the bargaining process in the permits market may lead to less-competitive outcomes in the product market when the number of participants is small. The reallocation of permits, hence abatement effort, can increase the dispersion of the sum of production and abatement costs and thus increase joint profits. Financial transfers among firms in the permits market can be used as a commitment mechanism to arrive at jointly more favourable outcomes in the product market.

The intuition underlying this subsection of the chapter is that Cournot oligopolists could have incentives to engage in cooperative cost-manipulating strategies. This is modelled as a two-stage process with permits trading occurring in the first stage and production in the second. Two recent papers, by Salant and Shaffer (1996) and Long and Soubeyran (1997), examine these cost manipulation strategies.[14] Assuming that the marginal cost of production is constant and demand is linear, both papers show that industry profits increase as the dispersion of marginal costs increases, keeping industry-wide total cost constant. Whether the dispersion of marginal costs, and thus market shares, is privately optimal depends on the costs of the first-stage actions. Both papers apply their results to emission control policies.[15]

Our discussion of cooperative cost manipulation strategies makes use of the diagrammatic exposition of Fershtman and de Zeeuw (1996). Consider again the case of two Cournot rivals facing a linear demand, operating under constant marginal cost of production and emitting a pollutant at a rate ρ per unit of output. Thus, the firms' emissions are $e_i(q_i) = \rho_i q_i$, $i = 1, 2$. Emissions are regulated under a tradable emissions permits system that grandfathers initially all permits to the two firms, each receiving l_i, $i = 1, 2$. If the firms' emissions exceed their respective allowances, they either engage in abatement or buy more permits. We follow Fershtman and de Zeeuw in assuming linear abatement costs. This facilitates the diagrammatic exposition shown in Figure 3.3. The thicker lines indicate the firms' reaction functions when no abatement is required. Point E_1 is the equilibrium when the permits allocation of each firm is such that neither has to engage in abatement. There is a level of output, $q_i = l_i/\rho_i$, above which firms are required to engage in abatement. This implies an increase in the marginal cost of production which results in an inward shift in each firm's reaction function. Point E_2 is the equilibrium when both firms are required to engage in abatement under the initial allocation of permits. Therefore, each firm's reaction function may exhibit a discontinuity the location of which depends on the initial allocation of permits.

By trading permits, the two firms can manipulate their reaction functions and thus both industry output and the distribution of market

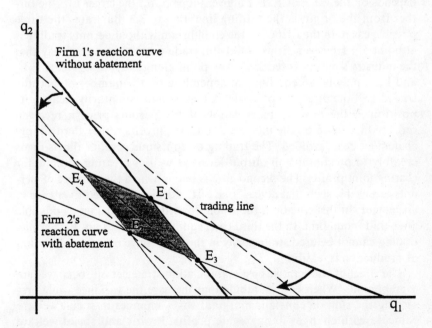

Figure 3.3   Profit-sharing agreements made possible by emissions permits trading

shares. The game is played in two stages; in the first, firms decide on permits trades through a cooperative Nash bargaining process that divides
the gains from trade equally between the two firms; in the second,
the two firms make their output decisions as Cournot duopolists.[16]
Although the firms in the market cannot condition trades of permits on
output outcomes (because of anti-trust considerations), they are aware
that the distribution of permits agreed upon in the first stage affects
their production costs and thus influences the second-stage product
market equilibrium. Therefore, the firms in the market try to use the permits trading process to arrive at a mutually beneficial allocation of
production. The price at which permits are traded in the game's first
stage is such as to facilitate the division of the anticipated increase in
profits resulting from both the restriction and the reallocation of output
in the second stage.

   The aggregate emissions ceiling $\bar{E}$, and the firms' technologies determine the constrained feasible set of trading equilibria. Regulation
requires that $\rho_1 q_1 + \rho_2 q_2 = \bar{E}$, which defines a constraint to possible permits trading equilibria, denoted by the dashed lines in Figure 3.3. The
position of the lines, hereafter called trading lines, relative to the origin
depends on the value of $\bar{E}$. For a given slope ρ_2/ρ_1, the larger is $\bar{E}$ the further from the origin is the trading line. Figure 3.3 illustrates the three
possible cases. In the first case, the equilibrium without permits trading is
at point E_1. However, firms could still trade permits in such a way that
the industry's output is reduced. Any point along the line segments E_1E_3
and E_1E_4 may be an equilibrium depending on the number of permits
traded and the direction of trade. A firm would voluntarily weaken its
position in the product market only if the permits price it received
reflected its share of the increased industry profits rather than simply
abatement costs avoided. The trading of emissions permits allows firms
credibly to precommit on output levels as well as creating a venue for
sharing joint profits. The second case is one in which the number of permits received is such that at least one of the firms is required to engage in
abatement. In this situation, the whole shaded area opens up as possible
after-trade equilibria. In the third case, equilibrium is at point E_2. Permits
trading cannot be used strategically in this case, since no other allocation
of production is feasible.

   The effect of cooperative cost manipulation strategies on social welfare
is ambiguous. When cost manipulations increase the variance while pre-
serving the sum of constant marginal costs, changes in social welfare
coincide with changes in aggregate profits. Profits and social welfare
increase when the decrease in aggregate production costs outweighs the
costs of manipulating production costs. Salant and Shaffer (1996) and

Long and Soubeyran (1997) specify the conditions under which the industry's profits increase. When cost manipulations change the sum of marginal costs, welfare analysis becomes more complex. In the simple case we considered above, following Fershtman and de Zeeuw (1996), the industry's output can decrease, since trades that leave unused permits are allowed. Since the industry's profits increase as output decreases, firms will choose to decrease the industry's output and they will start by decreasing the less-efficient firm's output. In this case, the inefficiency of reducing output contrasts the better allocation of production among firms. However, if larger reductions in output can be achieved by shifting production to the less-efficient firm then the inefficiency created by strategic actions in the permits market increases. Note that in all these cases the industry does not use all its emissions permits, which implies that the environmental quality improves further than the policy target. Therefore, the effect on social welfare depends on the emission damage function and the abatement and production technologies.

3.3.3 Non-cooperative Cost Manipulation Strategies in the Permits Market

In this subsection we examine cases in which one firm can influence the permits price by its purchases or sales of permits, while all other firms are price-takers in the permits market. The firm with power in the permits market, hereafter called the leader, can either use its power within the permits market to reduce its costs of compliance with the emissions standard (by reducing the price of permits) or use its advantage in the permits market to improve its position in the product market.

When the leader's motivation is permit cost minimization, its behaviour depends on its marginal cost of abatement. If its marginal cost of abatement is high (low) relatively to the other firms, it is a buyer (seller) of permits and thus it acts as a monopsonist (monopolist). In the former case the leader buys too few permits while in the latter case it buys too many permits relative to the efficient solution.[17] In both cases the number of transactions is limited and abatement cost minimization is not achieved, while the leader enjoys a higher share of the industry's profits.

The ability of the leader to use its power depends on the initial distribution of permits. When the leader acts as monopolist (monopsonist), the larger (smaller) its endowment of permits the greater will be the distortion in the allocation of abatement effort among firms, that is, the greater the inefficiency. This means that the initial allocation of permits is a powerful instrument for controlling the leader's power. If policy makers have sufficient information, they can eliminate the leader's advantage by the appropriate allocation of permits.

The permits market leader can also use its power in the permits market strategically in an attempt to increase its market share in the product market. Emission permits can be considered as an input with a fixed, exogenously determined supply. Each firm can substitute away from permits by engaging in abatement, which is costly. Since the amount and cost of abatement depend on output, decisions in the product and permits markets are linked. By affecting the permits price, the permits market leader affects its rivals' production costs and thus their market shares. This analysis is an extension of the concept of raising rivals' cost strategies to the emissions permits markets.[18]

To illustrate the effects of the strategic use of the permits market leader's power, we continue using the example of a Cournot duopoly. Figure 3.4 illustrates the effect of permits price manipulation on the permits market. Each firm's opportunity cost of permits equals its marginal abatement cost and thus firm i's demand for permits is given by its marginal abatement cost (MCA_i). The marginal cost of abatement increases as firms reduce emissions. For simplicity, we assume that the MCAs of both firms have the same slope but that they have different intercepts. The hori-

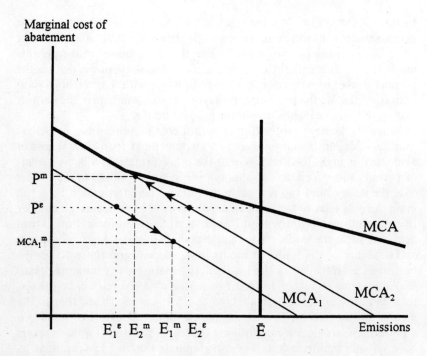

Figure 3.4   Permits price manipulation

zontal summation of the two firms' demands for permits is the market demand for permits. As before, we assume that all permits are distributed to the two firms in the market so that the supply of permits, $\bar{E}$, is perfectly inelastic. Under perfect competition in the permits market, the permits price would be P^e. Assuming that firm 1 is the leader in the permits market, it sets a price higher than the competitive permits price, P^m by holding more permits ($E_1^m - E_1^e$). It does that either by buying permits if its endowment is less than E_1^m or by asking for a high price when it is a seller of permits. The price-taker (follower) is forced to engage in a higher level of abatement while the leader undertakes less abatement relative to the efficient allocation. Since the leader's marginal cost of abatement is not equal to the permits price, the industry's abatement costs are not minimized.

Permits price manipulation also results in a change in industry output as well as a change in product market shares and profits. This is illustrated in Figure 3.5. The thicker lines depict each firm's reaction function when the permits market is perfectly competitive, while the thinner reaction functions reflect each firm's higher compliance costs under leadership. As a result of the higher permits price, both firms' marginal costs increase and thus their reaction functions are shifted inwards. However, the increase in the leader's marginal cost is smaller so that its

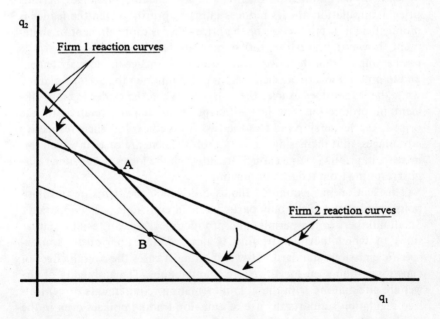

Figure 3.5   Product market shares under leadership

product market share increases. The product market equilibrium with competition in the permits market is at point A in Figure 3.5 while point B is the product market equilibrium under permits market price leadership. Figure 3.5 depicts a situation in which the increase in the price-taker's cost is so large relative to the leader that the leader not only increases its market share but also the volume of its production relative to the case of permits market competition. The extent to which the leader can increase its market share depends on its production and abatement efficiency relative to the price-taker.[19]

We now turn to the examination of the effect of permits market leadership on social welfare. Leadership in the permits market distorts the allocation of abatement effort between firms as well as both reallocating and changing the level of production. We have seen that the allocation of production when there is competition in the permits market is not efficient so that the output reallocation resulting from permits market price leadership might increase the industry's profits. The increase in profits might outweigh the losses in consumer surplus resulting from the restriction in industry output and lead to an overall increase in social welfare. Sartzetakis (1997a) finds that the change in industry profits depends on the abatement and production technologies of the firms in the market. When firms have similar production and abatement technologies, permits price manipulation always reduces industry profits. When the leader is more efficient in production or the price-taker is more efficient in abatement, however, industry profits increase. Leadership in the permits market implies that the price-taker is forced to engage in more abatement and to produce less than when there is competition in the permits market, while the leader does exactly the opposite. When the leader is more efficient in production but less efficient in abatement relative to the price-taker, leadership induces the two firms to exploit their respective advantages, thus increasing industry profits. There are cases in which this increase in profits is large enough to outweigh the losses in consumer surplus resulting from reduced production.

This section has examined the case in which the firms in an oligopolistic industry are the only participants in emissions permits markets. Small numbers in the permits and product markets can result in situations in which permits trading is not welfare-superior to source-specific emissions standards. However, in most cases the overall effect of emissions trading on social welfare is ambiguous. The ambiguity of the welfare effect along with the high information requirements of centralized regulation supports the use of emission trading policies even in the presence of market power.

3.4 CONCLUSIONS

Emissions trading is gathering increasing support among economists as well as policy makers mainly because in its idealized 'frictionless' form it has been shown to allocate abatement effort efficiently among sources of emissions while requiring relatively little information. Recently, however, the economics literature has identified a number of potential impediments to the efficient operation of emission permits markets. In this chapter we have examined the effects that 'frictions' associated with either product or permits market imperfections may have on both the efficiency of permits trading and the allocation of market shares among firms participating in the permits market.

We identify a number of ways in which the efficient allocation of abatement effort can be distorted when competition is imperfect. First, if only intra-industry permits trading is allowed, we have two possible cases. On the one hand, if one firm can dominate the permits market it has the option of either exploiting its power within the permits market (acting as a monopolist/monopsonist) or of extending its permits market power into the product market. On the other hand, if no one firm can dominate the permits market, permits trading can nevertheless facilitate agreements that increase joint profits by reducing competition in the product market. Second, if inter-industry trades are allowed and the permits market is competitive, a more efficient allocation of resources may not be achieved as long as one of the industries has an imperfectly competitive product market. The reason is that removal of an environmental externality while leaving an offsetting product market distortion in place may make matters worse.

Our focus on the potential limitations in the efficiency of permits trading does not imply a preference for source-specific standards over emission-permits trading. The reason is that source-specific standards are more efficient than permits trading only if the regulators have full knowledge of the respective abatement costs of all sources of emissions. With even limited information, however, permits trading regimes can be modified so as to mitigate many of the sources of inefficiency identified above. Thus, policy makers can enhance efficiency by using the available information to modify trading programmes when necessary rather than implementing source-specific standards regulations. Given limited information, permits trading is generally the superior regulatory instrument.

NOTES

We should like to thank James Boyd for helpful comments and suggestions on an earlier draft. We should also like to acknowledge financial support from the Ontario Natural Gas

Association in developing an earlier version of this chapter. E.S. Sartzetakis wishes to acknowledge financial support from SSHRC: 412-93-0005, ERA: Financing and Competitive Issues and UCC's Assisted Leave and Scholarly Activity Committees.

1.   See, for example, Hahn and Hester (1989) and Hahn and Noll (1983).
2.   See Tripp and Dudek (1989) and Stavins (1995).
3.   See Keeler (1991) and Egteren and Weber (1996).
4.   See Bohi and Burtraw (1992) and Laplante *et al.* (1997).
5.   In addition there are distributional issues associated with the initial allocation of permits. For example, Hausker (1992) discusses the political debate involved in the distribution of the sulphur dioxide (SO_2) permits under the 1990 Clean Air Act Amendments (CAAA).
6.   See Montgomery (1972).
7.   Assuming that the abatement cost functions are convex in the relevant range.
8.   The intuition underlying this powerful result is easier to grasp if the case in which the marginal abatement costs are not equalized across sources of emissions is considered. Marginal abatement costs are not equalized if the last dollar spent on abatement yields a greater reduction in emissions at source A than at source B. In this case, spending one dollar more on abatement at A and one dollar less at B reduces emissions at A by more than it increases emissions at B. Thus, reallocation between A and B of the same total abatement expenditure reduces their combined emissions. For a proof of this result in the case of taxation, see Baumol and Oates (1988: 165–9).
9.   Interpollutant trading has been suggested in Canada (1992). The possibility explored involves trading of permits allowing the emission of either sulphur dioxide (SO_2) or nitrogen oxide (NO_x), both of which contribute to the acid rain problem.
10.   Throughout the chapter we assume that regulators choose a fixed emissions ceiling. Alternatively, regulators might define the aggregate target based on a level of emissions that is normalized on a per-unit basis.
11.   In this chapter we concentrate on the effect that permits trading could have on firms' decisions concerning output levels and thus we ignore fixed costs. If fixed costs associated with abatement were considered, exit conditions under certain aggregate emission ceilings could be derived.
12.   In a Cournot oligopoly with a fixed number of firms and constant marginal costs, industry-wide output depends only on the sum of the respective marginal costs of the firms in the industry. Permits trading always decreases aggregate abatement costs but it could either decrease or leave unchanged the sum of marginal abatement costs. Thus, industry-wide output could either remain the same or increase as a result of permits trading.
13.   The manner in which market power is exercised depends on the particular market structure, the technological structure of the industry and the initial distribution of permits.
14.   For prior related work, see Dixit (1986) and Bergstrom and Varian (1985).
15.   Salant and Shaffer (1996) consider policy makers' optimal allocation of abatement effort under command and control policies, while Long and Soubeyran (1997) consider firms' emission permits trading within a cooperative Nash bargaining game that precedes the non-cooperative Cournot–Nash production game.
16.   Long and Soubeyran (1997) consider the same game within a different technological structure.
17.   Hahn (1984) first pointed to the importance of market power in the permits markets by examining the monopoly–monopsony cases. Misiolek and Elder (1987) developed a diagrammatical illustration of Hahn's arguments.
18.   See Salop and Scheffmann (1983, 1987); and Krattenmaker and Salop (1985, 1986, 1987). Recent contributions include Hart and Tirole (1990); Ordover *et al.* (1990); Gaudet and Long (1993).
19.   For more details, see Sartzetakis (1994).

REFERENCES

Baumol, W.J. and W.E. Oates (1988), *The Theory of Environmental Policy*, 2nd edn, Cambridge: Cambridge University Press.

Bergstrom, T. and H. Varian (1985), 'When are Nash equilibria independent of the distribution of agents' characteristics?', *Review of Economic Studies*, **52**, 715–18.

Bohi, D.R. and D. Burtraw (1992), 'Utility investment behaviour and the emission trading market', *Resources and Energy*, **14**, 129–53.

Borenstein, S. (1988), 'On the efficiency of competitive markets for operating licenses', *Quarterly Journal of Economics*, **103**, 357–87.

Buchanan, J. (1969), 'External diseconomies, correction taxes and market structure', *American Economic Review*, **59**, 174–7.

Canada (1992), *Economic Instruments for Environmental Protection*, Discussion paper, Canada's Green Plan. Ottawa: Minister of Supply and Services.

Dixit, A.K. (1986), 'Comparative statics for oligopoly', *International Economic Review*, **27**, 107–22.

Egteren, H. van and M. Weber (1996), 'Marketable permits, market power, and cheating', *Journal of Environmental Economics and Management*, **30**, 161–73.

Fehr, N.-H.M. von der (1993), 'Tradeable emission rights and strategic interaction', *Environmental and Resource Economics*, **3**, 129–51.

Fershtman, C. and A. de Zeeuw (1996), 'Transferable emission permits in oligopoly', CentER, Tilburg University, Netherlands, mimeo.

Gaudet, G. and N.V. van Long (1993), 'Vertical integration, foreclosure and profits in the presence of double marginalization', Université du Quebec à Montréal.

Hahn, R.W. (1984), 'Market power and transferable property rights', *Quarterly Journal of Economics*, **99**, 753–65.

Hahn R.W. and G.L. Hester (1989), 'Where did all the markets go? An analysis of EPA's emission trading program', *Yale Journal of Regulation*, **6**, 109–53.

Hahn R.W. and R.G. Noll (1983), 'Barriers to implementing tradable air pollution permits: problems of regulatory interaction', *Yale Journal of Regulation*, **1**, 63–91.

Hart, O. and J. Tirole (1990), 'Vertical integration, foreclosure and profits in the presence of double marginalization', *Brookings Papers on Economic Activity: Microeconomics*, **4**, 205–86.

Hausker, K. (1992), 'The politics and economics of auction design in the market for sulfur dioxide pollution', *Journal of Policy Analysis and Management*, **11**, 553–72.

Hung, M.N. and E.S. Sartzetakis (1997), 'Cross-industry emission permits trading', *Journal of Regulatory Economics*, **13**, 37–46.

Keeler, A.G. (1991), 'Noncompliant firms in transferable discharge permit markets: some extensions', *Journal of Environmental Economics and Management*, **21**, 180–89.

Krattenmaker, T.G. and S.C. Salop (1985), 'Anticompetitive exclusion: raising rivals' costs to achieve power over price', *Yale Law Journal*, **96**, 209–95.

Krattenmaker, T.G. and S.C. Salop (1986), 'Competition and cooperation in the markets to exclusionary rights', *American Economic Review, Papers and Proceedings*, **16**, 109–13.

Krattenmaker, T.G. and S.G. Salop (1987), 'Analysing anticompetitive exclusion', *Antitrust Law Journal*, **56**, 71–89.

Laplante, B., E.S. Sartzetakis and A. Xepapadeas (1997), 'Strategic behaviour of polluters during the transition from standard-setting to permits trading', Fondazione Eni Enrico Mattei, Nota di Lavoro 43.97.

Long, Ngo van and A. Soubeyran (1997), 'Cost manipulation in oligopoly: a duality approach', Department of Economics, McGill University, mimeo.

Malueg, D.A. (1990), 'Welfare consequences of emission credit trading programs', *Journal of Environmental Economics and Management*, **19**, 66–77.

Misiolek, W.S. and H.A. Elder (1987), 'Exclusionary manipulation of markets for pollution rights', *Journal of Environmental Economics and Management*, **16**, 156–66.

Montgomery, W.D. (1972), 'Markets for licenses and pollution control', *Journal of Economic Theory*, **5**, 395–418.

Ordover, J.A., G. Saloner and S.C. Salop (1990), 'Equilibrium vertical foreclosure', *American Economic Review*, **80**, 127–42.

Owen, N., A. Pototschnig and Z. Biro (1992), 'The potential role of market mechanisms in the control of acid rain', Research Report, London Economics, London: HMSO.

Requate, T. (1992), 'Permits or taxes? How to regulate Cournot duopoly with polluting firms', California Institute of Technology, Social Science working paper 792.

Requate, T. (1993), 'Pollution control under imperfect competition: asymmetric Bertrand duopoly with linear technologies', *Journal of Institutional and Theoretical Economics*, **149**, 415–42.

Salant, S.W. and G. Shaffer (1996), 'Unequal treatment of identical agents in Cournot equilibrium: private and social advantages', paper presented at the First International Conference in Industrial Economics, Universidad Carlos II de Madrid.

Salop, S.C. and D.T. Scheffman (1983), 'Raising rivals' costs', *American Economic Review, Papers and Proceedings*, **73**, 267–71.

Salop, S.C. and D.T. Scheffman (1987), 'Cost-raising strategies', *Journal of Industrial Economics*, **26**, 19–34.

Sartzetakis, E.S. (1994), 'Permits d'émission négotiables et réglementation dans des marchés de concurrence imparfaite', *L'Actualité économique*, **70**, 139–58.

Sartzetakis, E.S. (1997a), 'Raising rivals' costs strategies via emission permits markets', *Review of Industrial Organization*, **12**, 751–65.

Sartzetakis, E.S. (1997b), 'Tradeable emission permits regulations in the presence of imperfectly competitive product markets: welfare implications', *Environmental and Resource Economics*, **9**, 65–81.

Stavin R.N. (1995), 'Transaction costs and tradable permits', *Journal of Environmental Economics and Management*, **29**, 133–48.

Tripp, J.T.B. and D.J. Dudek (1989), 'Institutional guidelines for designing successful transferable rights programs', *Yale Journal of Regulation*, **6**, 369–91.

4. Experimental tests of market power in emission trading markets

Robert W. Godby, Stuart Mestelman and R. Andrew Muller

4.1 INTRODUCTION

The welfare benefits of emission trading programmes – the potential to minimize the aggregate cost of pollution control – seem clear. Several lines of research, however, cast doubt on the extent to which the benefits from emission trading can be realized. One line is represented by Oates (1995), who argues that introducing a market in emission rights might induce net welfare losses to the economy at large because exacerbation of pre-existing distortions in labour or capital markets could offset the gains in the emission markets alone. The second line of research addresses the effects of market power in the emerging markets for emission rights or in their related markets (Hahn 1984; Tietenberg 1985; Misiolek and Elder 1989). Market power may be of concern for at least two reasons. First, attempts to exploit market power will reduce the efficiency of emission permit markets, leading to lower gains than projected using theories of competitive markets. It is even possible that emissions trading could lead to net welfare losses if imperfections in emission permit markets are exploited to gain monopoly power in related product markets. Second, the exploitation of market power may alter the distribution of gains from emissions trading in a way that would reduce political support for it. This research underlies some objections made to emission trading during policy debates.[1]

Discussions of emissions trading generally fail to consider the market institutions under which trade will be conducted. Theorists have identified a great variety of these institutions. In a posted-offer market, each seller announces a single price–quantity combination and then buyers choose the quantity to purchase from each seller. In a posted-bid market the roles are reversed. In an English auction multiple buyers continuously offer rising bids for a single item until no further bids are forthcoming, at which point the single seller accepts the highest bid. In a Dutch auction the single seller makes continuously falling offers (asks) until one of the multiple buyers accepts. In a double auction buyers and sellers continuously make rising bids or falling asks until one side of the market accepts the outstanding bid or ask. In a call market supply and demand schedules are determined from price–quantity combinations submitted by buyers or sellers. When the market is called, successful buyers and sellers are matched and the price determined by some rule. Many other variants are possible.

It is by now well established that market institutions can have a marked effect on the market's efficiency. A theory's predictions may be validated under one institution but not in another. Thus, before deciding whether to implement an emissions trading system on the basis of theory alone, it is useful to investigate its performance in a more realistic, yet simple and controlled environment such as that provided by laboratory experiments. Laboratory methods in economics have proven successful both in testing basic economic theories and in *testbedding* specific policy proposals to determine those that appear best suited for a particular application. Flaws in proposed designs can be uncovered and corrected before implementation in the field, where such adjustments may require much greater expense (see reviews by Plott 1989 and Holt 1995).

In this chapter we review the considerable body of experimental literature which bears on the issue of market power in emissions trading markets. We begin with a brief introduction to laboratory methods and then review the results of a number of studies of market power in general. We then briefly review the economic theory of market power in emissions trading markets before finally turning to laboratory studies of market power in the specific context of emissions trading. We focus on two issues. First, what is known about the effect of trading institutions on the *actual* emergence of market power in those cases where it is *theoretically* possible for market power to emerge? Second, will market power emerge behaviourally in a laboratory environment that captures critical features of an emission trading programme when a single firm dominates the industry? Our goal is to determine whether there are known methods of organizing markets and designing trading institutions that will minimize the potential for exploitation of market power in emission trading markets and to provide direction for future research.

4.2 LABORATORY ECONOMICS[2]

Over the past 30 years laboratory experimentation has emerged as a substantial and vigorous subdiscipline of economics. Smith and Williams

(1992) provide a non-technical overview of the field. The current state of the discipline is well presented in Kagel and Roth (1995) and Davis and Holt (1993).

Experiments are conducted with human subjects, usually university undergraduates. There are many types of laboratory experiments in economics; here we concentrate on market experiments. Typically about eight to twelve subjects are recruited for each market session. At the beginning of each session, participants are instructed about the rules of the experiment and assigned roles as buyers, sellers or traders. Usually they are told they will be participating in a market for an abstract product in which they are to act either as buyer or seller. The session is divided into decision rounds or periods. In each round, buyers purchase the product in the experimental market and redeem it from the experimenter in return for laboratory money (lab dollars). They are given a schedule indicating the value of each coupon redeemed in the given period. For example, the first unit may be redeemed for 100 lab dollars, the second for 50 lab dollars, the third for 45 lab dollars, and so on. The buyer's profit on each unit is the difference between its redemption value and the price actually paid to the seller. Sellers incur a cost to acquire the product and gain revenue by selling it in the experimental market. They are given marginal cost schedules indicating what each unit they sell costs them and compute their profit as the difference between the selling price and the marginal cost of that unit. Trading may be done orally with manual record keeping, or it may be mediated by computer programs of varying complexity and sophistication. In most of the experiments reported here, subjects entered bids and offers for units at a computer terminal. At the end of a session, subjects' earnings are converted from lab dollars to local currencies at a previously announced exchange rate and the subjects are paid privately in cash. A typical undergraduate may earn about $30 for a two-hour session, well above the minimum wage.

Trading institutions and the redemption and cost schedules can be manipulated to test various hypotheses or testbed the performance of certain institutions. Price and quantity outcomes in laboratory markets can be compared to *a priori* predictions to determine the extent to which market performance conformed to expectations and the success of the traders in capturing gains from trade in the laboratory environment, since if economic theories are truly generally applicable they should also apply in the controlled laboratory environment.

One cardinal principle in experimental economics is to pay subjects sufficiently well to ensure that their decisions are motivated by market payoffs. Usually this is interpreted as providing potential remuneration well above the opportunity cost of the subjects' time. This has promoted the use of student subjects, since the opportunity cost of their time is less than that of employed adults, especially senior decision makers. The use of student subjects has been criticized on the grounds that they are unlikely to participate in the market in the same way that participants in field markets would. Fortunately, the experimental evidence shows little effect of subject pool on the outcome of market experiments (Davis and Holt 1993: 16–17). Moreover, if a particular hypothesis such as the emergence of market power is supported when using relatively unsophisticated student subjects, it is reasonable to presume that actual market traders would exploit such opportunities that may arise.

A second cardinal principle in experimental economics is never to deceive the subjects. All the rules of the experiment are announced in advance and followed strictly. The experimenters' interpretation of the data, however, may be different from the subjects'. For example, subjects are not usually told that the units they are trading represent permits to emit pollutants. In this way experimenters hope to avoid biases induced by the nature of the commodity being traded.

4.3   MARKET POWER IN THE LABORATORY

Laboratory studies have shown that market power is severely constrained by market institutions. For example, in posted-offer markets a single seller is usually able to maintain prices well above competitive levels, while in double-auction markets buyers quickly discover the monopolist's willingness to sell some units at low prices. Consequently, they withhold demand to force price reductions, resulting in outcomes much closer to the competitive level. The effect of market institution on exploitation of market power has been demonstrated in two experimental contexts: in pure monopoly or duopoly markets in which market power is created by limiting the number of sellers (or buyers) and in dominant firm markets in which it is profitable for some sellers to reduce the number of trades they engage in, thereby driving prices away from competitive levels.

The leading experiments in pure monopoly and duopoly environments were conducted by Smith (1981) and by Smith and Williams (1989). Smith compared the outcomes of double-auction, offer-auction and posted-bid markets with a single seller and posted-bid markets with two sellers using common demand and supply parameters. The efficient price (expected under perfect or Bertrand price competition) was $0.80, while the monopoly price (expected when market power is fully exploited) was $1.10. Standard economic theory suggests that the monopoly outcome should occur in single-seller markets, regardless of the trading rules used.

Table 4.1 shows that this was not the case. In a single-seller posted-offer market the monopolist was able to raise prices until they converged to the monopoly price and to maintain them for the rest of the session.[3] In the double-auction, offer-auction and posted-bid sessions, however, the single seller could only realize a small fraction (12.8 per cent to 30.9 per cent) of the potential increase in prices. Prices in the two-seller posted-bid market, however, approached the single-seller outcomes under the other institutions. Clearly, the pricing outcome depends on the type of trading institution used, with the double-auction and posted-bid markets showing the most potential for constraining market power.[4]

Smith and Williams (1989) further investigated the sensitivity of market outcomes to the number of sellers by comparing monopoly and duopoly outcomes in double-auction markets. Table 4.1 shows that all of their markets resulted in prices very close to the competitive price. Their work further demonstrates the resistance of double auctions to monopoly pricing. The mean final period market price calculated over five sessions implies that sellers were able to achieve only 6.6 per cent of the potential price increase.[5] Increasing the number of sellers to two resulted in competitive outcomes in the final period.[6]

A second set of experiments, summarized in Table 4.2, has investigated the emergence of market power in dominant firm markets. Holt *et al.* (1986) introduced a supply and demand configuration in which, due to their lower production costs, two of five sellers have the potential to realize market power by withholding output from buyers.[7] In effect, this action would shift the supply curve leftward, and result in an equilibrium price greater than the competitive level. Holt *et al.* observe this effect in three of five sessions in which sellers have market power. Over these three sessions, prices converged at about 8 per cent above competitive levels, compared to a 9.6 per cent increase predicted by theory. Davis and Williams (1991) replicate these results and also compare the performance of posted-offer and double-auction institutions using the same market design. They replicate the Holt *et al.* finding of supra-competitive prices in all of their double-auction markets (across the double auctions, prices converged to levels approximately 12 per cent higher than the competitive level). The prices in the posted-offer environments consistently converge to significantly higher levels than those found in the double auctions.[8]

Sbriglia and O'Higgins (1996) consider further the type of market power described by Holt *et al.* and Davis and Williams. They modify the Holt *et al.* design to sharpen the cost differences between sellers with and without market power and conduct four double-auction and six posted-offer markets to determine if the market power outcomes indicated in the previous experiments are robust to this parameteriza-

Table 4.1 Institutional performance in experiments where market power is caused by limiting the number of sellers[a]

Author	Trading institution	Number of sellers	Number of buyers	Number of sessions	Percentage deviation between competitive and monopoly price predictions[b]	Percentage of mean price deviation from competitive price (last period)[c]	Percentage of monopoly price increase attained (last period)[d]
Smith (1981)	Double auction	1	5	3	37.5	9.3	24.8
	Posted offer	1	5	1	37.5	37.6	100.2
	Posted offer	2	5	1	37.5	8.5	22.7
	Posted bid	1	5	3	37.5	4.8	12.8
	Offer auction	1	5	1	37.5	11.6	30.9
Smith and Williams (1989)	Double auction	2	5	1	7.9	0.8	10.2
	Double auction	2	6	1	9.1	0	0
	Double auction	2	10	2	4.8	-0.5	10.4
	Double auction	1	5	1	7.9	0	0
	Double auction	1	5	4	4.8	0.4	8.3

Notes
[a] All data taken from original articles.
[b] The absolute deviations between competitive and monopoly price predictions are the same in the Smith (1981) and Smith and Williams (1989) papers. In the latter experiment, redemption and cost schedules were displaced by a constant amount to create different nominal equilibrium prices across sessions. This is reflected in the different percentage deviations.
[c] Percentages reported have been calculated using the mean of the average prices reported for the last period in cases where more than one session was conducted.
[d] Calculated using previous data from previous two columns.

Table 4.2 *Institutional performance in experiments where market power is caused by the incentive for sellers to restrain trading activity*

Author	Number of double auction sessions	Number of posted-offer sessions	Difference between competitive and monopoly prices (%)	Double-auction markets		Posted-offer markets	
				Number of sessions with supra-competitive prices	Mean price deviation from competitive level (%)	Number of sessions with supra-competitive prices	Mean price deviation from competitive level (%)
Holt et al. (1986)[a]	5	0	9.6	3	7.7	0	Not applicable
Davis and Williams (1991)[a,c]	4	4	9.6	4	12.0	4	21
Sbriglia and O'Higgins (1996)[b,c]	4	6	0–200 30.0	4	5.0	4	19

Notes

[a] Competitive price is 260, monopoly price is 285. Davis and Williams use the same design as Holt et al. but displace the redemption and cost schedules to vary the equilibrium price across sessions. The results are normalized and reported to be comparable.

[b] Authors used two designs, both with a competitive price of 500, one with monopoly price range from above 500 to 1500, the other with monopoly price of 700.

[c] Estimated final period average price deviation from competitive price useing charted data included in the original article.

tion change or whether the severity of such outcomes is reduced by the use of double auctions instead of posted-offer markets. They found that the double auction appears to be more resistant to market power than the previous experiments of this sort indicated, with prices closer to the competitive level in three of four sessions. Using econometric analysis, they conclude that all of their double auctions appear to be converging to competitive outcomes.[9] Posted-offer markets, however, continued to exhibit strong market-power pricing, comparable in degree to those found in Davis and Williams. Convergence analysis of the data from these markets indicated at least four of the six markets were converging to non-competitive outcomes.

The data presented in Tables 4.1 and 4.2 indicate that monopoly and duopoly sellers are usually able to raise prices above competitive levels, but that posted-offer markets regularly result in greater increases than are found in double-auction markets. This appears especially true in posted-offer markets with a single seller. Most commentators ascribe the pro-competitive properties of the double auction to the extra power it delivers to the buying side. Thus Holt (1995: 398) concludes that 'market power that results from capacity constraints or shopping costs can produce supra-competitive prices reliably in posted-offer auctions' and 'sellers are sometimes able to exercise market power in double auctions, but the influence of seller market power is much weaker (in the double auction) because of the incentives to offer last-minute price concessions and the more active role that buyers have in this institution'. Plott (1989) similarly argues that in the double auction there is a countervailing buyer's market power at work which Porter (1991) attributes to the sequential nature of this trading institution. Since the monopolist cannot precommit to the monopoly price as trading progresses, it lowers its price when gains from trade still exist at the end of a trading period. As these price reductions become public knowledge, in succeeding periods more buyers wait for the price reductions, causing the monopolist's market power to be eroded further, as it may be more profitable for the monopolist to make some sales at competitive prices than no sales at all. This behaviour is discussed further in Godby (1999).

In summary, experimental economic evidence clearly indicates that the success with which market power opportunities are exploited depends on the trading rules employed in the market. Posted-price markets seem to allow the greatest opportunity to exploit market power. Double-auction markets seem to resist the exercise of market power, whether the opportunity is created by a limited number of sellers in the market or is due to cost and capacity advantages of dominant firms. In general, it seems that market power is most successfully deterred in those institutions that do not allow firms to precommit to their price and quantity offerings.[10]

4.4 SIMPLE ANALYTICS OF MARKET POWER IN EMISSION PERMIT MARKETS[11]

4.4.1 Introduction

Experimental tests of market power in emissions trading markets have generally been based on the models of simple manipulation and exclusionary manipulation developed by Hahn (1984) and Misiolek and Elder (1989) respectively. We provide a simple graphical exposition of the two models before reviewing laboratory tests.

We shall distinguish between command-and-control regulation and emissions trading. There are, of course, many ways to implement command-and-control regulation. In our stylized model, however, we shall consider only methods in which a regulator defines a total allowable discharge (a cap) for a specified group of firms and divides this target into discharge permits assigning the right to emit a specified quantity of emissions to individual polluters. Command-and-control regulation and market-based regulation will then differ only in whether or not the initial distribution of permits may be reallocated among firms through mutually agreed-upon trades. Unless the initial assignment minimizes the system cost of abatement, firms with lower marginal abatement costs will have an incentive to sell their permits to those with higher marginal abatement costs. This will be permitted under emissions trading but not under command-and-control regulation.

When incentives to trade exist, some firms will be net sellers of permits while others will be net buyers. Since the cost-minimizing allocation of permits is independent of the initial distribution, a firm's role as seller or buyer is determined exclusively by this initial distribution. Market power can arise when the initial allocation results in only one or a few net sellers or one or a few net buyers. Note that this can only occur when the initial allocation of permits does not minimize system abatement costs. In the examples that follow, market power may be realized by only one firm, who may be either a monopolist or a monopsonist in the market for emission permits.[12]

4.4.2 Simple Manipulation (Hahn 1984)

Consider Figure 4.1, in which a single firm (the monopolist) is a net seller of permits. The vertical axis indicates the price of a permit and the horizontal axis indicates the quantity of permits purchased from the monopolist by a group of small price-taking firms. The monopolist faces

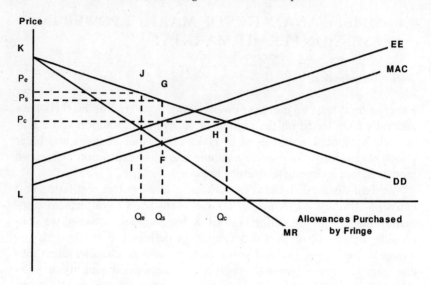

Figure 4.1   Simple and exclusionary manipulation by a monopolist in the allowance market

a derived demand for permits by the small firms, indicated by the line DD. It also faces a marginal opportunity cost of permit sales equal to its own marginal abatement cost (given by the line MAC).

The efficient (competitive) solution occurs if the monopolist does not attempt to influence the market price and sells permits at the price at which DD and MAC intersect. In equilibrium, Q_c units are sold at the price P_c. The efficiency gain over the initial command-and-control assignment is given by the area of triangle HKL. For all firms, price equals marginal abatement cost. No additional gains from trade are possible.

If the monopolist recognizes that the price it receives for permits depends on the quantity it sells, it will select the quantity at which its marginal revenue schedule (MR in Figure 4.1) intersects its marginal abatement cost schedule MAC. The resulting price is P_s (greater than P_c) and the quantity of permits sold is Q_s (less than Q_c). The monopolist sells fewer permits to keep price and profit higher than in the efficient outcome. Relative to the efficient outcome, the monopolist is emitting too much pollution and the small firms are emitting too little. The loss to society, relative to the efficient outcome, is indicated by triangle HGF. Note, however, that relative to the command-and-control outcome, there remains a net welfare gain given by the area LKGF.

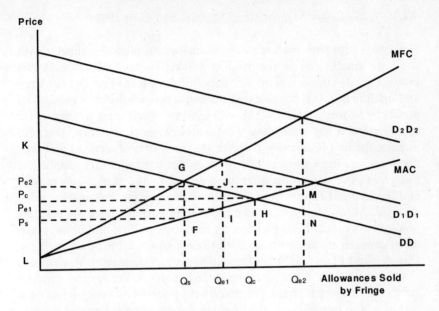

Figure 4.2   Simple and exclusionary manipulation by a monopsonist in the allowance market

Figure 4.2 describes the simple manipulation outcome in the market if the firm with market power is a monopsonist in the permit market. Note the horizontal axis now describes the number of permits purchased by the monopsonist from the small firms. As before, the derived demand for permits is given by the line DD; however, it is now derived from the abatement cost each permit saves the monopsonist. The supply curve of permits (denoted MAC) is the horizontal summation of the marginal abatement cost curves of the small firms. The efficient equilibrium is at Q_c and price P_c, with associated efficiency gain over the command-and-control assignment shown by the area HKL. If it recognizes that MFC reflects its marginal factor cost (associated with the average factor cost schedule MAC), the monopsonist can increase its profit by buying the monopsony output Q_s (where its marginal factor cost, MFC, equals its marginal benefit, DD) at the monopsony price P_s. Note that both the monopsony price and quantity traded are less than the competitive levels. The monopsony equilibrium represents a welfare improvement of area KLFG relative to the command-and-control allocation and a welfare loss of area FGH relative to the efficient outcome.

4.4.3   Exclusionary Manipulation (Misiolek and Elder 1989)

Suppose a firm with market power in the permit market competes with the same small firms in the product market (the manufacture of this product creates the emissions whose permits are traded among the large and small firms). It is possible that the market-power firm can increase its profits by hoarding permits. This will force the small firms to abate more of their emissions than they would otherwise do. In turn, this will increase the unit production costs for the small firms. Increased unit production costs force the small firms to reduce their quantity supplied at any given price. Given the quantity supplied by the market-power firm and the reduced supply from the small firms, the product market price will rise. Although hoarding behaviour may not maximize the market-power firm's profits from emission trading, total profit could be increased when considering profits from both the emission and product markets. Misiolek and Elder (1989) call this behaviour *exclusionary manipulation*.

Consider Figure 4.1. If the monopolist competes in the same product market as the small firms, the marginal opportunity cost of selling a permit will reflect not only the forgone abatement cost, but also the forgone opportunity of increasing a rival firm's costs and increasing the price in the product market. The effect of the exclusionary motive on the monopolist is shown by line EE, which is drawn as the vertical sum of the monopolist's marginal abatement cost and forgone exclusionary opportunity costs for each permit sold. The resulting equilibrium is characterized by even fewer permits sold (Q_e) at a higher price (P_e) than in the simple manipulation example. The additional efficiency loss in the emission market is measured by the area JGFI.

If the market-power firm is a monopsonist in the permit market (Figure 4.2), exclusion serves to raise the marginal gain from purchasing a permit by an amount equal to the marginal increase in profits obtained in the downstream market. The derived demand schedule for permits, DD, shifts upwards. With exclusionary manipulation, small firms may underutilize or overutilize abatement activities depending upon the incentive for the monopsonist to hoard permits due to their exclusionary effect in the product market. If permits have little effect on production costs for the small firms (including abatement costs), the incentive to exclude is weak, and the shift of DD is small (shown by line D_1D_1). The resulting equilibrium is shown at quantity Q_{el} and price P_{el}. Although small firms are still overabating, both measures have increased from the simple manipulation outcome to nearer the competitive outcome, increasing the cost-effectiveness of the market. The resulting efficiency loss is also smaller (area HIJ). If the incentive to exclude is stronger, the shift in the derived demand line will be greater, as described by line D_2D_2. Equilibrium now occurs at Q_{e2} and price P_{e2}. Both quantity and price exceed the competitive values. The efficiency loss relative to competitive equilibrium is shown by area HMN. Pollution control costs to society increase as the monopsonist abates too much and the small firms abate too little relative to the competitive outcome. For a sufficiently strong downstream effect, the efficiency loss in the emissions market could exceed the efficiency loss under simple manipulation.

To be effective, exclusionary manipulation can be profitable only if the market-power firm can use permit prices to influence the costs of its rivals in the product market. For this to be true, it must be the case that a significant share of the output in the product market is produced in the geographic region covered by the permit market and that the permit market is susceptible to the simple manipulation of the type described in Hahn (1984). Provided this is the case, the effects of simple and exclusionary manipulation (by the role of the market-power firm) on emission market cost-effectiveness relative to the competitive outcome are summarized in Table 4.3.

Table 4.3 Effect on market price by market power[a]

Dominant firm's market role	Cost-minimizing manipulation	Exclusionary manipulation	Net effect
Net seller	Decreasing	Decreasing	Decreasing
Net buyer	Decreasing	Increasing or decreasing	Undetermined

Note: [a] Relative to efficient (competitive) prediction.

The combined effect of emissions trading and market power on economic efficiency depends on whether exclusionary manipulation is possible. The analysis above indicates that in the case of simple manipulation, any emission trading is welfare increasing.[13] In the case of exclusionary manipulation, the motive to exclude could result in increased or decreased emission market efficiency relative to the case of simple manipulation. Overall efficiency is in question due to the effect of output restrictions in the product market. Once these are considered, Misiolek and Elder (1989) have shown that emission trading could reduce economic welfare relative to the outcome under command-and-control regulation.

4.5 LABORATORY INVESTIGATIONS OF MARKET POWER IN EMISSION TRADING MARKETS

Although a considerable body of experimental investigation into emission trading markets exists, not much of it has explicitly addressed the issue of market power. Early research (Hahn 1988; Franciosi *et al.* 1993) focused on the properties of different methods for auctioning permits. The earliest literature on emissions trading had envisaged the regulator auctioning off the total supply of permits, along the lines of a Treasury Bill auction. Because this plan would generate net revenue for the government and leave existing firms worse off than they would be under command-and-control regulation, many judged it politically infeasible. Hahn and Noll (1982) proposed a revenue-neutral auction (RNA) in which existing firms would be *grandfathered* by distributing to them the entire initial stock of permits. Although this would create an incentive for trade, there was concern that it would be necessary to force firms to enter the market. Under the RNA, all firms would offer their entire supply of permits for sale in a call auction, in which they would simultaneously submit a series of sealed-bid price–quantity combinations which would constitute their demand for permits. When the market was called the auctioneer would order the bids in descending order, match them with the available supply and set a uniform price at the lowest rejected bid. Permits would be distributed to the successful bidders and the revenue returned to the firms in proportion to their original supply of permits. Under this plan a firm could always maintain its initial allocation without any net cost while the regulator would maintain a thick market to ensure an efficient distribution of permits.[14] Franciosi *et al.* (1993) demonstrated that a laboratory implementation of the RNA generated high efficiencies, comparable to the equally high efficiencies of a naive double auction, in which permits were distributed to firms that were permitted but not forced to trade. Cronshaw and Brown-Kruse (1999) found excessive use of banking when this was permitted under rules similar to the US Environmental Protection Agency (EPA). Ledyard and Szakaly-Moore (1994, see below) found comparable results in their competitive sessions.

Subsequent research has focused on the efficiency properties of the rights conveyed by the emission permit and of alternative auction institutions in a competitive environment. Muller and Mestelman (1994) and Godby *et al.* (1997) investigated the performance of markets with *coupons* (actual discharge permits) and *shares* (time streams of coupons), banking, and uncertainty in control of emissions. They found that markets with shares and coupons showed particularly high efficiency and confirmed a result of Carlson *et al.* (1993) that some intertemporal substitution of permits is necessary to prevent price instabilities in the permit market. Bjornstadt *et al.* (1995) describe a number of experiments conducted to investigate the properties of auctions proposed for the US EPA sulphur dioxide allowance market developed under the Clean Air Act of 1990. Cason (1995) and Cason and Plott (1996) conducted two experiments which show that the discriminative price-call auction actually adopted by the EPA seriously biases both bids and offers downwards. Only Brown-Kruse *et al.* (1990), Brown-Kruse *et al.* (1995), Ledyard and Szakaly-Moore (1994) and Godby (1997, 1998, 1999) have conducted laboratory investigations directly addressing market power in emissions trading markets.

Ledyard and Szakaly-Moore (1994) argue that any politically feasible emissions trading plan must grandfather existing firms by distributing the initial stock of permits to them. They further argue that an unorganized system in which firms privately negotiate trades of their initial allocation would be inefficient due to the lack of a central clearing house, high transactions costs in finding trading partners and lack of price information. Accordingly, they describe the ordinary double auction and the Hahn and Noll (1982) RNA as the only efficient and politically feasible methods for trading emission permits. They compared these two institutions under monopoly and competitive market conditions. Under competitive market conditions, both institutions were very efficient, although the Hahn and Noll RNA was usually slightly out-performed by the double auction. Of more direct interest here is how these institutions compared in preventing the emergence of market power.

To investigate this issue, Ledyard and Szakaly-Moore provided the potential for market power by initially assigning ten permits to a single trader, who could then sell them through an auction market to five other subjects, each with abatement costs that exceeded the monopolist's. The seller's costs and the buyer's resale values schedules were the same as those used in Smith (1981). The high-cost subjects were assigned no permits. Seven sessions were conducted using an unchanging set of cost schedules and permit assignments. In four sessions the trading institution was the Hahn and Noll RNA; in three sessions the trading institution was the conventional double auction. Based on earlier laboratory work in which monopolists supplied output through a double-auction trading institution, the expectation was that market power would not be realized by the monopolist. The implications for the Hahn and Noll auction had not been explored. Since their experiment did not include downstream production markets, the more complex environment and predictions described by Misiolek and Elder (1989) were not explored.

On average, prices and quantities in the Hahn and Noll RNA converged towards the monopoly predictions by the end of the session. Double-auction outcomes varied across sessions. One session converged towards the monopoly outcome, while another converged towards the competitive prediction. In the remaining session, prices and quantities were between the competitive and monopoly predictions. Summary price data for these sessions are found in Table 4.4. Overall, the monopolists achieved 78.3 and 47.8 per cent of the potential price increase in the last period under the Hall and Noll RNA and double auction respectively.

Given that they used the same parameter set as Smith, it is surprising that Ledyard and Szakaly-Moore found the double auction less resistant to market power than Smith did. Two differences in the experimental design may explain this. Smith allowed subjects to buy or sell only, depending on their assigned market role. Ledyard and Szakaly-Moore allowed speculative trading, that is, they allowed buyers to resell units and sellers to re-buy them. Additionally, Ledyard and Szakaly-Moore conducted fewer market periods (ten) per session than Smith. Godby (1999) reports on double auctions where speculation is possible. He observed that such experiments take longer to converge. Given these differences in experimental procedures and the fact that the double-auction price paths reported by Ledyard and Szakaly-Moore appear to be still in the process of converging to a price level nearer the competitive level than the monopoly outcome, it is possible that with more time their results would not differ significantly from Smith's.

The Ledyard and Szakaly-Moore results do support Hahn's simple manipulation predictions, especially when the Hahn and Noll auction was used. It appears that prices may be expected to diverge from competitive levels when this is predicted by theory, although under double-auction trading rules the divergence is limited and perhaps temporary. The Hahn and Noll RNA is comparable to the posted-offer market in its relative inability to resist the exercise of market power. This is consistent with previous experimental findings, since both the RNA and the posted-offer markets allow sellers to commit themselves to a price schedule.

The work of Brown-Kruse *et al.* (1995) and Godby (1998) was designed to test the hypotheses of both simple manipulation and exclusionary manipulation.[15] The experimental designs incorporated a large firm and an industry fringe of small firms equal in aggregate to the size of the single large firm. All firms first participated in a double-auction market for permits and then made output decisions for their product market. Treatments varied in the nature of the product market and in the distribution of permits across subjects. In the simple manipulation condition, the price in the product market was fixed. In the exclusionary

Table 4.4 *Market-power pricing results from Ledyard and Szakaly-Moore (1994)*

Trading institution	Number of sessions	Number of sessions with supra-competitive prices[a]	Percentage deviation between competitive and monpoly price predictions	Percentage mean price deviation from competitive price (last period)[b]	Percentage of monopoly price increase attained (last period)
Double auction	3	2	37.5	17.9	47.8
Hahn and Noll auction	4	4	37.5	29.4	78.3

Notes
[a] As determined by average price in the last period of the experiment.
[b] Estimated using chart data in original article.

manipulation condition the product price was set at the price where the market demand for the product (defined by the experimenters) was equal to the aggregate output supplied by the firms in the industry. In the monopoly and monopsony conditions, all permits were distributed initially to the large firm and the fringe firms respectively. Godby (1998) introduced a third distribution condition in which the available permits were distributed proportionately to the large and small firms alike.

In Brown-Kruse *et al.*, the laboratory environment comprised one firm capable of producing ten product market units and ten small firms each capable of producing one product unit. Total production capacity of the market was 20 units. Production of one output unit created a unit of emissions. There were ten emission permits allocated in the market. Permits were called *coupons* and were described as an input which allowed subjects to avoid a part of each unit's production cost (called the *additional cost*) for each coupon held.[16] Direct production costs and additional costs (which together made up production cost) differed by firm, allowing gains to be made from trading coupons and reflecting the different production and abatement technologies in naturally occurring economies. These sessions also differed from the earlier monopoly double-auction sessions in giving information regarding the cost structure of the other firms in the industry to the large firm, though it was not explicitly given their permit demand.[17]

In the simple manipulation condition, subjects were informed that the product price would be 125 lab dollars. In the exclusionary manipulation condition, each subject was given a table describing what the product market price would be for all possible levels of total product market output. Because the product market price was determined by the total production of all firms, and firms made their production decision after engaging in coupon trade, the large firm had an opportunity to engage in exclusionary manipulation.

The combination of the two endowment conditions and two product market conditions created a 2×2 factorial design with each treatment testing for a unique type of coupon market manipulation. The predicted prices, assuming that the large firm exploits its market power, are reported in Table 4.5. Although exclusionary manipulation is possible in the exclusionary manipulation with monopsony treatment, it actually leads to lower profits for the large firm than this firm would realize if it constrained its actions to simple manipulation of the coupon market.

Each session consisted of ten decision periods using the parameter values associated with one of the cells in Table 4.2. Each period started with a coupon assignment to firms corresponding to the treatment followed by coupon trading using the MUDA computerized double auction

Table 4.5 Average price performance in market-power environments[a]

Experiment		Simple manipulation			Exclusionary manipulation		
		Monopsony	Monopoly	Proportional assignment[b]	Monopsony[c]	Monopoly	Proportional assignment
Brown-Kruse et al. (1995)	Number of sessions	3	3		3	3	
	Competitive price	105	105		105	105	
	Market-power price	90	110		75	180	
	Mean price[d]	**75**	**107**		**75**	**192**	
	Percentage of market-power price change attained[e]	166	40		100	116	
Godby (1998)	Number of sessions	3	3	3	3	3	3
	Competitive price	105	105	105	105	105	105
	Market-power price	90	110	105	75	180	127
	Mean price	**83**	**102**	**108**	**102**	**155**	**134**
	Percentage of market-power price change attained[e]	147	−60	Does not apply	10	66	132

Notes

a Mean coupon prices in the final period are reported in **bold** characters. The equilibrium coupon price is 105 lab dollars regardless of the initial assignment of coupons if market power is not exercised. The market-power prediction is less than 105 when the assignment is to the small firms and greater than 105 when assignment is to the large firm. Under proportional assignment, the market-power and competitive predictions differ only if exclusionary manipulation is possible. In this case, the market-power prediction is within the range of 125 and 127 lab dollars.

b There is no market-power prediction in this treatment.

c In Godby (1998), one session experienced what could be called a 'speculative bubble' where prices remained above rational levels throughout the experiment. If this session is ignored, the average price of the other two sessions' last periods are 55, or 167 per cent of the market-power price change predicted.

d Mean of final period prices across three sessions in each treatment.

e The percentage of the market-power price increase attained is calculated using price data from the last period of the experimental sessions only.

(Johnson *et al.* 1988). After the coupon market closed, each firm was asked to make a production decision. If the product market treatment in the session used a fixed market price, subjects then calculated their profits. If the product market price depended on total production of the industry, the decisions of the 11 firms were aggregated and the market price was announced. Subjects then computed their profits and the period ended. Note that coupons could not be banked: a new distribution of permits occurred in every period.[18] Three sessions were run for each of the four treatments. The resulting market prices and quantities were compared to the market power predictions and to the competitive prediction (the outcome consistent with the large firm not exploiting its market power in either market).

In analysing the results, the initial assignment of coupons was identified as the command-and-control assignment and the surpluses realized in the trading environments were compared to the surplus that would be realized if coupons were not traded but firms made profit-maximizing production decisions. This made it possible to compare total market efficiency under alternative allocations of permits and alternative opportunities for simple or exclusionary manipulation.

Godby (1998) investigated the effect of permitting speculative trading and of distributing permits proportionately so as to eliminate the incentives for simple manipulation. A slightly modified parameter set was used. The ten small firms in the Brown-Kruse *et al.* (1995) design were reduced to five firms, each with a production capacity of two units. The production costs of these ten units were comparable to the production costs of the ten units from the small firms in use by Brown-Kruse *et al.*[19] Product market treatments were identical to those used in Brown-Kruse *et al.*, however, an additional assignment treatment was included. The new treatment had each of the small firms initially receiving an endowment of one coupon while the large firm received five. This corresponds to an equal proportional reduction in pollution emission entitlements across all firms.[20]

In both experiments, market prices and quantities systematically deviated from the competitive equilibrium in the direction predicted by Hahn (1984) and Misiolek and Elder (1989). Table 4.5 reports the mean contract price in the last period of each treatment averaged over the three replications. In nine of the ten treatments the competitive and market-power price predictions differ. In six of these nine treatments, the average coupon price more closely conformed to the market-power prediction than to the competitive prediction. The exceptions occurred in the simple manipulation/monopoly treatment (both experiments) and in the exclusionary manipulation/monopsony treatment (Godby only). In one of the sessions of the latter case, a severe speculative bubble (where prices remained above all rationally predicted levels throughout the session) drastically reduced the price deviation reported for the treatment. Ignoring this anomaly, the average coupon price in the last period was 55, implying a price deviation 67 per cent greater than predicted by the market-power hypothesis. In the remaining two cases there was only scope for simple manipulation, the difference between competitive and monopoly predictions was small, and the results were either intermediate between the market-power and competitive predictions (Brown-Kruse *et al.*) or slightly below the competitive prediction. Since this treatment corresponds to the type of market power previously investigated in other experimental double auctions, it is not surprising that the competitive result should be realized.

Overall, the Brown-Kruse *et al.* and Godby results strongly suggest that manipulative behaviour will arise in emission markets which permit it. Moreover, the double-auction institution was surprisingly unable to resist the exploitation of market power. Across all sessions where a market-power prediction existed, the firm with market power achieved an average of 80 per cent of the potential deviation from competitive price levels.

Such price deviations imply serious losses in efficiency. Table 4.6 shows that this is the case. In this case efficiency is measured by the increase in aggregate profits (relative to the command-and-control allocation) as a fraction of the potential gain. Both Brown-Kruse *et al.* and Godby find similar patterns across treatments. Market efficiency is highest when the large firm receives all the permits and only simple manipulation is feasible (96 per cent and 81 per cent for Brown-Kruse *et al.* and Godby respectively). Efficiency falls somewhat when the large firm is the sole buyer (71 per cent and 63 per cent respectively). When exclusionary manipulation is feasible, the surplus realized by the subjects was less than that which they would have realized if making profit-maximizing production decisions under command-and-control regulation. The loss is severe in the case of monopsony power (losses of 42 per cent in both experiments) and even worse in the case of monopoly power, with losses of 140 per cent and 119 per cent of the potential gain, respectively. When permits are distributed to minimize the potential for market power, coupon trading allows subjects to realize nearly all (94 per cent) of the available gains.

The poor performance of the double auction in these experiments seems surprising at first, given that previous market experiments indicated that this institution limits market power. On further consideration, however, some of the results do conform to previous interpretations of the success of the double auction. In particular, in the exclusionary

Table 4.6 Efficiency of laboratory emission trading markets by market-power treatment and assignment of coupons[a]

Experiment	No market power Proportional assignment	Simple manipulation			Exclusionary manipulation		
		Monopsony	Monopoly	Proportional assignment	Monopsony	Monopoly	Proportional assignment
Godby et al. (1997)	0.94						
Brown-Kruse et al. (1995)		0.71	0.96		-0.42	-1.4	
Godby (1998)		0.63	0.81	0.32	-0.42	-1.19	-0.33

Note: [a]Efficiency reported in this table represents the proportion of the potential gains from coupon trading in a competitive environment that is realized.

manipulation environment the firm with market power can commit to a specific quantity in the product market. Commitment to initial strategies was advanced as an explanation for the success of monopolists in posted-bid institutions. This does not, however, explain the poor performance of the double auction in the simple manipulation environments. Here the biggest surprise is the substantially poorer performance of the double auction in the monopsony case. Why should it be easier for a monopsonist to avoid purchasing marginal units at a high price than for a monopolist to avoid selling marginal units at a low price? This is fertile ground for future research. Godby's results show that the Brown-Kruse *et al.* findings are robust to changes in the number of fringe firms and opportunities for speculative trade. All of this suggests that the double auction may not be nearly as robust an institution for resisting market-power pricing as had been previously thought.

4.6 CONCLUSIONS

The laboratory experiments reported in this chapter suggest that regulators should take seriously the threat that market power may emerge in emissions trading markets, particularly those which may affect competition in related markets. Trading institutions should also be carefully considered. Although the double auction has been shown to limit the exercise of market power, recent experiments suggest that it may not afford as much protection as previous work has suggested. In addition, the opportunity to engage in exclusionary manipulation poses serious concern for the social feasibility of a trading scheme. Although the theory underlying exclusionary manipulation only suggests that welfare losses are possible, the behavioural results of the few laboratory studies that have been completed show dramatically that the threat is real.

A characteristic of the Brown-Kruse *et al.* (1995) and Godby (1998) experiments which is not necessarily characteristic of the field is that the firm with market power has complete information about its rivals' cost schedules. It is important to investigate whether this complete information is essential for market power to emerge. If market-power results emerge even with less than complete information, it will be particularly important to develop alternative trading institutions to limit price distortions. Laboratory evaluation of these new institutions can provide useful insights into their validity.

Although needing replication and extension, laboratory experiments show that the effects of market power predicted by economic theory tend to emerge in controlled environments, although their quantitative significance depends importantly on the institutions governing trading. They suggest that concerns regarding market power in emissions trading markets are well founded, especially when firms compete in both emissions and downstream product markets. They also validate the use of experimental methods in market design, especially in cases where no fully developed theory exists to guide policy makers as they try to implement new regulatory methods that both are politically viable and increase the economic efficiency of an economy.

NOTES

1. American markets have usually been large enough to avoid such concerns and therefore little attention has been given to market power. See, for example, the sulphur dioxide (SO_2) market proposals (US Environmental Protection Agency 1991). Even in Canada, where markets could be much smaller and therefore more susceptible to such manipulation, however, little concern for market power has been shown in various policy documents (for example, see Nichols 1992, where even though in Ontario alone one firm, Ontario Hydro, accounts for over 45 per cent of emissions, no mention is made of the potential for market power). If mentioned at all, it is usually assumed that existing anti-competitive practices legislation will deter uncompetitive activity (see Recommendation 38, in Introduction, Summary of Recommendations, NRTEE 1993: 4, where no design responses are recommended to deter market power in the presence of existing legislation). Greenhouse gas trading as envisaged under the Kyoto Protocol to the United Nations Framework Convention on Climate Change could also be influenced by market power as the former Soviet Union is expected to be the principal seller in the proposed market (see US Inter-Agency Analysis Team 1997).
2. Parts of this section have been taken from Muller and Mestelman (1998). More details about conducting laboratory sessions can be found in Davis and Holt (1993) and Friedman and Sunder (1994).
3. Experimental market outcomes often take time (typically up to four periods in market experiments) to converge as subjects become familiar with their task or the environment. No satisfactory theoretic descriptions exist to explain this process. Only the final period is reported to allow for this process; however, the general results presented in Table 4.1 do not change if one looks at the pricing results over the whole experiment or after some time is allowed for the convergence process to occur.
4. Holt (1995: 381) summarizes a number of experiments that also find that monopolists are successful at keeping prices above the competitive price in the posted-offer environment.
5. This result is computed by taking data from the last two rows and last column of Table 4.1 and weighting the price results by the number of sessions.
6. Using the data in Table 4.1, the average price deviation from competitive levels is –0.1 per cent over the three duopoly markets.
7. These authors also induce buyer market power of the same type in two sessions; if two of five buyers were to withhold purchases they could reduce the equilibrium market price. In these sessions, one observed competitive results while the other found prices below the competitive outcome.
8. Davis and Williams also conducted a series of post-offer markets using computerized (non human) buyers. These sessions are not reported here.
9. One session exhibited price levels higher than the competitive levels in all periods, but, by both casual inspection and econometric analysis, prices appear to be converging on the competitive price.

10. A possible test of the importance of precommitment is indicated by Smith's results. His results indicated that posted-offer markets were very susceptible to single *seller* market-power pricing, yet posted-bid markets were not. The precommitment argument supports this result. As an extension one could compare the performance of these institutions in monopsony settings. If the precommitment hypothesis holds, the posted-offer market should outperform the posted-bid market. Such an experiment has not been reported in the literature.

11. Parts of this section have been taken from Godby (1997).

12. In general, the results are applicable to a number of firms who might act in concert. Theoretically, a small number of firms could each have market power and act strategically and with respect to the other's actions. Such outcomes are not considered here, although they are described in Sartzetakis (1992, 1993). His results are comparable to those derived in the more simple environment described here.

13. This assumes that the product markets remain relatively unaffected by any possible changes in production by firms in the permit market due to reallocation of their permit endowment and subsequent production decisions. It may be reasonable to assume such an outcome would occur if these product markets were competitive.

14. It could always submit a very high (and presumably successful) bid for its initial distribution and no bid for any additional permits. Regardless of the final price, the cost of the permits acquired would equal the revenues from the permits sold).

15. The design was introduced by Brown-Kruse and Elliott (1990), who conducted one session per treatment cell. Brown-Kruse *et al.* (1995) report 12 additional sessions (three per cell). Godby (1998) extended the design to test for additional effects.

16. To avoid *framing* effects, subjects were not told that the market in which they were participating was a pollution emission market. By not referring to pollution, emission coupons or abatement, actions by subjects in the markets observed should reflect only their desire to earn trading profits; it should avoid effects due to personal beliefs regarding pollution emission trading.

17. This reflects the implicit theoretic assumption made in section 4.4 that the market-power firm has the information available to exploit its power. In reality, large firms could have the resources to discover their competitors' costs and thus estimate the permit demand or abatement values. The market-power firm was not given the demand information, only enough knowledge to construct such relationships if it chose to. In the actual experiments none did, with all market-power subjects appearing to ignore the other firms' cost information contained in their experiment folders.

18. Banking refers to saving permits from one period to be used in the next. Allowing permits to be saved in this way, it is possible that market power could be exacerbated or mitigated in emission trading drawing upon the results found in theoretic futures markets for commodities (see Anderson 1991 for a survey of this literature). The interaction of market power and the possible properties of the permit traded have not been considered theoretically or experimentally.

19. Costs were modified to ensure each firm had increasing production and abatement costs.

20. If the initial permit distribution is defined to be the command-and-control assignment, this new endowment treatment could be considered more representative of the type that would be expected under actual regulatory conditions than the extreme assignments used in previous experiments.

REFERENCES

Anderson, R.W. (1991), 'Futures trading for imperfect cash markets: a survey', in Louis Phelps (ed.), *Commodity, Futures and Financial Markets*, Boston, MA: Kluwer Academic, pp. 249–71.

Bjornstadt, D.J., S.R. Elliott and D.R. Hale (1995), 'Understanding experimental economics and policy analysis in a federal agency: the case of marketable emission permits', Oak Ridge, Tenn.: Oak Ridge National Laboratory and US Department of Energy, MS.

Brown-Kruse, J. and S. Elliott (1990), 'Strategic manipulation of pollution permit markets: an experimental approach', Boulder, Col.: University of Colorado, Department of Economics Working Paper.

Brown-Kruse, J., S. Elliott and R. Godby (1995), 'Strategic manipulation of pollution permit markets: an experimental approach', Hamilton, Ontario: McMaster University, Department of Economics Working Paper 95-10.

Carlson, D., N. Olmstead, C. Foreman, J. Ledyard, C. Plott, D. Porter and A. Sholtz (1993), *An Analysis and Recommendation for the Terms of the RECLAIM Trading Credit: Report Submitted to the South Coast Air Quality Management District*, Contract R-C93074.

Cason, T.N. (1995), 'An experimental investigation of the seller incentives in the EPA's emission trading auction', *American Economic Review*, **85**, 905–22.

Cason, T.N. and C.R. Plott (1996), 'EPA's new emissions trading mechanism: a laboratory evaluation', *Journal of Environmental Economics and Management*, **30**, 133–60.

Cronshaw, M.B. and J. Brown-Kruse (1999), 'An experimental analysis of emission permits with banking and the Clean Air Act Amendments of 1990', in M. Issac and C. Holt (eds), *Emissions Permits Experiments. Research in Experimental Economics, Volume 7*, Greenwich, CT: JAI Press, 1–24.

Davis, D.D. and C.A. Holt (1993), *Experimental Economics*, Princeton, N.J.: Princeton University Press.

Davis, D.D and A.W. Williams (1991), 'The Hayek hypothesis in experimental auction: institutional effects and market power', *Economic Inquiry*, **29**, 261–274.

Franciosi, R., R.M. Isaac, D.E. Pingry and S. Reynolds (1993), 'An experimental investigation of the Hahn–Noll revenue neutral auction for emissions licences', *Journal of Environmental Economics and Management*, **24**, 1–24.

Friedman, D. and S. Sunder (1994), *Experimental Methods*, New York: Cambridge University Press.

Godby, R. (1997), *The Effect of Market Power in Emission Permit Markets*, PhD thesis, McMaster University.

Godby, R. (1998), 'Market power, vertical markets and laboratory emission permit double auctions', Laramie: University of Wyoming, MS.

Godby, R. (1999), 'Market power in emission permit double auctions', in M. Isaac and C. Holt (eds), *Emissions Permit Experiments. Research in Experimental Economics, Volume 7*, Greenwich, CT: JAI Press, 121–62.

Godby, R., S. Mestelman, R.A. Muller and J.D. Welland (1997), 'Emission trading with shares and coupons when control over discharges is uncertain', *Journal of Environmental Economics and Management*, **32**, 359–81.

Hahn, R.W. (1984), 'Market power and transferable property rights', *Quarterly Journal of Economics*, **99**, 753–65.

Hahn, R.W. (1988), 'Promoting efficiency and equity through institutional design', *Policy Sciences*, **21**, 41–66.

Hahn, R.W. and R. Noll (1982), 'Designing a market for tradable emissions permits', in W.A. Magat (ed.), *Reform of Environmental Regulation*, Cambridge, Mass.: Ballinger, 119–46.

Holt, C.A. (1995), 'Industrial organization: a survey of laboratory research', in J.H. Kagel and A.E. Roth (eds), *The Handbook of Experimental Economics,* Princeton, N.J.: Princeton University Press, 349–443.

Holt, C.A., L. Langan and A. Villamil (1986), 'Market power in oral double auctions', *Economic Inquiry*, **24**, 107–23.

Johnson, A., H.-Y. Lee and C.R. Plott (1988), 'Multiple unit double auction user's manual', Social Science Working Paper 676, Pasadena: California Institute of Technology.

Kagel, J.H. and A.E. Roth (eds) (1995), *The Handbook of Experimental Economics*, Princeton, N.J.: Princeton University Press.

Ledyard, J.O. and K. Szakaly-Moore (1994), 'Designing organizations for trading pollution rights', *Journal of Economic Behavior and Organization*, **25**, 167–96.

Misiolek, W.S. and H.W. Elder (1989), 'Exclusionary manipulation of markets for pollution rights', *Journal of Environmental Economics and Management*, **16**, 156–66.

Muller, R.A. and S. Mestelman (1994), 'Emissions trading with shares and coupons: a laboratory experiment', *Energy Journal*, **15**, 185–211.

Muller, R.A. and S. Mestelman (1998), 'What have we learned from emissions trading experiments?', *Managerial and Decision Economics*, **19**, 225–38.

National Roundtable on the Environment and Economy (NRTEE) Economic Instruments Collaborative (1993), *Achieving Atmospheric Quality Objectives Through the Use of Economic Instruments*, Ottawa: NRTEE.

Nichols, A.L. (1992), *Emissions Trading Program for Stationary Sources of NOx in Ontario*, Cambridge, Mass.: National Economic Research Associates.

Oates, W.E. (1995), 'Green taxes: can we protect the environment and improve the tax system at the same time?', *Southern Economic Journal*, **61**, 915–22.

Plott, C.R. (1989), 'An updated review of industrial organization: applications of experimental methods', in R. Schmalensee and R.D. Willig (eds), *Handbook of Industrial Organization*, Vol. II, Amsterdam: North-Holland, 1109–76.

Porter, R.H. (1991), A review essay on *Handbook of Industrial Organization, Journal of Economic Literature*, **29**, 553–72.

Sartzetakis, E.S. (1992), *Emissions Trading Under Imperfect Competition in Both the Emission Permit and Product Market*, Ottawa: Carleton Industrial Organization Research Unit, Department of Economics, Carleton University.

Sartzetakis, E.S. (1993), *The Use of Emission Permits in Deterring Entry in the Product Market*, Ottawa: Carleton University and GREEN, Department of Economics, Carleton University.

Sbriglia, P. and N. O'Higgins (1996), 'Collusion and market power in experimental auction markets', *Economic Notes*, **3**, 541–72.

Smith, V.L. (1981), 'An empirical study of decentralized institutions of monopoly restraint', in G. Horwich and J. P. Quirk (eds), *Essays in Contemporary Fields of Economics in Honor of Emanuel T. Weiler (1914–1979)*, West Lafayette, IN: Purdue University Press, pp. 83–106.

Smith, V.L. and A.W. Williams (1989), 'The boundaries of competitive price theory: convergence, expectations, and transaction costs', in L. Green and J.H. Kagel (eds), *Advances in Behavioral Economics*, vol. 2, Norwood, N.J.: Ablex Publishing.

Smith, V.L. and A.W. Williams (1992), 'Experimental market economics', *Scientific American*, **267** (6), 116–21.

Tietenberg, T. (1985), *Emissions Trading: An Exercise in Reformulating Pollution Policy*, Washington, D.C.: Resources for the Future.

US Environmental Protection Agency (1991), 'Auctions, direct sales, and independent power producers written guarantee regulations and request for delegation of proposals to administer the auctions and direct sale; rule and notice', *Federal Register*, 65592-65609 (17 December) (40 CFR) Part 73.
US Inter-Agency Analysis Team (1997), 'Draft report on the economic effects of global climate change policies', June, Washington, DC.

5. The competitive implications of facility-specific environmental agreements: the Intel Corporation and Project XL

James Boyd, Janice Mazurek, Alan Krupnick and Allen Blackman

5.1 INTRODUCTION

As part of its regulatory reinvention initiatives, the Environmental Protection Agency (EPA) has begun to experiment with voluntary initiatives that provide industrial facilities with relief from certain regulatory requirements in return for superior overall environmental performance. Facility-specific permitting can be thought of as part of a larger 'tailored' approach to environmental regulation. The regulation is tailored in the sense that it rejects rigid, one-size-fits-all emissions standards in favour of standards that reflect the unique characteristics of specific production processes, products and industrial sites.

There is a broad literature on the economics and effectiveness of voluntary approaches to regulation (OECD *et al.* 1997; Storey *et al.* 1997; Léveque 1996; OECD and Storey 1996; Glachant 1994). However, the topic of voluntary *facility-specific* regulation remains relatively unexplored. This chapter describes the economic and institutional characteristics of tailored regulation in order to highlight the distinctions between it and more conventional forms of regulation. A particular focus is on the way in which this form of voluntary agreement can affect competition. By its very nature, tailored regulation is not applied uniformly to firms in a given industry. This lack of uniformity, in principal, can have significant consequences for competition and market structure.

To illuminate these issues we examine the case of a facility-specific permit covering an Arizona microprocessor manufacturing facility owned and operated by the Intel Corporation. The permit arose as part of the EPA's Project XL, a voluntary initiative whose mission has been to experiment with innovative forms of environmental regulation. Because Intel's market is dynamically competitive, but oligopolistic, the case provides a particularly clear illustration of the way in which tailored regulation can affect business strategy and, in turn, market-level outcomes and social welfare in general.[1]

The next section describes tailored regulation in more detail and compares it to command-and-control (CAC) and incentive-based environmental regulations. The potential benefits of facility-specific permitting and the challenges associated with implementation are highlighted. The section concludes with a discussion of potential market-level effects. Sections 5.3–5.5 present the Intel case study. Section 5.3 describes the XL permit. Section 5.4 explores the value of accelerated product introductions for Intel and places particular emphasis on the strategic benefits associated with the permit. Section 5.5 considers the larger consequences of the permit for social welfare. Section 5.6 offers conclusions.

5.2 FACILITY-SPECIFIC, TAILORED REGULATION

Under a system of tailored regulation firms volunteer to negotiate site-specific, performance-based pollution control agreements. Agreements contain both legally binding and non-binding elements. Parties to the negotiation include not only the firm and regulator, but also a broad set of community and environmental stakeholders. In essence, tailored regulation is a deal struck between a firm and environmental interests, including the regulator. The regulator grants the firm some type of flexibility. This regulatory flexibility is translated into financially advantageous production changes. In exchange, the firm agrees to superior *overall* environmental performance. The fact that the process is voluntary and negotiated guarantees that there are net gains to the parties to the deal.[2]

5.2.1 Tailored versus Command-and-control Regulation

The rationale for experimentation with this type of regulation is the widely held belief that CAC regulations inhibit the pursuit of manufacturing efficiency and stifle innovative abatement strategies. Still the most common form of pollution control in the US, CAC regulation features extensive government influence over the technologies used and the degree of abatement undertaken by firms.[3] Not only does CAC often mandate specific technologies, but technical constraints also arise because emission standards are applied to individual substances rather than to broader categories of effluent. Because of this, limits on the output of a single substance can significantly constrain the design of a production process. Finally, because of its emphasis on abatement procedures and specific effluent streams, firms must continually re-permit as their production processes change. This re-permitting is a costly and time-consuming exercise in and of itself – and particularly costly for firms whose production processes must change frequently

The uniformity of CAC regulation is a virtue since it is easier to monitor technology or emissions standards that are fixed and common to many firms. However, given the unique characteristics of most firms, the constraints imposed by uniform standards are increasingly viewed as an overly blunt and costly way to control pollution.

5.2.2   Flexibilities Created by Tailored Regulation

Tailored regulation creates flexibility by shifting to a more 'performance-based' measure of environmental compliance. Instead of judging environmental compliance on the basis of technological inputs or narrowly defined emissions standards, tailored regulation relies on more holistic measures of a facility's performance. It is important to distinguish between two conceptually distinct types of flexibility: namely, flexibility geared towards cost reduction and flexibility geared towards speeded product introductions. It is most common to think of regulatory flexibility as an opportunity for cost reduction. But regulatory flexibility can also be aimed at reducing delays associated with regulatory compliance.

First, consider flexibilities leading towards cost reduction. Instead of placing strict numerical limits on individual hazardous air pollutants, for example, a tailored permit may instead define an aggregate limit on all hazardous air pollutants. This aggregate limit, or cap, may be more stringent than the aggregate limit implied by the pre-existing limits on individual pollutants. Nevertheless, the ability to exceed a pre-existing limit in exchange for reductions in other emissions may allow for production changes that are financially valuable.

The above example is illustrative only. The flexibility sought by firms can take a variety of forms specific to their products and production processes. The general principle, however, is that tailored regulation judges compliance on the basis of broader, aggregate (facility- or process-wide) emission targets. Within those targets, firms are granted greater freedom to meet them in the most cost-effective manner.

Note that the cost-reducing production flexibilities allowed under tailored regulation are similar in flavour to the production efficiencies brought about by incentive-based, cap-and-trade programmes such as the United States' sulphur dioxide (SO_2) allowance trading programme. Both systems create incentives to reduce pollution and both allow firms a degree of freedom in deciding how best to make reductions. In effect, both tailored regulation and allowance trading programmes allow firms to substitute cheaper pollution reductions for more expensive ones. In the case of allowance trading programmes, this substitution occurs between firms in an industry. In the case of tailored regulation, the substitution occurs across pollutants, and possibly across media, but within a single facility.

Now consider another important form of flexibility. Tailored regulation creates opportunities, not only for cost reductions, but for speeded product introductions as well. Regulatory permitting often moves at a slow pace. In general, any production change that modifies air or water emissions requires a new permit or formal regulatory review. Permitting delays can significantly penalize firms in highly innovative markets where production process changes are frequent. Tailored regulation promises a *dynamic* form of flexibility. Specifically, facility-specific permitting may allow a firm to change a production process (and thus its emissions profile), or even build a new process plant, without re-permitting.

Performance-based, rather than narrow, technical compliance allows for this dynamic flexibility. Relatively long-horizon, multi-year permits can be designed. As long as the firm complies with broad, pre-approved measures of environmental performance, it need not seek approval for production changes. The ability to avoid repeated re-permitting removes a potential source of production delays. In many of today's innovative product markets avoided delay can translate into significant financial and strategic advantage.

5.2.3 Challenges

While the conceptual benefits of facility-specific regulation are significant, there are a set of practical challenges to the implementation of such a programme. First, the need to demonstrate superior environmental performance under a tailored permit requires the definition of baseline environmental performance. This issue is more complex and controversial than it might appear. The most obvious baseline is the level of pollution mandated by CAC regulations. However, CAC regulations are notoriously complex and vary from jurisdiction to jurisdiction. In many instances, a 'bright line' CAC baseline is difficult to define. Also, the stakeholder negotiation process may lead to definitions of environmental performance that are broader than those implied by regulatory programmes themselves. Finally, CAC standards are in a constant process of redefinition, particularly when they are being applied to new production processes. Thus, the CAC baseline is itself a kind of moving target.

Second, baseline issues highlight the potentially contentious nature of the stakeholder negotiation process. The number of parties involved and the diversity of viewpoints likely to be represented raise the possibility of protracted, and thus costly, negotiation. Legal challenges to a permit are also likely to arise since permit terms will, by definition, often be at odds with underlying CAC standards. Statutory reforms may remedy some of these problems, but negotiated permitting will almost certainly remain a contentious process.[4]

Third, it is often more difficult to monitor environmental compliance associated with a tailored permit. Because permits are facility-specific, monitoring procedures and technologies have to be facility-specific as well. And in many cases performance-based monitoring is more difficult than the technology-based monitoring typically associated with CAC regulation.

Finally, facility-specific regulation has the potential to affect competition in a material way.

5.2.4 Implications for Competition

By design, tailored regulation enhances the competitiveness of a participating firm. After all, the motivation to participate comes from the cost reductions, public relations benefits or dynamic advantages described above. If no advantage is created, firms will not have an incentive to participate.[5] Moreover, because tailored regulatory agreements are firm-specific, in most cases a permit's advantage will not be fully transferable to its competitors. Even if production processes are comparable, firm A's ability to secure a permit does not imply that its competitor, firm B, will be granted a similar permit.[6] Because the agreements are facility-specific, the benefits of a tailored regulatory permit are likely to be non-uniform across an industry.[7] Tailored regulation's impact on competition, therefore, is likely to be non-uniform as well.

Tailored permitting benefits firms that are already in positions of environmental leadership. This is because, in practice, the EPA favours permit applications made by firms with established reputations as environmental leaders.[8] The rationale for this is largely sound. Because tailored permitting operates outside more-established systems of regulation there is an element of trust involved in the granting of innovative regulatory approaches. Proven environmental track records are a natural basis for that trust. From a firm's standpoint, participation in a tailored permit is a potentially daunting task. The intensive stakeholder negotiation process, in particular, favours firms with extensive public relations, political and regulatory expertise. The financial resources required for that kind of expertise are most commonly associated with companies in positions of market leadership.

This means that access to, and the consequences of, tailored regulation are unlikely to be competitively neutral. Access to the programme and its competitive advantages are in practice likely to be limited to firms that are already market leaders. In some sense, tailored regulation has the potential to let 'the rich get richer'.[9] From the perspective of social welfare this need not be a bad thing; after all, the competitive advantages created by the programme are the carrot that is used to induce superior environmental performance. It is necessary to consider the competitive consequences of tailored regulation in judging its overall welfare effects, however. While firm-specific competitive advantages create a powerful inducement to environmental innovation and pollution reduction, this benefit must be weighed against any anti-competitive consequences.

Note that the welfare tradeoff just described is reminiscent of the welfare tradeoff associated with the patent system. In the latter case, a 'static' competitive advantage (monopoly power) is granted to create an incentive for innovations with 'dynamic' welfare benefits. Similarly, tailored regulation may be a particularly effective way of encouraging environmental innovation precisely because it promises the innovator a competitive advantage.

5.3   THE INTEL–XL AIR PERMIT

The three-year-old Project XL programme is an experiment for both the US EPA and participating firms. It is hoped that the programme can confront implementation challenges and begin to reap the benefits of a tailored permitting system that is sensitive to the unique characteristics of regulated firms. The Intel case is the first air permit approved under Project XL.

The permit is of particular interest because its value to Intel may largely derive from its ability to speed product introductions via reduced permitting delay. Intel's market is oligopolistic but highly competitive in a dynamic, innovative sense. Because of this, the case has interesting implications for the kind of competitive advantages that can flow from a system of tailored regulation.

5.3.1   Characteristics of the Permit

Intel's XL agreement governs air, water and waste issues at a semiconductor fabrication facility (fab) in Arizona. This analysis focuses on the air permitting portion of Intel's XL agreement, because it is under that portion that the principle regulatory flexibilities arise. The five-year permit relieves Intel from a set of standard provisions in the Clean Air Act Amendments (CAAA), which require manufacturers to notify regulators, and in some cases seek approval from regulators, in order to make routine process changes.

There are three general categories of benefit to Intel. The first is advanced approval of production changes. Under a conventional permit, an Intel facility would be required to file up to 28 air permit notifications per year for each fab.[10] The second is plant-wide emissions caps. The permit replaces some individual emissions limits with aggregate limits. Caps give the firm greater flexibility to modify its production and abatement processes and equipment. Third, Intel is allowed to expand operations – including the construction of another facility on-site – without re-permitting.

The permit achieved 'superior environmental performance' by decreasing allowable emissions under the caps. The conventional and hazardous air pollutant caps are, in aggregate, more stringent than is required by federal law. To achieve this goal, Intel must design its equipment and processes so that not one, but potentially two, facilities produce fewer emissions than are allowed for a comparable, existing facility.[11] Intel also agreed to testing and public notification provisions beyond those required under a traditional permit. Because of this, it is possible that Intel's overall abatement costs under the agreement are actually higher than they otherwise would have been.

5.4 THE VALUE OF TECHNICAL AND MARKETING LEADERSHIP

It is possible that Intel will achieve some cost savings from the flexibility permitted under the hazardous and conventional air caps. However, in our view, the agreement's principle benefit arises from the firm's ability to minimize permitting delays. It is to the value of this form of flexibility that we now turn.

5.4.1 The Semiconductor Industry's Sensitivity to Delay

In the past, Intel has suggested that regulation-based delays are a serious source of competitive disadvantage. In one instance, the firm cautioned that lengthy state reviews would cause the company to 'seriously question whether it could remain committed to the construction and expansion of our US sites' (Hatcher 1994: 4). Intel's sensitivity to delay is a function of both its market and its technology.

For the manufacturers of high-end semiconductors, such as Intel, profitability is closely connected to their ability to release new chip products in advance of competitors. Intel is currently the world's leading supplier of microprocessors, controlling between 80 and 90 per cent of the US market. Advanced Micro Devices (AMD) and, until recently, Cyrix Corp., are Intel's few close competitors. Despite Intel's seemingly secure market position, continuous technological innovation is not enough to preserve its market dominance. It must continue to be the first to introduce new product capabilities to the market.

The slimness of Intel's marketing leads is indicated by the rapid pace of innovation and production facility turnover. In five years, an average Intel facility using the latest process technology will introduce at least two new generations of technology; make 30 to 45 process chemical changes *per year*; and install 5 to 15 new equipment types and/or new processes (Hatcher 1994: 7). Intel constructs a new wafer fab roughly every nine months (Kirkpatrick 1997: 62). To grasp the financial stakes involved, consider that the price tag for new fabrication plant construction is over $2 billion per plant (Hutcheson and Hutcheson 1996). With this amount at stake, delays of weeks or months can have very significant financial consequences.

In addition to the pace of change, the complexity of the technologies involved contributes to the risk of delay. To design and optimize its production process Intel must constantly modify process chemistries and equipment. Each new generation of chip typically requires radically different design characteristics. Moreover, microprocessor production typically involves more than 300 distinct manufacturing steps. Continual experimentation and refinement is required. In turn, this implies the need for frequent equipment and process chemical changes, each of which has the potential to alter a plant's pollution emissions profile.[12]

The pace of process change is clearly a challenge to regulators – a challenge that is not particularly well met by conventional permitting procedures. Delays associated with notification and review processes can be significant. Federal, state and local agencies can subject even routine process changes to review. These reviews can impose delays of several days or several months, depending on whether regulators require public notice and comment periods (which themselves can take up to 60 days).

The pre-approval of an environmental permit, such as that provided by Intel's XL permit, can avoid such delays and speed Intel's time to market. The financial and strategic consequences of that advantage are likely to be significant both for Intel and its competitors.

Intuitively, it seems better to bring a product to market sooner rather than later. But exactly why is that so? And if a single firm achieves a quicker time to market, how does that affect other firms and society generally? This section analyses the dynamic, or intertemporal, effects of the XL permit using insights from business and economic theory. Understanding these benefits is necessary in order to evaluate the ultimate performance of the XL agreement for Intel and for society generally. There are a number of competitive advantages that arise when a firm can get a product to market more quickly. Several of these relate to the semiconductor industry's market structure and unique characteristics of demand for computer-related products.

5.4.2   Accelerated Income

Perhaps the most obvious benefit of accelerated product introductions is the financial benefit associated with earning income sooner rather than later. More formally, the benefit is equal to the financial return that could have been earned on the profits over the period of delay. Whether income is disbursed to shareholders or is used to retire debt or to finance capital expenditures, there is always an opportunity cost associated with delays in collecting that income. Because of Intel's huge capital requirements, and because delayed income increases the cost of holding debt and new capital investment, speeded product introductions are highly valuable to the company.

It should also be noted that consumer demand, which is clearly related to the firm's ability to generate income, is time-sensitive. The time-sensitivity of demand depends upon the degree to which consumption in a later period of time is a substitute for consumption in an earlier period of time. Two polar cases help to illuminate the concept. First, assume that any unsatisfied demand in period 1 is perfectly transferred to period 2. If so, delay does not affect a consumer's willingness to pay. The second case is that in which there is only demand for the product in period 1. There is no willingness to pay in period 2. In this case, the inability to satisfy demand in period 1 means that revenue from such a sale is not just delayed, as in the previous case, but is forgone altogether. This example does not account for the presence of competing products, but underscores the way in which a firm's income is related to the timing of product introductions.[13]

5.4.3   Price Premiums

Empirical research on firm profitability suggests that technological 'first-movers', that is, firms which are the first to introduce a technology into the market place, gain a significant competitive advantage in terms of market share and sustainable price premiums. This is true in a variety of industries and for a variety of reasons.[14] By definition, innovative products are unlike any others, at least for some period of time. This uniqueness implies a strategic advantage. Because there are fewer substitutes for innovative products, price competition is relatively weak. Thus, innovation provides a temporary window of monopoly power.[15] Within this window, the prices a firm may charge are relatively unconstrained by competition.[16] Moreover, being a first-mover can be valuable because it allows the firm to pursue strategies that deter the entry of competitors. Deterred entry, in turn, can mean a further relaxation of price competition and higher profits for the leader.[17]

5.4.4 Strategic, First-mover Advantages

While the benefit of leadership may seem self-evident, several aspects of market leadership of the microprocessor industry make it particularly valuable. Three characteristics of the computer chip market are critical: (a) the need for technical coordination between firms producing complementary products; (b) the predominance of standardized operating systems; and (c) manufacturer cost savings due to 'learning-by-doing'.

Affiliation with complementary producers
The value of more rapid product introductions depends not just on a firm's direct competitors (other chip manufacturers), but also on the development of complementary products used in conjunction with microprocessors, such as software applications and computer hardware. Intel's chips are integrated, in both a technical design and commercial sense, with the products of other firms. These other product markets are themselves characterized by intense product competition, featuring high rates of innovation.

An important advantage of leadership in this market is the ability to define technical protocols (standards) that promote the design integration of complementary products. Because computers are a bundled product, a software manufacturer which wishes to reap the benefits of being first to market must be technically and commercially affiliated with chip designers and hardware manufacturers which will also be first to market. This creates a tendency for first-movers to create complementary design protocols that speed the movement of the bundled product to market.

'Later-movers' also have access to these technical protocols but lack the ability to affect their technical characteristics. It is natural for the designer of technical protocols to set them in a way that minimizes the designer's costs; a particularly creative designer may also consider ways to maximize its rivals' costs of complying with the protocol. Technical standardization required by the need to integrate hardware and software favours the first-mover.

Operating system standardization

Intel's products enjoy a close commercial and technical integration with the Microsoft Windows operating system, which dominates its market. While this dominance is due in part to the quality of Microsoft's and Intel's products, it is also due to some special economic characteristics of computer operating systems, notably network externalities. A network externality describes the situation in which a product becomes more valuable as more consumers use it. By its nature, a network externality can create a market dominated by a single firm. If consumers value the use of a single, standard product, this can undermine a market's competitiveness by deterring rival, non-standard products. Such deterrence is clearly beneficial to the firm whose product defines the standard.

A formal example will help to illustrate. Let $U(n)$ and $V(n)$ denote the benefits to a consumer of using two potentially competing products. If both products exhibit a network externality, these benefits are an increasing function of n, the number of people who consume them. For simplicity, assume that there are only two consumers. It follows that $U(2) > U(1)$ and $V(2) > V(1)$. Further, assume that $V(2) > U(1)$ and $U(2) > V(1)$. This means that the consumers are strictly better off if they coordinate, and both use the same product. This emphasizes the desirability of a technological standard. Without such a standard, one consumer may purchase the U product, while the other purchases the V product, and both would be worse off.[18]

This example also highlights the strategic benefits of being a first-mover. By setting the standard, a first mover can assure itself of a market free from competition. To see this, assume that if there were agreement on the standard, the U product would be preferred to the V product, that is, $U(2) > V(2)$. But consider what happens if the V product is brought to market first and is purchased by one of the consumers. The presence of the network externality means that it is in the interest of the second consumer to also purchase the V product, because $V(2) > U(1)$. The network externality, combined with V's first-mover advantage results in V's emergence as the standard, even though U would have been unanimously preferred (Farrell and Saloner 1985). In this way, first-movers are able to deter strategically the emergence of a rival standard.

The pervasiveness of the Microsoft operating system (OS) and the problems for its rivals are due, at least in part, to the successful employment of this strategy. Computer operating systems exhibit a network externality because users value compatibility with other users. Software applications that run on different operating systems are not typically compatible. In turn, this means that documents and databases constructed on one OS cannot be 'read' by applications associated with another OS. Moreover, it is costly for users to maintain parallel systems. There are significant 'switching costs' involved with moving between operating systems. These include hardware costs (since different operating systems typically have different hardware needs) and the need to learn how to use the second operating system (a daunting proposition for many users). Microsoft's open architecture and focus on market share has led to the emergence of its operating system as the market standard. Given switching costs and the presence of a network externality, Microsoft is in a strong position to deter and stifle rival operating systems.

Intel has contributed to Microsoft's market dominance by providing it with hardware innovations necessary to the performance of Microsoft's software innovations. In turn, Microsoft's ability to dominate its market translates into strong, consistent demand for Intel's products. Microsoft enjoys significant market power via its possession of the dominant operating system standard. Intel shares in that market power because of its technical integration with Microsoft's products. This has two conflicting implications for the benefits of accelerated product development. Even if a competitor were to be first to market with an innovative chip, Intel would probably be insulated from the threat due to its integration with the OS standard. This is true since innovations which are not integrated with the standard OS platform tend to be resisted by consumers. If this insulation effect dominates, then the benefits of accelerated product introduction may not be large, or even present. However, this insulation is likely to be effective only in the short term. If a competing chip manufacturer consistently beat Intel to market, Microsoft would undoubtedly seek product integration with the competitor. Also continued integration with the Microsoft OS is very valuable to Intel. Accelerated product introduction enhances the firm's ability to remain in innovative lockstep with Microsoft and thus profit from the dominance of their bundled product.

Learning-by-doing
Consider now a first-mover advantage that arises from the manufacturing side of the market. As a firm produces greater quantities of a product, it learns to produce it more efficiently and with higher levels of quality. Production experience leads to the rationalization of processes, reduced waste and greater labour force expertise. Average production

costs decrease over time and with increases in the firm's cumulative output.[19] This effect is referred to as the 'learning curve' or 'learning-by-doing'. Learning-by-doing raises entry barriers by creating a persistent cost advantage for first-mover firms, which may deter the entry of competitors. Any initial first-mover cost advantage increases market share, which in turn, leads to even greater learning, cost reductions and competitive advantage.[20]

There is a pronounced learning curve associated with the manufacture of computer chips. Consider the 'yield rate', or the ratio of usable chips to total chips on a wafer. This yield rate has been shown in several studies to be an increasing function of production experience. Unusable chips are costly, so as the yield rate improves the average cost of usable chips falls. Gruber (1994) finds evidence of firm-specific learning-by-doing in the semiconductor industry.[21] Flamm (1994) considers the question of whether learning takes place primarily within a given product line, within a given firm, or across different firms. Using statistical techniques, he finds that learning-based cost reductions are best explained by facility-specific experience.[22]

Given learning-by-doing, speeded product introduction clearly benefits a firm such as Intel. By enhancing its ability to be a first-mover, speed allows for the capture of initial market share. This triggers the virtuous circle of lower manufacturing costs, greater market share, even more learning-by-doing, lower costs, and so on. The end result of this cost advantage is the ability to price aggressively and/or sustain healthy profit margins.

Reduced risk of knowledge appropriation
The design and development of new products requires investment in new scientific, technical and manufacturing knowledge. Because these investments are costly, they will be made only if the firm expects some competitive reward for doing so. This reward may take the form of reduced production costs, which increase profit margins or allow the firm to undercut competitors' prices. In the case of a firm such as Intel, the reward comes from producing a new, 'differentiated' product. Differentiated products are those which have no close substitutes. The lack of close substitutes means relatively weak price competition, or a kind of temporary monopoly. The promise of such a monopoly, even if it is only brief, motivates innovation.

The benefits of innovation are significantly reduced, however, if competitors can appropriate the innovator's ideas. The patent system guards against appropriation, but it does so imperfectly: first, some ideas cannot legally be patented; second, even if a patent is granted, competitors may be able to 'innovate around' the patent using slightly different techniques; third, patenting requires the innovator to reveal publicly the substance of its new idea. Together, these problems can undermine the patent system's ability to assure an innovator of adequate rewards. Evidence of the rapid dissemination of semiconductor technologies suggests that patent system protections in this industry are relatively weak (Lamond and Wilson 1984: 46).

Because of weaknesses in the patent system, innovators must often rely on a delay in their competitors' ability to appropriate. Imitation, while much easier than innovation itself, may nevertheless be difficult. New ideas, jealously guarded by their originators, must be acquired. Engineering personnel must educate themselves regarding the new ideas (or be hired away from the innovator) and designs and production processes must be altered. This creates an 'imitation lag', or a window of time during which the original innovator can expect to be in sole possession of the fruits of its innovation. Innovation lags are important in the semiconductor industry, but are also vanishingly brief. Intel's two to three month lead on its closest competitors is illustrative.[23]

Speeded product introduction is particularly valuable in a market environment in which imitation lag times are short. Speeded introduction lengthens the period of time during which the innovator's product is unique within the market place and thus not subject to competitive pricing pressures. Appropriation can begin to occur long before a product comes to market. If imitation begins with the development of new designs, for instance, a delay in manufacturing will not delay imitators, it will simply reduce the time span over which the innovator can market its unique (and thus relatively profitable) product.

5.5   WELFARE IMPLICATIONS

Up to this point, our focus has been on the implications of speeded permitting – and accelerated time to market – for Intel itself. What is good for Intel may not be good for society. Thus, special attention must be paid to costs and benefits not captured or borne by Intel.

On the benefits side, consumers are made better off by having access to products sooner. The accelerated consumption benefit corresponds to the gain in utility that consumers experience from being able to consume the product earlier. This accelerated consumption benefit is the analogue of the accelerated income benefit described in the previous section. In general, the more rapid the pace of product quality innovations, the greater the increase in consumer utility.[24] Regulatory delays can reduce the value of products to consumers by truncating the number of periods over which the product's benefits can be realized.

In a market such as Intel's, however, this benefit may be offset by competitive effects that reduce consumer welfare. Earlier adoption may yield a competitive advantage significant enough to reduce competition. In principle, earlier product introduction could yield a large private benefit but create a net social cost. Even if speeded product introduction unambiguously benefits Intel, and even if the environmental implications of the permit are positive, a more cautious declaration of improved social welfare is required.

First, economic analyses suggest that competition in innovation can lead to excessively *early* adoption of new technologies. Fudenberg and Tirole (1985), for instance, develop a model in which firms choose the optimal timing for new product adoptions. One of the strategies explored in the model is for a technological innovator to pre-empt its rival by adopting an innovation sooner than it otherwise would. Early adoption is potentially undesirable because it is almost certainly more costly than later adoption. Because part of the benefits of being a first-adopter come at the expense of rival firms, the private benefit of early adoption exceeds its social benefit. As a result, competition can result in earlier – and more costly – adoption times than would be socially optimal.

Second, analyses of product variety (Scherer 1979; Spence 1976) suggest that some markets may produce excessive product variety. If we draw an analogy between product variety and multiple product generations, this type of result suggests that computer manufacturers may introduce product upgrades too frequently. A monopolist may deter rivals by offering a range of products to fill niches that would otherwise invite entry. The value of filling such niches is higher to a monopolist than to its competitors since the monopolist does not face competitive price pressures. As a consequence, brand proliferation or excessively frequent upgrades can be a sustainable, entry-deterring strategy.[25]

Third, potentially anti-competitive consequences of a first-mover advantage are exacerbated by factors that already contribute to a high degree of market concentration. Because of the need for technical compatibility, consumers' desire for standardization and the existence of manufacturing learning effects, firms that capture initial market share possess a distinct, and valuable, strategic advantage. Analyses of first-mover strategies suggest that they can have a positive effect on market power. By definition, firms with market power can sustain price levels that exceed production costs. It must be emphasized, however, that market power is a powerful reward for innovation. Without it, socially valuable innovations may be inhibited. On the other hand, market power by definition creates a loss to society associated with higher prices and/or lower quality.

Theoretically, then, product introductions can be too early, too numerous and lead to anti-competitive outcomes. This suggests that the effect on social welfare of speeded product introductions is complex and is certainly not equivalent to the private benefits enjoyed by the market leader itself.[26]

5.6 CONCLUSION

The conclusions of this analysis must be generalized with some caution. Facility-specific permitting is a regulatory tool with a much broader potential application than is reflected by this one case. The characteristics of Intel (as a market leader in a dynamically competitive industry) and the regulatory flexibility being gained (accelerated permitting) are somewhat special to this case. Nevertheless, there are lessons worth emphasizing. First, dynamic flexibilities are potentially valuable to firms and thus may represent an important direction for future regulatory reforms. Because of their value, these kinds of flexibilities can lead to significant environmental improvements, as part of the tailored regulation bargaining process. Second, effects on competition should be considered when evaluating the desirability of flexible regulations. Because of their firm-specific nature, tailored agreements skew the competitive playing field. First-mover advantages that can be translated into market power may be enhanced by this type of regulation. Of course, it is the promise of those advantages that prompts firms to propose and implement environmental innovations, innovations with potentially significant social value. Thus, attempts to speed the diffusion of an XL agreement's provisions to other firms (or circumscribe the kinds of agreements that can be reached) may threaten the environmental benefits sought by this type of programme.

APPENDIX: THE TIME-SENSITIVITY OF DEMAND

It is socially desirable to achieve gains from trade sooner rather than later. This appendix depicts two sources of benefit from speeded product introductions: accelerated income and accelerated consumption benefits. The discussion is highly stylized and does not attempt to depict the important, but significantly more complex, issues that arise in models with strategic interactions between firms in product rivalry.

From product to product, consumers differ in their tastes for the timeliness of consumption. In the case of microprocessors, business consumers in most cases value timely access to computing speed more highly than do household consumers. Thus, the value of a product can be expressed as a function of both the product's price and the time at which consumers are able to begin using it. Let this value, or consumer demand D, be defined as follows:

$$D(t, \phi, p) = A - \phi t - p$$

where A is a constant, p the product's price, t the date of consumption, and ϕ a taste parameter. Note that demand is a decreasing function of both price and the length of time before consumption. All prefer access to the product sooner, but high-ϕ-type consumers, such as businesses that require high-volume data processing, value timeliness more highly than low-ϕ types, such as households.

Given this framework, what is the benefit of accelerated product introduction? To answer the question assume that the product is either sold immediately ($t = 0$) or is delayed one period ($t = 1$). Also, assume n consumers, a marginal production cost c, and a discount factor δ. Without delay, and assuming for simplicity that the monopolist can extract all consumers' surplus, the firm can set its price so that $p = A$. This follows since $D = A - p$. Profits are therefore $\Pi_0 = n (A - c)$.

Now, if the firm is forced to delay the product's introduction, it can only charge a price $p = A - \phi$. And since revenues are earned in the future period, the value of the profit must be discounted. Profits from a sale that is delayed are therefore $\Pi_1 = \delta n (A - \phi - c)$. The difference in profits, and therefore the benefit of accelerated introduction, is:

$$(1 - \delta)\Pi_0 + \delta n\phi.$$

This expression depicts both the accelerated income and the accelerated consumption benefits. To isolate the accelerated income benefit, assume that $\phi = 0$, so that consumers are completely insensitive to the timing of consumption. Note that, even though consumer utility is unaffected by delay, delay still creates a cost. Specifically, the firm is $(1 - \delta)\Pi_0$ worse off than if its product introduction had not been delayed. This is the cost of achieving profits later, rather than sooner. It is equivalent to the financial return that could have been earned on the profits over the period of delay. Thus, irrespective of its effect on consumer utility, acceleration always implies an income-based benefit.

When $\phi > 0$, we see the benefit of accelerated consumption. This benefit corresponds to the gain in consumer utility that arises due to accelerated consumption. To isolate this benefit, assume no discounting

($\delta = 1$) so that there is no accelerated income benefit. The accelerated consumption benefit is then simply $n\phi$. In extreme cases, where ϕ is large (specifically, when $\phi > A - c$) delay can reduce the product's utility so significantly that the product's market is eliminated altogether. This would imply a very large benefit to accelerated introduction.

NOTES

1.   Project XL is one example of tailored regulation. However, our goal is not to evaluate that specific programme. Instead, we use the Intel-XL case to illuminate issues that arise under tailored regulation more generally.
2.   Note, however, that if not all affected interests are represented in the negotiation, there is no guarantee that the process will lead to a socially superior outcome.
3.   Emission standards may not explicitly dictate a technology choice. However, they often carry an implicit incentive to employ a standard technology. This is because standards are usually developed based upon the emission characteristics of specific technologies. Firms can minimize their likelihood of being found in violation of standards by employing the technologies on which the standards were based. Innovative approaches run a higher risk of generating permit violations or triggering permitting delays.
4.   There is currently a bill under consideration in the US Senate (S. 1348, 105th Cong., 1st session) that precisely delineates time limits for notice and response and rules governing participation in the negotiation process.
5.   Recall that participation is completely voluntary.
6.   Firm B can apply for its own permit, but in general there is no automatic transferability of the permit's terms to other firms – although diffusion of such innovations is a stated goal of the Project XL programme.
7.   If the EPA is able to diffuse the permitting innovations to other firms in the industry, this non-uniformity may only be temporary. Immediate transferability of flexibility would also quickly erode any competitive advantage received by the original innovator. In practice, however, with so many site-specific and stakeholder-specific issues to address in each negotiation, the diffusion process is likely to be very slow.
8.   The EPA favours proposals from firms 'that have already taken voluntary measures to achieve a level of environmental performance far better than is required by applicable regulations' (Federal Register, 23 April 1997, Notice of Modifications to Project XL, FRL-5811-7). Also consider the language of the statute being considered in the Senate (supra n. 2, sec. 7). In deciding whether to enter into an agreement with a given firm, the EPA shall consider, among other things, whether the facility 'has a strong record of compliance' and 'reflects historic demonstration of leadership in environmental performance'.
9.   Arora and Cason (1995) come to a similar conclusion in their analysis of the EPA's voluntary '33/50' programme.
10.   See Boyd *et al.* (1998).
11.   As indicated in the previous section, demonstrating superior environmental performance is complicated by the difficulty of establishing the relevant emission baseline. For more detail on the way in which this baseline was calculated, see ibid. That paper also includes a more detailed analysis of the permit, including its technical characteristics, financial benefits, history and implementation.

12. The source of emissions is due to chemicals used both to affix transistors to the silicon wafer and to 'sterilize' the chip, lack of sterility being the leading cause of chip failure.

13. The appendix provides a more formal description of the way in which income and consumer welfare are related to the timing of product introductions.

14. See Schmalensee (1982) and Bond and Lean (1977). Also, note that the so-called 'Porter hypothesis' – that regulation can enhance competitiveness by forcing innovation – is derived from the theory of first-mover advantage (Porter 1990).

15. Our use of the term 'monopoly' should not be taken to imply that Intel behaves anti-competitively in a legal sense. Instead, the term points to strategic advantages possessed by a product innovator.

16. The pattern for Intel is to be first to market, sell at a relatively high price until competitors such as Cyrix or Advanced Micro Devices enter the market, and then innovate again while exiting the older market. In this way, Intel stays ahead of its competitors, but also stays ahead of price competition. For example, a leading-edge Pentium® may initially sell for $1 000. As Intel's output increases and competitors enter the market, Intel will continuously lower the product price until it hovers just over $200. Such product release and pricing strategies earn the manufacturer gross margins of around 60 per cent.

17. Profitability itself has been shown to be positively correlated with market share. This is true holding things such as product quality constant (Buzzell and Gale 1987).

18. This situation is evocative of the competition between the competing video cassette player formats, VHS and Betamax, in the early 1980s. Before VHS emerged as the standard, video distributors had to choose between supplying tapes formatted for only one standard (which meant lost sales) and manufacturing tapes for both formats (which increased costs). Consumers faced a corresponding dilemma in terms of which type of player to purchase. The lack of a uniform standard resulted in costly duplication, unavailable video titles for many consumers and investment in ultimately useless products based on the failed Betamax standard.

19. Airframes and Ford's Model T are classic examples.

20. For economic analyses of learning-by-doing and its competitive implications, see Arrow (1962); Spence (1981); and Fudenberg and Tirole (1983).

21. He also develops a theoretical model to explore the effect of learning-by-doing on firm profitability in the industry. The model confirms the value of being a first-mover by showing that profits are decreasing in the order of entry into the market.

22. For another empirical examination of learning-by-doing in the industry, see Dick (1994).

23. Appropriation, while ethically problematic, is an inescapable reality in all industries. The discussion in this section, however, should not be taken to suggest any specific allegations of appropriation by Intel's competitors.

24. The appendix includes a more formal description of the accelerated consumption benefit. Note that if Intel could price discriminate it could capture all of the benefits realized by consumers; but in a competitive market, most of these benefits remain inappropriable.

25. See also Gilbert and Newberry (1982). They demonstrate that a monopolist's incentive to innovate and remain a monopoly is greater than an entrant's incentive to innovate and become a duopolist (that is, one of two leading firms), since competition reduces the industry's aggregate profits.

26. It is also worth noting that semiconductor manufacture is an internationally competitive industry. There is evidence, for instance, that Japanese firms are particularly adept at optimizing the production process (that is, learning-by-doing effects are significant). In one study (OECD 1985: 35), the average yield rate on chips was twice that of US firms in the first two years of a product cycle. Global competitive threats strengthen the desirability – domestically – of accelerated product introductions but the benefits from a world perspective are not necessarily positive.

REFERENCES

Arora, S. and T. Cason (1995), 'An experiment in voluntary environmental regulation: participation in EPA's 33/50 program', *Journal of Environmental Economics and Management*, **28**, 271–86.

Arrow, K. (1962), 'The economic implications of learning by doing', *Review of Economic Studies*, **29**, 155–73.

Bond, R. and D. Lean (1977), *Sales, Promotion, and Product Differentiation in Two Prescription Drug Markets*, Staff Report to the US Federal Trade Commission, Washington, D.C.

Boyd, J., A. Krupnick and J. Mazurek (1998), *Intel's XL Permit: A Framework for Evaluation*, Discussion Paper 98-11, Washington, D.C.: Resources for the Future.

Buzzell, R. and B. Gale (1987), *The PIMS Principles Linking Strategy to Performance*, New York: Free Press.

Dick, A.R. (1994), 'Accounting for semiconductor industry dynamics', *International Journal of Industrial Organization*, **12**, 35–51.

Farrell, J. and G. Saloner (1985), 'Standardization, compatibility, and innovation', *Rand Journal of Economics*, **16**, 70–83.

Flamm, K. (1994), 'Strategic arguments for semiconductor trade policy', *Review of Industrial Organization*, **7**, 295–325.

Fudenberg, D. and J. Tirole (1983), 'Learning by doing and market performance', *Bell Journal of Economics*, **14**, 522–30.

Fudenberg, D. and J. Tirole (1985), 'Preemption and rent equalization in the adoption of new technology', *Review of Economic Studies*, **52**, 383–402.

Gilbert, R. and D. Newberry (1982), 'Preemptive patenting and the persistence of monopoly', *American Economic Review*, **72**, 514–26.

Glachant, M. (1994), 'The setting of voluntary agreements between industry and government: bargaining and efficiency', *Business Strategy and the Environment*, 3(2), 43–9.

Gruber, J. (1994), *Learning and Strategic Product Innovation: Theory and Evidence for the Semiconductor Industry*, Amsterdam: North-Holland.

Hatcher, J. (1994), Comments by Intel Corporation on the Proposed Amendments to the Criteria for Interim Approval of Title V Programs before the United States Environmental Protection Agency, 28 September.

Hutcheson, G. Dan and J.D. Hutcheson (1996), *Technology and Economics in the Semiconductor Industry*, San Jose, Cal.: VLSI Research.

Kirkpatrick, D. (1997) 'Intel's amazing profit machine', *Fortune*, 17 February, 60–72.

Lamond, A. and R. Wilson (1984), *The Competitive Status of the US Electronics Industry*, Washington, D.C.: National Academy Press.

Léveque, F. (1996), *Environmental Policy in Europe: Industry, Competition and the Policy Process*, Cheltenham, UK: Edward Elgar.

OECD (1985), *The Semiconductor Industry: Trade Related Issues*, Paris: Organization for Economic Cooperation and Development.

OECD and M. Storey (1996), *Demand Side Efficiency: Voluntary Agreements with Industry, Policies and Measures for Common Action*, Working Paper 8, prepared for Annex 1 Expert Group on the UNFCCC, December.

OECD, J. Newman, R. Segal and G. Dinkelmann (1997), 'Utility voluntary agreements to reduce greenhouse gas emissions', in *Electricity Sector, Policies and Measures for Common Action*, Working Paper 15, prepared for the Annex I Expert Group of the UNFCCC, November.

Porter, M. (1990), *The Competitive Advantage of Nations*, New York: Free Press.

Scherer, F. (1979), 'The welfare economics of product variety: an application to the ready-to-eat cereals industry', *Journal of Industrial Economics*, **28**, 113–34.

Schmalensee, R. (1982), 'Product differentiation advantages of pioneering brands', *American Economic Review*, **72**, 346–65.

Spence, M. (1976), 'Product selection, fixed costs, and monopolistic competition', *Review of Economic Studies*, June, 217–35.

Spence, M. (1981), 'The learning curve and competition', *Bell Journal of Economics*, **12**, 49–70.

Storey, M., G. Boyd and J. Dowd (1997), 'Voluntary agreements with industry', 26.97, special issue on *The Economics and Law of Voluntary Approaches*, Milan: Fondazione Eni Enrico Mattei.

6. Environmental policy and time consistency: emission taxes and emissions trading

Peter W. Kennedy and Benoit Laplante

6.1 INTRODUCTION

A key consideration in the choice of pollution control instruments is the incentive for regulated firms to adopt cleaner technologies. The adoption of less-polluting production techniques holds the key to long-term consumption growth with limited accompanying environmental damage. More immediately, it allows firms to achieve pollution reduction targets at lower cost and with potentially smaller impact on their international competitiveness. These issues are of particular importance to many developing countries where high growth rates mean that a large number of key industrial technology choices are being made on a daily basis. It is essential that those choices are the right ones if the net benefits of growth are to be maximized.

Of course, the right technology is not necessarily the cleanest technology available. This is especially true when an existing production technology is already employed and the associated investment has been sunk. Retooling with a less-polluting production method or the retrofitting of abatement equipment can be very costly; that cost must be carefully weighed against the benefits of reduced pollution from technological change. Thus, it is not enough that policy instruments create incentives for technological change; they must create the *right* incentives, in the sense that they induce technology adoption decisions which correctly balance the benefits and costs of alternative technologies.

There is a wide array of pollution control policies available to regulators and each of them has different properties with respect to incentives for technological change. In this chapter we focus on emission taxes and emissions trading. These market-based instruments are becoming increasingly popular in practice due in part to their dynamic incentives. By attaching an explicit price to emissions, these policy instruments create an ongoing incentive for firms continually to reduce their emission volumes. In contrast, command-and-control type emission standards create incentives to adopt cleaner technologies only up to the point where the standards are no longer binding (at which point the shadow price on emissions falls to zero). However, the ongoing incentives created by market-based instruments are not necessarily the right incentives. In particular, time consistency constraints on the setting of these instruments can potentially limit the ability of the regulator to set policies that implement efficiency as rational expectations equilibria with respect to technology adoption choices. This chapter explores these time consistency issues for Pigouvian emission taxes and emissions trading.

We examine the policy problem under a range of conditions relating to the structure of the 'pollution market' and the nature of the environmental damage. We show that time consistency constraints do not limit the ability of the regulator to achieve a first-best outcome if there is a continuum of regulated firms or if environmental damage is linear in aggregate emissions. However, if there are relatively few regulated firms, such that there is strategic interaction between firms and the regulator, and environmental damage is strictly convex in aggregate emissions, then time consistency problems do arise. In particular, the rational expectations equilibrium under emission taxes exhibits excessive incentives for the adoption of a new technology while the equilibrium under emissions trading exhibits incentives for adoption that are too weak.

Our chapter contributes to a broad existing literature on incentives for technological change under environmental regulation.[1] Downing and White (1986) examine the incentive effects of an emissions tax but they do not take account of time consistency issues and whether or not the outcomes examined can in fact be rational expectations equilibria. Malueg (1989) argues that emissions trading may not create the right incentives for new technology adoption but his analysis is also flawed by a failure to examine incentives in equilibrium. The firms in his paper do not base their investment decisions on a rational expectation of equilibrium prices. Milliman and Prince (1989) similarly neglect equilibrium considerations in their comparative analysis of emission taxes and emissions trading.

Biglaiser *et al.* (1995) examine incentives in a rational expectations environment and claim that an emissions tax does *not* suffer from a time consistency problem. Their result is correct in the context of their model but they restrict attention to the case of linear damage. They also claim that technology adoption is distorted under emissions trading because of a time consistency problem for the regulator. However, this problem arises in their model only when the investment decisions of individual firms have a significant effect on aggregate emissions. This possibility is not consistent with their assumption of price-taking behaviour on the permit market. If firms are small players in the permit market then there is no time inconsistency problem in their model (which assumes damage is linear) and no associated distortion of technology investment decisions.

Laffont and Tirole (1996a, b) also examine technological change under emissions trading. A primary focus of their work is the time consistency problems arising from a non-unitary cost of public funds. They show that incentives for innovation are weakened if the regulator cannot commit to distort future permit prices for the purpose of raising revenue.

Jung *et al.* (1996) compare the incentive effects of emission taxes and emissions trading but they fail to account for time consistency issues. In particular, they assume that firms expect the tax rate to remain unchanged after adoption of a cleaner technology even though this tax rate is suboptimal *ex post*. Similarly, they assume that firms expect the supply of permits to remain unchanged even though that supply is suboptimal *ex post*. In their model these expectations are fulfilled in equilibrium but only because the regulator fails to make the optimal adjustments. Thus, the regulator is assumed to be able to commit to a policy that is not time consistent. This also raises a problem with their comparative analysis of taxes and permits because the implicit objective of their regulator varies with the instrument used to implement it. The implicit objective under a tax policy is to maintain the tax rate constant while the implicit objective under permits is to achieve a given level of emissions. These objectives are not consistent.

Our analysis focuses on the time consistency of policy and its implications for the importance of examining incentives in equilibrium. Our rational expectations framework allows a direct and consistent comparison of emission taxes and emissions trading. The rest of the chapter is organized as follows. Section 6.2 describes the model on which our analysis is based. Section 6.3 characterizes efficiency with respect to technology adoption in the context of that model. Sections 6.4 and 6.5 then examine the circumstances under which efficient technology choices can and cannot be implemented through a Pigouvian emissions tax and emissions trading respectively. Section 6.6 concludes.

6.2 THE MODEL

Time is divided into two periods. In period 1 each of n firms uses a production technology with associated abatement cost function $c_0(\bar{e}_0 - e)$, where e denotes emissions, and $\bar{e}_0$ is the level of emissions corresponding to no abatement. Thus, $\bar{e}_0 - e$ represents abatement. Abatement may involve a variety of measures, including a reduction in output, a change in inputs or some end-of-pipe remedial action. The abatement cost function measures the least-cost mix of abatement measures. Abatement cost has the following important properties: $c_0' > 0$ and $c_0'' > 0$.

A cleaner technology becomes available at the beginning of period 2. It can be adopted by any firm at some fixed installation cost K. This technology has an associated abatement cost function $c_1(\bar{e}_1 - e)$ with $c_1' > 0$ and $c_1'' > 0$, where $\bar{e}_1 \leq \bar{e}_0$ and $c_1' < c_0'$ for any $e \leq \bar{e}_0$. Thus, any positive level of abatement can be achieved at lower cost with the new technology.

Polluting firms are assumed to be price-takers on the product market. This means that private and social marginal abatement costs coincide. It is important to note that this assumption can hold even if the number of polluting firms in the regulated region is small, since the regulated firms do not necessarily constitute the whole industry. Such is the case, for example, when polluting firms take world prices as given.

Environmental damage D(E) in any period is an increasing function of aggregate emissions E in that period. That is, attention is restricted to the case of a dissipative pollutant that is uniformly mixed relative to the regulated region. Two cases are considered with respect to the damage function: $D''(E) > 0$ (strictly convex damage) and $D''(E) = 0$ (linear damage).[2]

6.3 EFFICIENCY

We begin with an analysis of a single firm since this helps to illuminate the key issues with respect to efficiency in technology adoption. We then examine the case with many firms.

6.3.1 A Single Firm

Figure 6.1 illustrates the marginal damage schedule drawn for the case of linear damage. Marginal damage is denoted by δ. Also illustrated are the marginal abatement cost schedules associated with the old and new technologies, labelled $c_0'(\bar{e} - e)$ and $c_1'(\bar{e} - e)$ respectively. The efficient level of emissions if the firm uses technology i is e_i^* such that $c_i'(\bar{e}_i - e_i^*) = \delta$.[3]

The shaded area in Figure 6.1 represents the social benefit obtained if the firm adopts the cleaner technology. This social benefit comprises the reduction in damage associated with the fall in emissions from e_0^* to e_1^*, represented by area (A + C) plus any reduction in abatement cost associated with switching to the cleaner technology, represented by area (B − C)

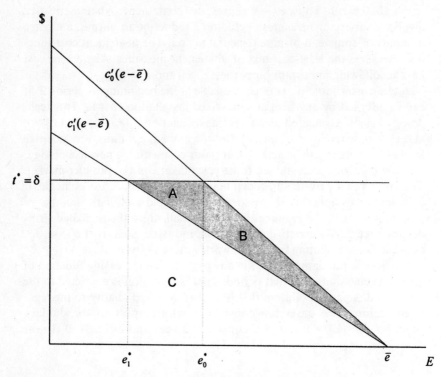

Figure 6.1   Social benefit from technology adoption (linear damage)

in the figure. Note that abatement cost could be *higher* under the cleaner
technology since efficiency requires that more abatement is undertaken
for that technology. However, the overall social benefit is necessarily positive. Let G denote that social benefit.

Figure 6.2 illustrates an increasing marginal damage schedule, labelled
D'(E). The efficient level of emissions for the firm if it uses technology i is
e_i^* such that $c_i'(\bar{e}_i - e_i^*) = D'(e_i^*)$. The shaded area in Figure 6.2 represents
the social benefit obtained if the firm adopts the cleaner technology. It
has the same interpretation as in the constant marginal damage case.

Whether or not adoption of the cleaner technology yields a positive
net social benefit depends on the size of the adoption cost K. Adoption is
worthwhile if and only if G > K. It is clear from Figures 6.1 and 6.2 that
adoption of the cleaner technology is most likely to be worthwhile if
marginal damage is high and the difference between marginal abatement
costs is significant.

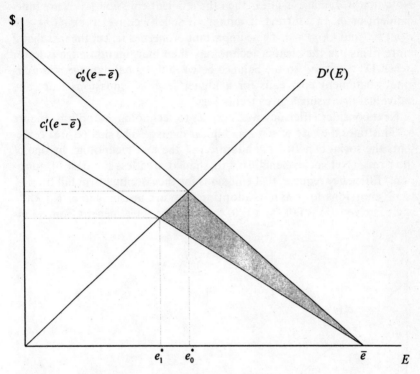

Figure 6.2 Social benefit from technology adoption (strictly convex damage)

6.3.2 Many Firms

Now suppose there are $n > 1$ regulated firms. Let m denote the number of firms to adopt the cleaner technology. Efficient emission levels for a given value of m are given by $e_0(m)$ and $e_1(m)$ such that:

$$c_0'(\bar{e}_0 - e_0(m)) = c_1'(\bar{e}_1 - e_1(m)) = D'(E(m)) \tag{6.1}$$

where:

$$E(m) = m e_1(m) + (n - m) e_0(m) \tag{6.2}$$

Note that if damage is linear then the efficient emission levels are independent of m. In contrast, if damage is strictly convex then $e'_0(m) > 0$, $e'_1(m) > 0$ and $E'(m) < 0$. These important properties reflect the fact that if more firms use the cleaner technology then marginal damage is lower (when $D'' > 0$), and so the balance between marginal damage and marginal abatement cost calls for a higher level of emissions from any individual firm using a given technology.

Next consider efficiency with respect to technology adoption. Figure 6.3 illustrates the case of $n = 2$ and linear damage. The shaded area represents the social benefit from adoption of the new technology by one of the firms. (Net social benefit is this shaded area less the cost of adoption.) Efficiency requires that emissions for the adopting firm fall from e^*_0 to e^*_1; emissions for the non-adopting firm are unchanged at e^*_0, while aggregate emissions fall from $E(0)$ to $E(1)$. The social benefit from adop-

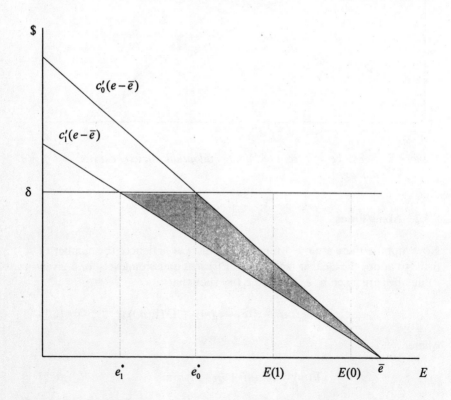

Figure 6.3 Social benefit from technology adoption by one firm (linear damage)

tion comprises the reduction in damage associated with the fall in aggregate emissions plus any reduction in abatement cost for the adopting firm.

The picture is somewhat more complicated when damage is strictly convex. Figures 6.4(a) and 6.4(b) illustrate the adoption of the new technology by one of the two firms. Efficiency requires that emissions for the adopting firm fall from $e_0(0)$ to $e_1(1)$, and that emissions for the non-adopting firm rise from $e_0(0)$ to $e_0(1)$. The efficient level of aggregate emissions falls from $E(0)$ to $E(1)$. The shaded areas in Figure 6.4(a) reflect the reduction in abatement cost for the adopting firm: area $(B - A)$. The shaded areas in Figure 6.4(b) represent the other components of the social benefit from adoption: area D is the reduction in damage associated with the fall in aggregate emissions; area C is the reduction in abatement cost for the *non-adopting firm* associated with the rise in its emissions. Note that this latter component of social benefit does not arise

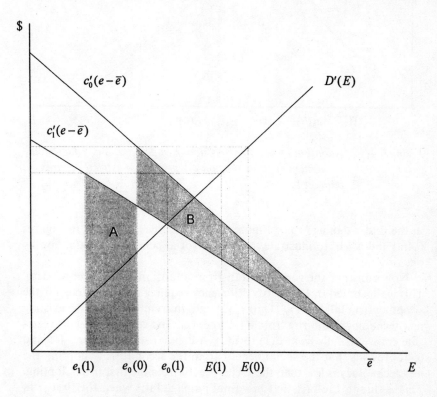

Figure 6.4(a) Adoption by one firm: reduction in abatement cost for the
                adopting firm (strictly convex damage)

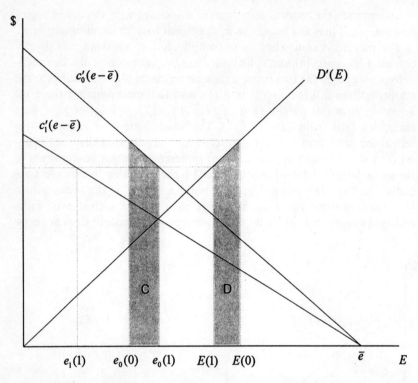

Figure 6.4(b)   Adoption by one firm: reduction in damage and reduction in
*   abatement cost for the non-adopting firm (strictly convex*
*   damage)*

in the linear damage case. Figure 6.4(c) combines the areas in Figures
6.4(a) and 6.4(b) to illustrate the overall social benefit from adoption by
one firm.

Now consider the social benefit from adoption by the second firm.
This is illustrated in Figure 6.5. Efficiency requires that emissions for the
adopting firm fall from e_0 (1) to e_1 (2), and that emissions for the existing
new technology firm rise from e_1(1) to e_1 (2). The efficient level of aggregate emissions falls from E(1) to E(2). A comparison of Figures 6.5 and
6.4(c) reveals that the social benefit from the second firm adopting the
new technology is less than the social benefit from the first firm adopting.
This is due to the fact that marginal damage falls when the first firm

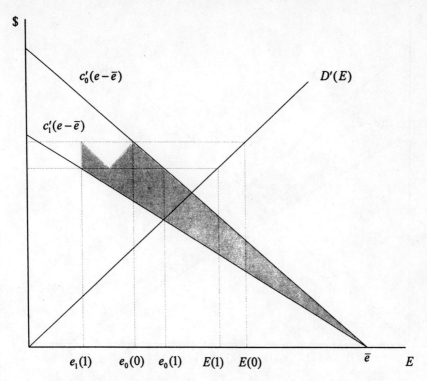

Figure 6.4(c) Social benefit from adoption by one firm (strictly convex damage)

adopts, so the social benefit from the second firm adopting is smaller. Since the cost of adoption is constant, this means that efficiency may require strictly partial adoption: some firms should adopt the cleaner technology and some firms should retain the old technology, even though all firms are identical *ex ante*.

In contrast, strictly partial adoption is never efficient when damage is linear since marginal damage is constant in that case, and so the social benefit from adoption by one firm is independent of how many firms adopt. Efficiency in that case requires adoption of the cleaner technology either by all firms (if K is relatively small) or by no firms (if K is relatively large). Of course, a corner solution can also be efficient in the strictly convex damage case if K is large enough or small enough.

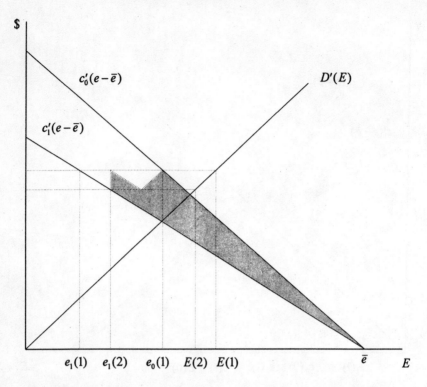

Figure 6.5   Social benefit from adoption by the second firm (strictly convex damage)

6.4   IMPLEMENTATION WITH AN EMISSIONS TAX[4]

The timing of the game between the firms and the regulator is as follows. In period 1 the tax is set according to the Pigouvian rule for the prevailing technology. The new technology arrives at the beginning of period 2 and the regulator announces a tax rate for that period. Firms then decide whether or not to adopt the cleaner technology, taking as given the simultaneous technology adoption decisions of other firms. The regulator cannot commit to a tax rate that is time inconsistent. That is, the tax rate announced for period 2 must be consistent with the technology choices that the tax induces.

6.4.1   A Single Firm

The equilibrium to the game between the firm and the regulator depends importantly on whether damage is linear or strictly convex. We examine each case in turn.

Linear damage

The unit tax rate on emissions is set equal to marginal damage: $t^* = \delta$. This is illustrated in Figure 6.1. Note that this optimal tax rate is independent of which technology is in place because marginal damage is constant. The firm responds to the tax by setting its emissions level to equate its marginal abatement cost with the tax rate: $c_i'(\bar{e}_i - e_i) = t^*$. Thus, the firm chooses e_0^* if it uses the old technology and e_1^* if it uses the new technology. That is, the emissions tax implements static efficiency for any given technology.

The private benefit to the firm from adopting the cleaner technology comprises the reduction in tax payments, $t^*(e_0^* - e_1^*)$, plus any reduction in abatement cost. Note that the reduced tax payments correspond exactly to the reduced environmental damage since $t^* = \delta$. It follows that the private benefit to the firm from adopting the new technology is identical to the social benefit. Thus, the emissions tax also implements efficiency with respect to technology adoption.

Strictly convex damage

The regulatory problem is somewhat more complicated when marginal damage is increasing. For an emissions tax to implement the efficient level of emissions for any given technology i, the tax rate must be set equal to marginal damage evaluated at the efficient level of emissions; that is, $t_i^* = D'(e_i^*)$. Thus, the tax rate required depends on which technology is in use. This creates a potential time consistency problem for the regulator. If adoption of the new technology is efficient then the regulator would like to announce a tax rate t_i^* for period 2. Conversely, if adoption of the new technology is not efficient, then the regulator would like to announce a tax rate t_0^* for period 2. The problem is that a tax rate of t_0^* may actually induce the firm to adopt the *new* technology, while a tax rate of t_1^* may induce the firm to retain the *old* technology. In both cases the announced tax rate would not be optimal *ex post* and hence could not be committed to *ex ante*.

Under what conditions will this time consistency problem arise? Suppose adoption of the new technology is not efficient; that is, $G \leq K$. Then the first-best tax rate for period 2 is t_0^*. Figure 6.6 illustrates the private benefit to the firm from adoption of the new technology at this fixed

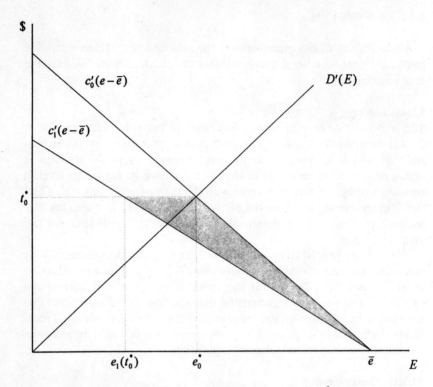

Figure 6.6 Private benefit from technology adoption (at t_0^*)

tax rate. If the firm retains the old technology, then it sets emissions equal to e_0^*. Conversely, if it adopts the new technology, then it sets emissions equal to $e_1(t_0^*)$. Let $B(t_0^*)$ denote the private benefit from adoption at t_0^*. Comparing Figures 6.2 and 6.6 reveals that $B(t_0^*) > G$. That is, the private benefit from adoption at t_0^* exceeds the social benefit from adoption. This does *not* necessarily create a time consistency problem. In particular, if $B(t_0^*) \leq K$ then adoption of the new technology is not privately worthwhile for the firm, and so t_0^* is optimal *ex post*. In this case the announced t_0^* tax rate is credible, and the Pigouvian tax policy implements efficiency with respect to technology adoption.

However, if $B(t_0^*) > K$ then t_0^* will induce adoption of the new technology, and so t_0^* will not be optimal *ex post*. In this case the regulator cannot commit to the first-best tax rate. The best the regulator can do in this case is to announce that it will set the tax at t_0^* if the firm does not adopt the new technology, and set the tax at t_1^*, if the firm does adopt the new technology; no other Pigouvian tax strategy is time consistent. Milliman and Prince (1989) refer to this policy as *tax ratcheting*.

Figure 6.7 illustrates the private benefit to the firm from adoption of the new technology under the tax ratcheting policy. If the firm retains the old technology then it faces a tax rate of t_0^* and sets emissions at e_0^*. Conversely, if it adopts the new technology it faces a tax rate of t_1^* and sets emissions at e_1^*. Let $B(t_0^*, t_1^*)$ denote the private benefit from adoption in this case. Comparing Figures 6.3 and 6.7 reveals that $B(t_0^*, t_1^*) > B(t_0^*)$. It follows that if $B(t_0^*) > K \geq G$ then $B(t_0^*, t_1^*) > K \geq G$. Thus, if efficiency calls for retention of the old technology but t_0^* is not time consistent, then the only time consistent policy is ratcheting, and this policy induces the *inefficient* adoption of the new technology.

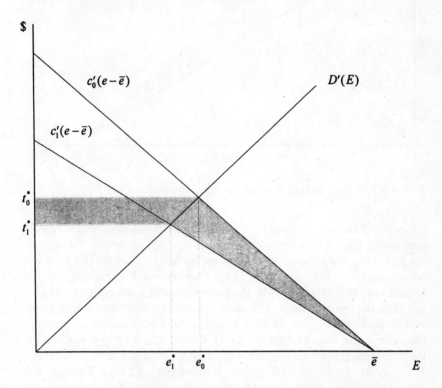

Figure 6.7 Private benefit from technology adoption under ratcheting

There is no corresponding problem if efficiency calls for adoption of the new technology (that is, if $G > K$). In this case, the first-best tax rate for period 2 is t_1^*. Figure 6.8 illustrates the private benefit to the firm from

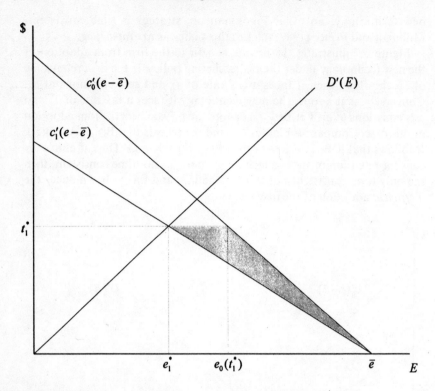

Figure 6.8 Private benefit from technology adoption (at t_1^*)

adoption of the new technology at this tax rate. If the firm retains the old technology then it sets emissions equal to $e_0(t_1^*)$. Conversely, if it adopts the new technology then it sets emissions equal to e_1^*. Let $B(t_1^*)$ denote the private benefit from adoption at t_1^*. Comparing Figures 6.2 and 6.8 reveals that $B(t_1^*) < G$. That is, the private benefit from adoption at t_1^* is less than the social benefit. This does not create a time consistency problem if $B(t_1^*) > K$ since in that case the firm will adopt the cleaner technology at t_1^* even though $B(t_1^*) < G$. Conversely, if $B(t_1^*) < K$ then t_1^* is not time consistent and the only time consistent policy is tax ratcheting. However, if $G > K$ then $B(t_0^*, t_1^*) > K$ since $B(t_0^*, t_1^*) > G$. Thus, if efficiency calls for adoption of the new technology then ratcheting will always implement that outcome.

These results indicate that the emissions tax cannot induce too little technological change but it can induce too much technological change. This problem with the emissions tax stems from the fact that it does not discriminate across units of emissions according to the damage they cause. The tax rate is set equal to the damage caused by the *marginal* unit of emissions and this tax rate is applied to every unit of emissions. This means that when marginal damage is increasing the total tax payment exceeds the total damage done. In assessing the private benefit to adopting a cleaner technology, the firm thinks in terms of reduced tax payments, but what matters from a social perspective is reduced damage. Since the reduction in tax payments under ratcheting exceeds the reduction in damage, the firm's incentive is distorted in favour of cleaner technology adoption. This generates the wrong technology choice if efficiency calls for retention of the old technology.

It is important to note that the dynamic incentive problem associated with the emissions tax is *not* due to the assumed timing of the game between the regulator and the firm. We have assumed that the regulator moves first by announcing a tax rate to which the firm responds with a technology choice. An alternative timing of the game would have the firm leading with a technology adoption decision and the regulator responding with the announcement of a tax rate. Under this timing the only time consistent strategy the regulator can ever play is ratcheting. The outcome to this differently timed game corresponds to the outcome of the game we have examined where the regulator moves first but the time consistency constraint is binding.

6.4.2 Many Firms

We now turn to the case of many firms. For any given m, where m is the number of firms that adopt the new technology, the optimal tax rate is equal to marginal damage evaluated at the efficient level of aggregate emissions:

$$t(m) \; D'(E(m)) \tag{6.3}$$

Thus, if $D'' = 0$ then $t'(m) = 0$, and if $D'' > 0$ then $t'(m) < 0$. This tax induces the efficient emission levels for *given* technologies; that is, a firm with technology i chooses its emissions $e_i(t(m))$ such that:

$$c_i'(\bar{e}_i - e_i(t(m))) = t(m) \tag{6.4}$$

This implements equation (6.1); that is, $e_i(t(m)) = e_i(m) \; \forall i$.

Whether or not the tax implements efficiency with respect to cleaner technology adoption depends again on whether damage is linear or strictly convex. We consider each case in turn.

Strictly convex damage

Recall from the single-firm case that the first-best tax rate may not be time consistent when damage is strictly convex. The same potential problem arises in the case of many firms and is in fact more acute. In particular, if efficiency requires strictly partial adoption of the new technology ($0 < m^* < n$) then the corresponding first-best tax rate is never time consistent. Why? If an announced fixed tax rate of $t(m^*)$ induces adoption of the new technology by *any* firm then it will induce adoption by *all* firms; it cannot induce strictly partial adoption among *ex ante* identical firms. Thus, if efficiency calls for strictly partial adoption then the associated first-best tax rate, $t(m^*)$, cannot be time consistent.

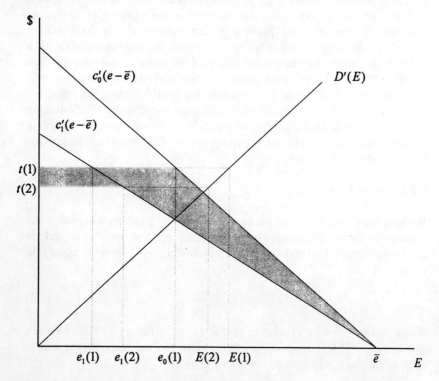

*Figure 6.9   Private benefit to the second adopting firm (strictly convex
damage)*

If the first-best tax rate is not time consistent then the only time consistent tax Pigouvian policy is ratcheting. Ratcheting in the context of many firms simply means announcing that the *ex post* tax rate will be set according to equation (6.3), based on the number of firms that adopt the new technology. The equilibrium induced by ratcheting exhibits excessive incentives for the adoption of the new technology. This is illustrated in Figure 6.9 for the case of $n = 2$ and $m^* = 1$. The shaded area in Figure 6.9 represents the private benefit to the second firm from adopting the new technology. This private benefit comprises the reduction in tax payments plus any reduction in abatement cost. Comparing Figures 6.9 and 6.5 reveals that the private benefit exceeds the social benefit. Thus, there is an excessive incentive for the second firm to adopt. The basic intuition behind this result is the same as for the case of a single firm: the total tax payments made under the Pigouvian emissions tax exceed the true external cost of emissions when damage is strictly convex.

Linear damage

When damage is linear the optimal tax rate is independent of the technologies used and so there is no potential time consistency problem for the regulator. Thus, the Pigouvian emissions tax policy implements efficiency with respect to technology adoption. The intuition behind the result is straightforward. When damage is linear the tax payments by a firm are exactly equal to the damage caused by its emissions. It follows that the private and social benefits from cleaner technology adoption coincide.

6.4.3 A Continuum of Firms

It is worth noting that when there is a continuum of firms, the Pigouvian emissions tax policy implements efficiency with respect to technology adoption even if damage is strictly convex. The reason is straightforward: if there is a continuum of firms then each firm is insignificant relative to the aggregate, and so each firm perceives that its own technology adoption choice has no impact on the tax rate chosen by the regulator.

6.5 IMPLEMENTATION WITH EMISSIONS TRADING

We now turn to the potential time consistency problems associated with emissions trading. It is important to note at the outset that we assume that the regulator is committed to adjusting the aggregate supply of permits to maintain an efficient balance between marginal damage and marginal abatement costs. Thus, we assume that the regulator has the same objective whether the policy instrument of choice is an emissions tax or an emissions trading programme. This ensures a consistent comparison between the two instruments.

We examine a tradable permit programme that operates in the following way. At the beginning of period 1 the regulator issues an aggregate number of permits corresponding to the efficient level of emissions based on the existing technology (used by all firms in period 1). It is not important for the problem at hand whether permits are issued by auction or through some sort of grandfathering scheme, provided that the initial distribution does not create asymmetric market power. Each permit allows one unit of emissions during period 1. We assume that no banking is allowed (which means that permits unused in period 1 cannot be carried forward to period 2).[5] The new technology arrives at the beginning of period 2 and the regulator then issues permits for use in period 2. The regulator may or may not then have to readjust that supply of permits in response to the technology adoption that actually occurs in equilibrium, depending on whether or not the first-best permit supply is time consistent.

Recall that the first-best tax rate under an emissions tax is the tax rate that induces efficiency with respect to technology adoption and at the same time generates the efficient level of aggregate emissions given the technologies in place. If this tax rate is not time consistent then the regulator must use tax ratcheting. Similarly, the first-best supply of permits (and associated equilibrium permit price) is that which induces efficient technology adoption choices and at the same time corresponds to the efficient aggregate level of emissions, given those technology choices. If this first-best permit supply is not time consistent then the regulator must use a responsive policy, akin to tax ratcheting, whereby the supply of permits is set at the beginning of period 2 and then adjusted *ex post* in response to equilibrium technology choices. As in the case of an emissions tax, the time consistency of the first-best solution depends on the nature of the damage function and on the number of regulated firms. We begin with a situation in which there is a continuum of firms and then consider a situation where the number of firms is small enough that each firm has some market power in the permit market. In both cases we examine a situation with linear damage and a situation with strictly convex damage.

6.5.1   A Continuum of Firms

Linear damage
Recall from section 6.4 that when damage is linear the regulator does not need to respond to technological change if an emissions tax is used. The tax rate is simply set equal to marginal damage and no adjustment is required. Moreover, this tax rate creates the correct incentives for technological change to occur. Thus, the regulator does not need to respond to the advent of a cleaner technology.

In contrast, the advent of a new technology requires a reassessment of the permit supply under an emissions trading programme even when damage is linear. In particular, the aggregate supply of permits that is efficient for an existing technology will generally *not* be efficient if a new technology is adopted; the first-best permit supply depends on the technologies in use. Recall from section 6.3 that when damage is linear, efficiency requires either adoption of the new technology by all firms or retention of the old technology by all firms, depending on the magnitude of the adoption cost. If efficiency calls for universal adoption then the first-best aggregate permit supply is $E_1^* = ne_1^*$ such that $c_1'(\overline{e}_1 - e_1^*) = \delta$. In contrast, if efficiency calls for universal retention of the old technology then the first-best permit supply is $E_0^* = ne_0^* > E_1^*$, such that $c_0'(\overline{e}_0 - e_0^*) = \delta$.

Consider first the case where efficiency calls for universal adoption. If the regulator issues the corresponding first-best number of permits, then adoption by all firms is the equilibrium response and the permit supply is efficient *ex post*. The key to this result is the fact that the *ex post* equilibrium price of permits is equal to marginal damage; thus, the private benefit from adoption to any individual firm is, in equilibrium, exactly equal to the social benefit.

Similarly, if efficiency calls for retention of the old technology and the permit supply is left unchanged from period 1, then the *ex post* price of permits in an equilibrium with no adoption is equal to marginal damage, and so the private benefit to adoption in that equilibrium is equal to the social benefit. Thus, leaving the supply of permits unchanged between periods is time consistent and induces efficiency.

It is important to emphasize that leaving the supply of permits unchanged in response to the advent of a new technology ensures efficiency with respect to the adoption of that technology only if efficiency calls for no adoption. If the regulator does not adjust the supply of permits *ex ante* then the permit price in a candidate equilibrium in which all firms adopt the new technology would be lower than marginal damage and so the private benefit to adoption in that candidate equilibrium would be less than the social benefit. The private benefit to adoption in the candidate equilibrium could therefore be less than the cost of adoption, in which case adoption by all firms could not in fact be an equilibrium even though adoption by all firms is efficient. Thus, ensuring efficiency when efficiency calls for the adoption of the new technology generally requires an adjustment to the supply of permits in response to the advent of that new technology even when damage is linear.

Strictly convex damage

Recall from section 6.4 that when damage is strictly convex the regulator faces a time consistency problem with an emissions tax when there is a relatively small number of firms but that the problem vanishes when there is a continuum of firms because each firm is insignificant relative to the aggregate and so perceives an independence between its own choices and the policies implemented by the regulator. The same is true in the case of emissions trading with a continuum of firms: there are no time consistency problems associated with implementation of the first-best policy even when damage is strictly convex.

The policy problem for the regulator in this case is in fact somewhat simpler under emissions trading than under an emissions tax. Recall that strictly convex damage means that efficiency may require strictly partial adoption of the new technology. In that case the regulator must use tax ratcheting, since committing to the first-best tax rate *ex ante* cannot induce asymmetric technology choices by *ex ante* symmetric firms, as required for an efficient equilibrium. In contrast, under emissions trading the regulator can set the first-best permit supply at the beginning of period 2, without the need for *ex post* adjustment, and none the less induce an asymmetric and time consistent equilibrium.

The key to this result is the flexibility of the permit price to respond to technology adoption choices in equilibrium. The equilibrium price of permits is decreasing in the number of firms that adopt the new technology since the demand for permits is lower when more firms use the new technology. This equilibrating role of the permit price means that the private benefit to any firm from adopting the new technology is decreasing in the number firms using that technology, and this in turn allows an equilibrium to exist in which some firms adopt but additional potential adopters find it unprofitable to do so. No comparable automatic adjustment to the price of emissions occurs under a fixed tax rate policy; hence the need for explicit tax ratcheting.

The equilibrium induced by the first-best supply adjustment is efficient. Each firm takes the permit price as independent of its own action and, since each firm is insignificant relative to the aggregate, marginal damage is effectively constant with respect to the emissions of each individual firm. Thus, the saving to the firm from having to hold fewer permits at the first-best equilibrium price fully reflects the reduction in damage.

6.5.2   A Small Number of Firms

The conditions required for a 'perfectly competitive' permit market break down when there are only a 'small' number of firms. However, emissions trading can still yield valuable efficiency gains under such circumstances and can still be an effective regulatory instrument if potentially destructive collusive and predatory practices can be controlled. Our approach here is to abstract from these potential 'anti-competitive' problems and focus on the implications of strategic interaction between firms, and between individual firms and the regulator, for the time consistency of permit supply adjustment policy. We begin with the case of linear damage.

Linear damage
The key issue of interest is the same as in the case with a continuum of firms: is it a time consistent policy for the regulator to issue the first-best number of permits at the beginning of period 2 without the need for *ex post* adjustment?

Consider first the case where efficiency calls for retention of the old technology by all firms. (Recall that efficiency requires 'all or nothing' when damage is linear.) Suppose the regulator issues permits corresponding to the associated first-best level of aggregate emissions: $E(0) = ne_0(0)$. Retention of the old technology by all firms will be an equilibrium response to this policy if no firm has an incentive to deviate from that equilibrium by adopting the new technology.

Consider the incentives for a potentially deviating firm. This firm is not a price-taker since the permit market is not characterized by perfect competition. The firm must instead sell permits through individual bargaining with other firms. The specific trading schedule the potential deviant faces depends on the number of firms in the market and the nature of the bargaining game between firms. However, that schedule must have two general properties. First, the trading schedule cannot lie above δ since no firm will be willing to purchase a permit if the asking price is higher than its marginal abatement cost. Since $c_0'(\overline{e}_0 - e_0(0)) = \delta$ at the candidate equilibrium, and since $c_0'' > 0$, it follows that the potential deviant cannot sell a permit for a price higher than δ. Second, the trading schedule cannot be downward sloping (since $c_0'' > 0$). An example schedule satisfying these two properties is illustrated as SS in Figure 6.10. Faced with this trading schedule the deviating firm sets emissions at $\tilde{e}_1$, and the private benefit from its new technology adoption is the shaded area in Figure 6.10. A comparison with Figure 6.1 reveals that the private benefit to the deviating firm cannot be greater than the social benefit from that deviation (and will generally be less). Since the social benefit is less than the cost of adoption (by nature of the fact that efficiency here by construction involves no adoption), it follows that the private benefit is also less than the cost of adoption, and so the deviation is not privately optimal. Thus, universal retention of the old technology is a time consistent equilibrium response to the first-best permit supply policy when universal retention of the old technology is efficient.

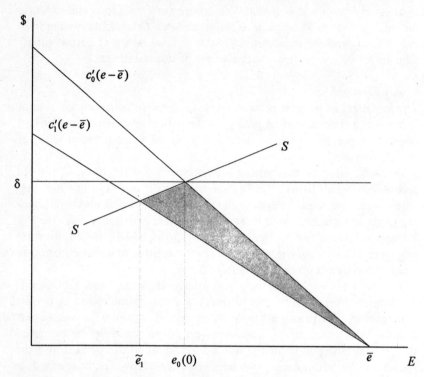

*Figure 6.10   Private benefit to a deviating firm that adopts the new
technology (linear damage)*

The first-best policy is also time-consistent when efficiency calls for
universal adoption of the new technology. The argument is exactly analogous to the one just made. Figure 6.11 illustrates the private benefit to a
deviating firm which retains the old technology when all other firms
adopt the new technology. The deviating firm cannot purchase permits
for less than the lowest marginal abatement cost of the other firms, and
so the deviating firm's trading schedule cannot lie below δ for permit purchases. Thus, the private cost (or forgone benefit) of retaining the old
technology for the deviating firm (the shaded area in Figure 6.11) must
exceed the social benefit from adoption, which in turn exceeds the cost of
adoption. Thus, the avoided cost of adoption for the deviating firm is less
than the cost of the deviation, and so the deviation is not worthwhile.
Thus, universal adoption of the new technology is a time consistent equilibrium response to the first-best permit supply policy when universal
adoption is efficient.

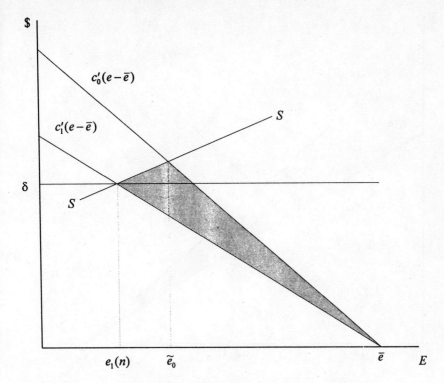

Figure 6.11 Private benefit to a deviating firm that retains the old technology (linear damage)

Strictly convex damage

In section 6.4 we argued that strictly convex damage combined with relatively few firms means that a Pigouvian emissions tax is generally not able to implement efficiency with respect to technology adoption. In particular, unless efficiency involves a corner solution, the only time consistent tax policy is ratcheting, and this policy creates excessive incentives for technology adoption. A similar problem arises under emissions trading but with the opposite implication for incentives.

Figures 6.9 and 6.12 illustrate the comparison between the tax policy and the emissions trading policy for the case of two firms and where $m^* = 1$. Recall that the shaded area in Figure 6.9 represents the private benefit (under ratcheting) to the remaining old technology firm if it deviates from the first-best solution. In comparison, the shaded area in Figure 6.12 illustrates the maximum private benefit to the remaining old technology firm if it deviates from the first-best solution under emissions

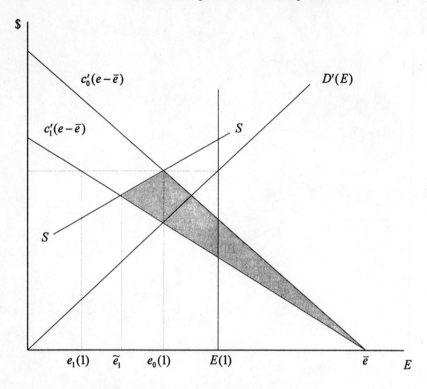

Figure 6.12   Private benefit to the second adopting firm at the first-best permit supply (strictly convex damage)

trading, where the supply of permits has been fixed at its first-best level. This area can be explained as follows. The maximum price the deviating firm can obtain for permits sold to the new technology firm is the latter firm's marginal abatement cost. The schedule labelled SS in Figure 6.12 plots that maximum price. Faced with this trading schedule, the deviating firm will set emissions at $\tilde{e}_1$, and so derive a private benefit from the deviation equal to the shaded area. A less favourable bargaining solution for the deviating firm will mean a smaller benefit than the shaded area. Comparing Figures 6.9 and 6.12 shows that the private benefit to the deviating firm is strictly less under emissions trading than under an emissions tax. Thus, the private benefit to deviation under emissions trading is less likely to exceed the cost of adoption than under the emissions tax. This means that under some conditions the first-best permit supply policy will be time consistent (and so implement efficiency) while the emissions tax policy leads to excessive technology adoption.

When the private benefit to deviation from the first-best solution does exceed the cost of adoption, the first-best permit supply policy will not be time consistent: the permit supply corresponding to the first-best technology choices will not implement those choices and so will not be optimal *ex post*. In such cases the only time consistent permit supply policy is a type of ratcheting, whereby the regulator initially issues the same number of permits in period 2 as in period 1 but then buys back permits to adjust the supply in response to technology adoption choices. Suppose the regulator cannot expropriate permits but must repurchase permits from willing sellers. Then the only time consistent policy is to announce that permits will be repurchased at a price equal to marginal damage evaluated at the optimum, given the technologies in place.

This is illustrated in Figure 6.13. At the beginning of period 2 both firms are using the old technology and the regulator issues $E(0)$ permits accordingly. Suppose one of the firms then adopts the new technology, in

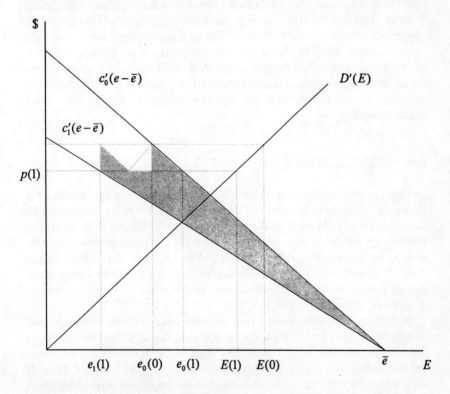

Figure 6.13 Private benefit from adoption by one firm under permit supply ratcheting (strictly convex damage)

which case the efficient level of aggregate emissions falls to $E(1)$. The regulator then offers to buy permits at price $p(1) = MD(E(1))$. At that price the adopting firm is willing to sell $e_0(0) - e_1(1)$ permits. The non-adopting firm is willing to pay a price higher than $p(1)$ for $e_0(1) - e_0(0)$ permits and so the adopting firm sells this many permits to the non-adopting firm. The remaining $E(0) - E(1)$ permits are sold back to the regulator. The resulting equilibrium is efficient, given the technologies in use. No other repurchase price will induce an efficient supply adjustment and so no other policy is time consistent.

The shaded area in Figure 6.13 represents the maximum private benefit to the single adopting firm under the permit supply ratcheting policy. This benefit comprises the payment received from the regulator for repurchased permits, plus the maximum possible payment from the adopting firm for traded permits, plus any reduction in its own abatement costs. In comparison, recall from Figure 6.4(c) the social benefit from adoption by one firm. It is clear that the private benefit under-represents the social benefit. Thus, the permit supply ratcheting policy tends to create an underincentive for the adoption of the new technology. Recall that the opposite result obtains for an emissions tax but the underlying reason is of the same nature. The ratcheting policy under emissions trading creates an underincentive for adoption because the payment received from the regulator for the repurchased permits understates the social value of the reduced damage.

6.6   CONCLUSION

In this chapter we have examined the time consistency properties of a Pigouvian emissions tax and emissions trading. Our main results can be summarized as follows. If damage is linear, then efficiency with respect to technology adoption involves either universal adoption of the new technology or universal retention of the old technology, depending on the cost of adoption. The first-best tax policy and the first-best permit supply policy are both time consistent under these conditions, and the induced equilibrium is efficient.

If damage is strictly convex, then efficiency may require strictly partial adoption of the new technology. In this case the first-best tax policy is not time consistent and tax ratcheting must be used. Ratcheting will none the less induce an efficient equilibrium if there is a continuum of firms. If there are relatively few firms, then ratcheting creates excessive incentives for adoption of the new technology. Thus, the resulting equilibrium may involve too much adoption.

The first-best permit supply policy is time consistent if there is a continuum of firms and induces the efficient solution. If there are relatively few firms, then the first-best policy may not be time consistent and the regulator must use permit supply ratcheting. This policy creates an under-incentive for firms to adopt the new technology. Thus, the resulting equilibrium may involve too little adoption.

Since both the Pigouvian emission tax and emissions trading potentially fail to induce efficiency when damage is strictly convex and there are relatively few firms, our results do not speak strongly in favour of one instrument over the other. However, it should be noted that if an emissions trading programme is intended to implement technological efficiency, then it is necessary to adjust the supply of permits continually in response to technological change, even when damage is linear. This continual adjustment is not needed for an emissions tax when damage is linear, a distinction that gives the emissions tax a possible advantage over emissions trading.

NOTES

1. See Kemp (1997) for a survey of this literature.
2. Some environmental problems are possibly characterized by concave damage at very high pollution levels but we have not examined that case here.
3. For clarity, all graphs are drawn for the case where $\bar{e}_0 = \bar{e}_1 = \bar{e}$.
4. The main results in this section are reported in more detail in Kennedy and Laplante (1997).
5. Allowing banking makes no difference at all since the arrival of a new technology in period 2 with lower abatement costs means that the option to bank would never be exercised.

REFERENCES

Biglaiser, Gary, John K. Horowitz and John Quiggin (1995), 'Dynamic pollution regulation', *Journal of Regulatory Economics*, **8**, 33–44.

Downing, Paul B. and Lawrence J. White (1986), 'Innovation in pollution control', *Journal of Environmental Economics and Management*, **13**, 18–29.

Jung, Chulho, Kerry Krutilla and Roy Boyd (1996), 'Incentives for advanced pollution abatement technology at the industry level: an evaluation of policy alternatives', *Journal of Environmental Economics and Management*, **30**, 95–111.

Kemp, Rene (1997), *Environmental Policy and Technical Change*, Cheltenham, UK and Brookfield, US: Edward Elgar.

Kennedy, Peter W. and Benoit Laplante (1997), 'Dynamic incentives and the Pigouvian tax', University of Victoria Discussion Paper 97–01.

Laffont, Jean-Jacques and Jean Tirole (1996a), 'Pollution permits and compliance strategies', *Journal of Public Economics*, **62**, 85–125.

Laffont, Jean-Jacques and Jean Tirole (1996b), 'A note on environmental innovation', *Journal of Public Economics*, **62**, 127–40.

Malueg, David A. (1989), 'Emission credit trading and the incentive to adopt new pollution abatement technology', *Journal of Environmental Economics and Management*, **16**, 52–7.

Milliman, Scott R. and Raymond Prince (1989), 'Firm incentives to promote technological change in pollution control', *Journal of Environmental Economics and Management*, **17**, 247–65.

7. Does government precommitment promote environmental innovation?

Emmanuel Petrakis and Anastasios Xepapadeas

7.1 INTRODUCTION

Recently, the theoretical literature has reflected a growing interest in issues related to the credibility of government policies. The credibility of government policies has mainly been analysed in the context of macro-economic policies,[1] however, more recently credibility issues related to microeconomic policies have come under consideration.[2] A basic question raised in the policy context is whether the ability of the government to precommit to a specific policy measure has beneficial effects on various aspects of the economic activity, such as the innovation rate, economic growth, or welfare. Despite the importance that the credibility of government policies may have for environmental innovation and hence pollution control, this issue has not been addressed in the context of environmental economics so far.

This chapter is a first attempt to analyse and compare the effects of environmental policies on environmental innovation and social welfare when the government can, or cannot, precommit to a specific level of emission taxes. For this purpose, we compare two scenarios: in the first the government precommits to an emission tax, and then a monopolist selects its abatement effort and output. This is the case that has been analysed in the literature so far. In the second, the monopolist chooses its abatement effort first, then the government sets an emission tax, and finally the monopolist decides its output. The second scenario emerges whenever the government's policy is non-credible. If the government is unable to commit to an emission tax in the first stage, firms will rationally anticipate that the government will adjust its emission tax in response to their own environmental innovation efforts, hence it is as if the government were choosing the emission tax in the second stage. Moreover, in this case firms can strategically select their abatement efforts in order to influence the emission tax the government will eventually set.

Using specific functional forms for demand, cost of environmental innovation, production costs and emission functions, we compare equilibrium environmental innovation, emission taxes and welfare when the government can, or cannot, commit to a specific policy. Our main result is that the government's inability to commit to a level of emission tax has a beneficial impact on environmental innovation. In this case the monopolist spends more on abatement than if the government had pre-committed to a specific emission tax. The monopolist, by exhibiting environmentally friendly behaviour, can strategically induce the government to substantially decrease its emission tax, or even to provide emission subsidies, and thus increase its profits. As a result, the emission tax set by the government is lower in the time consistent equilibrium than under precommitment. However, welfare is *always* lower if the government cannot precommit to a specific policy. The higher consumer surplus (due to the monopolist's output expansion) and the lower level of pollution are not sufficient to compensate for the increase in abatement expenditures due to the monopolist's overinvestment in clean technologies.

The rest of the chapter is organized as follows. Section 7.2 introduces the general model. In section 7.3, our main results axe derived for specific functional forms. Finally, section 7.4 concludes.

7.2 THE GENERAL MODEL

We consider a monopolist producing a homogeneous good and facing a standard demand curve, $p(q)$. Pollution is a byproduct of its production process. The monopolist, faced with a tax on its emissions t, can undertake an abatement effort (environmental innovation) w to reduce its emissions level, and thus reduce its tax burden. Environmental innovation increases costs but reduces emissions. Thus the cost function for the monopolist is defined by the strictly increasing convex function $c = c(q, w)$, while its emission function is defined as $s = s(q, w)$. The emission function is increasing and convex in q for fixed w, and decreasing and convex in w for fixed q.

We compare two alternative scenarios: the traditional scenario, where the government precommits to an emission tax and then the monopolist, taking this tax as given, chooses its abatement and output. However, due to both the investment characteristics of abatement expenses, which imply that abatement represents a long-term decision as compared to the short-term output decision, and also the ability of the government to change the emission tax following normal legislative procedures, the tax structure determined in this scenario cannot be credible unless the government possesses a specific commitment mechanism. Once the abatement effort has been chosen by the monopolist, the emission tax determined through precommitment is not *ex post* optimal and therefore is not time consistent. The monopolist rationally anticipates a change in the emission tax once its abatement expenses are already sunk.

Therefore, when the government cannot credibly commit to a policy and is expected to change the emission tax after abatement expenses have been chosen, then a time consistent emission tax implies that the tax is *ex post* optimal, given abatement expenses and the firm's future output response to the emission tax. To determine this time consistent tax, we consider the following scenario. The monopolist first selects its abatement effort, then the government sets the emission tax, and finally the monopolist chooses its output. We begin our analysis with this second scenario.

7.2.1 Non-credible Environmental Policies

Output stage
The monopolist treats the emission tax t as given and chooses output, given its own abatement expenses, w, that are sunk at this stage, by solving the problem:

$$\max_q p\,(q)\,q - c\,(q,\,w) - t^*s\,(q,\,w)$$

with first-order conditions for an interior solution:

$$p + q\,\frac{\partial p}{\partial q} = \frac{\partial c}{\partial q} + \frac{\partial s}{\partial q}\,t^* \tag{7.1}$$

The profit-maximizing level of output is a function of the tax t^* and the abatement effort w. That is, $q^* = g\,(t^*,\,w)$. Standard comparative static analysis indicates that:

$$\frac{\partial q^*}{\partial t^*} < 0,\,\frac{\partial q^*}{\partial w} > 0$$

Thus, an increase in taxation reduces output, while an increase in abatement increases the profit-maximizing output level.

Emission tax stage
The government's objective function is determined as the sum of consumer and producer surplus less environmental damages which are

defined by a convex, in emissions, damage function D (s (q, w)). Given the profit-maximizing output $q^* = g$ (t^*, w), the government chooses the tax rate t^* by maximizing its objective function. Thus, the government solves:

$$\max_{t^*} \int_0^q p\,(u)\,du - c(q^*, w) - D\,(s(q^*, w)); \; q^* = g\,(t^*, w)$$

The first-order condition for this problem is:

$$\left(p - \frac{\partial c}{\partial q} - D'\frac{\partial s}{\partial q}\right)\frac{\partial q}{\partial t^*} = 0, \text{ or } p - \frac{\partial c}{\partial q} - D'\frac{\partial s}{\partial q} = 0 \qquad (7.2)$$

since $\dfrac{\partial q}{\partial t^*} < 0$.

Solving (7.2) for the optimal tax t^*, we determine this tax as a function of the abatement effort w, or $t^* = \tau\,(w)$. Comparative static analysis indicates that:

$$\frac{\partial t^*}{\partial w} < 0$$

Thus increased abatement effort reduces the optimal emission tax.

Innovation stage
In this stage the monopolist chooses abatement but treats the emission tax not as a fixed parameter but as a function of its own abatement effort. The monopolist solves the problem:

$$\max_{w} p\,(g\,(\tau\,(w),\,w))\,g\,(\tau\,(w),\,w) - c\,(g\,(\tau\,(w),\,w),\,w) - \tau\,(w)\,s\,(g\,(\tau\,(w),\,w),\,w)$$

The first-order condition for this, after some simplification, is:

$$\frac{\partial c}{\partial w} = -t^*\frac{\partial s}{\partial w} - \frac{\partial t^*}{\partial w}\,s, \; t^* = \tau\,(w) \qquad (7.3)$$

7.2.2 Government Precommitment

The tax structure in the case of precommitment is well known (Barnett 1980). Solving the problem backwards, the monopolist chooses output and abatement and then the government sets the optimal emission tax.[3]

Output–innovation stage

The monopolist treats the emission tax t as given and solves the problem:

$$\max_{q,w} p\,(q)\,q - c(q,\,w) - \tilde{t}s\,(q,\,w)$$

with the usual first-order conditions for interior solutions:

$$p + \frac{dp}{dq} = \frac{\partial c}{\partial q} + \tilde{t}\frac{\partial s}{\partial q} \tag{7.4}$$

$$\frac{\partial c}{\partial w} = -\tilde{t}\frac{\partial s}{\partial w} \tag{7.5}$$

Optimal output and abatement are determined as $\tilde{q} = \tilde{q}(\tilde{t})$ and $\tilde{w} = \tilde{w}(\tilde{t})$.

Emission tax selection

Given $\tilde{q} = \tilde{q}\,(\tilde{t})$ and $\tilde{w} = \tilde{w}\,(\tilde{t})$, the government determines the optimal tax to maximize total welfare (as above):

$$\max_{\tilde{t}} \int_0^q p\,(u)\,du - c(\tilde{q},\,\tilde{w}) - D\,(s(\tilde{q},\,\tilde{w}));\quad \tilde{q} = \tilde{q}\,(\tilde{t}),\ \tilde{w} = \tilde{w}\,(\tilde{t})$$

Using the monopolist's profit-maximizing conditions (7.4) and (7.5), the optimal tax is determined as:

$$\tilde{t} = D' - \frac{p}{|\varepsilon|}\frac{\partial \tilde{q}}{\partial s}$$

where ε is the elasticity of demand.

Comparing condition (7.3) with (7.4) reveals the basic difference between the case of non-credible environmental policies and the case where the government is able to precommit to a policy. In the latter, optimal abatement is determined at the level where marginal abatement cost equals marginal tax savings due to abatement. On the other hand, in the discretionary case optimal abatement is determined through (7.3) at the level where marginal abatement cost equals marginal tax savings due to emission reduction from abatement, $-t^*(\partial s)/(\partial w)$, plus marginal tax savings due to tax rule reduction from an increase in abatement, $-s(\partial t^*)/(\partial w)$. Therefore, in the non-credible policy case the choice of abatement is affected by the effect that the abatement itself has on the emission tax, through the term $\partial t^*/\partial w$, while in the precommitment case no such effect exists. This second-round effect on abatement causes deviation between optimal environmental innovation and optimal emission taxes in the pre-commitment and time consistent cases.

7.3   THE LINEAR-QUADRATIC CASE

In this section, for tractability reasons, we shall consider specific functional forms. Assume that market demand is linear, $P(q) = a - q$. The cost function is assumed to be additively separable in production costs and environmental innovation costs, that is, $c(q, w) = cq + \gamma(w^2/2)$. There are constant returns to scale in production, that is, the marginal production cost c is constant. On the other hand, innovation costs are quadratic in innovation effort w, that is, the marginal innovation cost is increasing in w, with γ representing the degree of decreasing returns to scale of innovation effort. Further, total emissions are proportional to output, $s(q, w) = q(v - w)$, where v are the emissions per unit of output with the current technology. The monopolist, by investing an amount of $\gamma(w^2/2)$ in environmental R&D, can reduce its unitary emissions by w. Finally, the damage function is assumed to be linear in total emissions, that is, $D(q, w) = d(v - w)q$, where d represents the marginal damage.[4]

As environmental R&D effort is a long-run decision variable for the monopolist, we shall assume that abatement effort is chosen first, and then follows the decision on output.[5] In subsection 7.3.1 we analyse the case of time consistent emission taxes, while in subsection 7.3.2 the pre-commitment case is treated. Finally, subsection 7.3.3 compares the results when the government can, or cannot, precommit to an emission tax.

7.3.1   Non-credible Environmental Policies

Output selection
In the last stage, the monopolist chooses its output to maximize profits:

$$\max_q [(a - q)\, q - cq - \tfrac{1}{2}\gamma w^2 - t\,(v - w)q]$$

where t is the tax per unit of emissions. The first-order condition is:

$$a - q^m - c - t(v - w) = q^m \qquad (7.6)$$

Let A = $a - c$, where A is a measure of the market size. From (7.6) the optimal output is:

$$q^m = \tfrac{1}{2}(A - t(v - w)) \qquad (7.7)$$

and the monopolist's profits are:

$$\pi^m = (q^m)^2 - \tfrac{1}{2}\gamma w^2 \qquad (7.8)$$

Note that the monopolist's output and profits decrease with the emission tax, t, and increase with the market size, A. Further, output (and gross profits) increase with the monopolist's abatement effort, w.

Government's choice of emission tax
In the second stage, the government chooses the emission tax that maximizes total welfare, taking into account the monopolist's reaction in the subsequent output selection stage. The total welfare is defined as the (unweighted) sum of consumer surplus, monopolist's profits and environmental damages due to the monopolist's emissions. Given that the monopolist selects output according to (7.7), the government solves:

$$\max_{t^*} \int_0^{q^m} (a - c - x)dx - d(v - w)q^m - \tfrac{1}{2}\gamma w^2$$

which is equivalent to:

$$\max_{t^*} [\, Aq^m - \tfrac{1}{2}(q^m)^2 - d(v - w)q^m - \tfrac{1}{2}\gamma m^2 \,] \qquad (7.9)$$

The first order condition is:

$$\left[A - q^m - d(v - w)\frac{dq^m}{dt} = 0 \right] \qquad (7.10)$$

where $dq^m/dt = -\tfrac{1}{2}(v - w) < 0$. Then, from (7.7), we get the optimal tax on the monopolist's emissions:

$$t^* = 2d - \frac{A}{v - w} \qquad (7.11)$$

Note that the optimal emissions tax increases with the marginal damage, d, and the unitary emissions with the current technology, v, and decreases with the market size, A. More interestingly, it decreases with the monopolist's abatement effort, w. Therefore, the monopolist, by increasing its environmental innovation expenditures, can *strategically* induce a lower tax on its emissions.

Now, substituting (7.11) into (7.7) and (7.8), we get the monopolist's output and profits:

$$q^m = A - d(v - w) \tag{7.12}$$

$$\pi^m = (A - d(v - w))^2 \tfrac{1}{2}\gamma w^2 \tag{7.13}$$

That is, the monopolist's output (and gross profits) increase with its abatement effort. Finally, by (7.9), total welfare is:

$$TW^* = \tfrac{1}{2}(A - d(v - w))^2 - \tfrac{1}{2}\gamma w^2 \tag{7.14}$$

Environmental innovation selection
In the first stage, the monopolist chooses its abatement effort to maximize its profits, taking into account that its decision will affect the government's optimal policy in the subsequent stage. Thus, the monopolist solves (see (7.13)):

$$\max_w [A - d(v - w)]^2 - \tfrac{1}{2}\gamma w^2$$

The first-order condition is:

$$2(A - d(v - w^m))d - \gamma w^m$$

hence, the optimal abatement effort for the monopolist when the government cannot credibly commit to an emissions tax is:

$$w^m = \frac{2d(A - dv)}{\gamma - 2d^2} \tag{7.15}$$

To simplify the analysis, define $r = 2d^2/\gamma$ and $s = vd/A$. Observe that r is a measure of marginal pollution damage relative to the degree of decreasing returns of abatement costs; r increases with the marginal pollution damage and decreases as the abatement cost function becomes more convex. On the other hand, s is the per unit of output damage when producing with the current technology relative to the market size; s decreases with the market size, and increases with the marginal pollution damage and the initial unitary emissions of the monopolist. Note that for an interior solution to exist in our problem, that is, $0 < w^m < v$, the following condition must hold: $r < s \leq 1$. In what follows, we shall also assume that $s > \underline{s}(r) > 0.25$, where $\underline{s}(r)$ solves $4s^2 - 2s + r = 0$, hence $\underline{s}$ is decreasing in r.[6] We can now express optimal innovation effort, emission tax, output, profits and total welfare as functions of s and r:

$$w^m = \frac{r(1-s)}{s(1-r)} v \qquad (7.16)$$

$$t^* = d - \frac{d(1-s)}{s-r} = d\frac{2s-r-1}{s-r} \qquad (7.17)$$

$$q^m = \frac{\gamma}{2d} w^m = \frac{(1-s)}{1-r} A \qquad (7.18)$$

$$\pi^m = \frac{(1-s)^2}{1-r} A^2 \qquad (7.19)$$

$$TW^* = \frac{(1-2r)\,(1-s)^2}{2(1-r)^2} A^2 \qquad (7.20)$$

Note that if $s \leq (1+r)/2 < 1$ then $t^* \leq 0$, that is, the time consistent tax is negative. As the monopolist has decreased substantially its unitary emissions by overinvesting in abatement technology, the government, through emission subsidies, partially corrects for the inefficiency provoked by the monopolist's market power. Note further that, when $r > 0.5$ (for instance, if γ is relatively small and d sufficiently high), total welfare turns out to be negative. Innovation expenditures are so high that they do not compensate for the decrease in the environmental damages and the increase in the consumer surplus.

7.3.2 Government Precommitment to an Emissions Tax

The output selection stage is the same as above. Thus, the optimal output
and profits are given by (7.7) and (7.8).

Environmental innovation selection
The monopolist chooses its abatement effort to maximize profits:

$$\max_{w}[(q^m)^2 - \tfrac{1}{2}\gamma w^2]$$

The first-order condition is:

$$2q^m \frac{dq^m}{dw} = \gamma w \tag{7.21}$$

where from (7.7) we have that $dq^m/dt = t/2$, hence (7.21) becomes:

$$t(A - t(v - \tilde{w}^m)) = \gamma \tilde{w}^m$$

Solving, we obtain the optimal environmental innovation effort,
output and profits for the monopolist. Let $t_n = t/d$, that is, t_n is the emission tax relative to marginal damage. Then:

$$\tilde{w}^m = \frac{t\,(A - tv)}{2\gamma - t^2} = \frac{vt_n\,(1 - t_n s)}{s\left(\dfrac{4}{r} - t\,^2_n\right)} \tag{7.22}$$

$$\tilde{q}^m = \frac{\gamma}{t}\,\tilde{w}^m = \frac{\gamma\,(A - tv)}{2\gamma - t^2} \tag{7.23}$$

$$\tilde{\pi}^m = \frac{\gamma\,(A - tv)^2}{2(2\gamma - t^2)} = \frac{(1 - t_n s)^2}{r\left(\dfrac{4}{r} - t\,^2_n\right)} \tag{7.24}$$

Optimal emissions tax

The government chooses the emissions tax that maximizes total welfare, taking into account how the monopolist will react to its environmental policy:

$$\max_{t} \int_{0}^{\tilde{q}^{m}} (a - c - x)dx - d(v - \tilde{w}^{m})\,\tilde{q}^{m} - \tfrac{1}{2}\gamma(\tilde{w}^{m})^{2}$$

Equivalently,

$$\max_{t} [A\,\tilde{q}^{m} - \tfrac{1}{2}(\tilde{q}^{m})^{2} - d(v - \tilde{w}^{m})\,\tilde{q}m - \tfrac{1}{2}\gamma(\tilde{w}^{m})^{2}]$$

Substituting output and innovation effort from (7.23) and (7.22) we obtain the total welfare as a function of t:

$$\widetilde{TW} = \frac{\gamma(A - tv)\,[vt^{3} - 3At^{2} + (2\,Ad + \gamma v)t + (3A - 4dv)\gamma]}{2\,(2\gamma - t^{2})^{2}}$$

$$= \frac{A^{2}\,(1 - t_{n}s)\left[st_{n}^{3} - 3t_{n}^{2} + 2\left(1 + \dfrac{s}{r}\right)t_{n} + \dfrac{2}{r}\left(3 - 4s\right)\right]}{r\left(\dfrac{4}{r} - t_{n}^{2}\right)^{2}} \qquad (7.25)$$

The first-order condition after some manipulations becomes:

$$\frac{d\widetilde{TW}}{dt} = \frac{\gamma A^{2}d^{3}}{(2\gamma - t_{n}^{2}d^{2})^{3}}\;[\mu_{4}t_{n}^{4} - \mu_{3}t_{n}^{3} + \mu_{2}t_{n}^{2} - \mu_{1}t_{n} + \mu_{0}] = 0 \qquad (7.26)$$

where:

$$\mu_{4} = 2s \qquad \mu_{3} = 3 + 2s + \frac{10s^{2}}{r} \qquad \mu_{2} = 3\left(1 + \frac{6s}{r} + \frac{4s^{2}}{r}\right)$$

$$\mu_{1} = \frac{8s}{r}\left(3 + \frac{s}{r}\right) \qquad \mu_{0} = \frac{4}{r^{2}}\,(4s^{2} - 2s + r)$$

This fourth-degree equation in (s, r) cannot be solved analytically, and thus there is no explicit expression for the optimal precommitment emission tax. Note however that, if $4s^2 - 2s + r > 0$, then $d\widetilde{\text{TW}}/dt\,|_{t=0} > 0$, and thus $\tilde{t} > 0$. This condition holds for all $s \geqslant 0.5$. On the other hand, if $0.25 < s < 0.5$, it holds as long as s is sufficiently large, that is, $s > \underline{s}$, where $\underline{s}$ solves $4s^2 - 2s + r = 0$, with $\underline{s}$ decreasing in r. Finally, it never holds for $s \leqslant 0.25$. As we said above, we shall restrict attention to the cases where total welfare increases with a tax on emissions, that is, $s > \underline{s}(r) > 0.25$.

7.3.3 Non-credible versus Precommitment Policies

In this subsection we compare optimal time consistent and precommitment emission taxes and innovation efforts, as well as monopolist's profits and total welfare in these two cases. The following proposition compares emission taxes in the two regimes:

Proposition 1 The optimal time consistent emission tax is always lower than the optimal precommitment emission tax, that is $\tilde{t} > t^*$.

Proof Note first that if $\underline{s} < s < (1+r)/2$, then $t^* < 0 < \tilde{t}$. It remains to prove that this is also true for $s > (1+r)/2$. To do this we need to evaluate $d\text{TW}/dt$ at $t = t^*$. First, the denominator of (7.26) is positive, since it can be written as:

$$2\gamma - (t^*)^2 = 2\gamma \left[1 - \frac{s\left(s - \dfrac{r+1}{2}\right)^2}{(s-r)^2} \right] > 0$$

Thus the sign of $d\text{TW}/dt\,|_{t=t^*}$ is the same as the sign of the expression in square brackets in (7.26) evaluated at $t_n = t^*/d$. Substituting t^* from (7.17) and plotting the expression in square brackets for all (s, r) such that $0 < r < s \leqslant 1$ and $s \geqslant (r+1)/2$, we can see that $d\text{TW}/dt\,|_{t=t^*} > 0$. Hence, $\tilde{t} > t^*$. QED

We now turn to the comparison of innovation efforts under non-credible and precommitment policies. w^m is given by (7.16). However, to obtain $\tilde{w}^m$, we need first to solve (7.26) for t_n, select the appropriate root t_n^* and then substitute t_n^* into (7.22). Since we cannot solve (7.26) analytically for the optimal precommitment emission tax, the only way to compare w^m and $\tilde{w}^m$ is by numerical simulations. As we are able to evaluate[7] w^m and $\tilde{w}^m$ on a fine grid $(r/s, s)$, simulations do not limit the generality of our results. In particular, since $0 < r < s \leqslant 1$, with $s > \underline{s} > 0.25$, we define a grid $(r/s, s)$, with $s = 0.3, 0.4, \ldots, 0.9$ and $r/s = 0.1, 0.2, \ldots, 0.9$.[8] Normalize $w_n^m = w^m/v$ and $\tilde{w}_n^m = \tilde{w}^m/v$. Then w_n^m and $\tilde{w}_n^m$ depend only on the parameters r/s and s.

The results for n the normalized values of the innovation efforts are reported in Table 7.1. The following summarizes the results:

Result 1 The monopolist's environmental innovation is always higher when the government cannot credibly commit to an emission tax, that is $w^m > \tilde{w}^m$.

The intuition is straightforward. When the government selects its environmental policy after the monopolist's decision on environmental innovation, the monopolist has a strategic incentive to increase its abate-

Table 7.1 Environmental innovation efforts

$\frac{s}{r/s}$	0.3	0.4	0.5	0.6	0.7	0.8	0.9	
0.1			0.0526	0.0426	0.0323	0.0217	0.011	w_n^m
			0.0019	0.0069	0.0086	0.0076	0.0046	$\tilde{w}_n^m$
0.2			0.1111	0.0909	0.0698	0.0477	0.0244	w_n^m
			0.0061	0.0142	0.0172	0.0155	0.0096	$\tilde{w}_n^m$
0.3			0.1764	0.1463	0.1139	0.0789	0.0411	w_n^m
			0.0118	0.0218	0.0258	0.0237	0.015	$\tilde{w}_n^m$
0.4			0.25	0.2105	0.1667	0.1176	0.0625	w_n^m
			0.0184	0.0296	0.0344	0.0320	0.0208	$\tilde{w}_n^m$
0.5		0.375	0.333	0.2857	0.2308	0.1667	0.0909	w_n^m
		0.0063	0.0257	0.0378	0.0431	0.0405	0.027	$\tilde{w}_n^m$
		0.4737	0.4286	0.375	0.3103	0.2308	0.1304	w_n^m
0.6		0.0137	0.0337	0.0461	0.0518	0.0492	0.0338	$\tilde{w}_n^m$
0.7		0.5833	0.5385	0.4828	0.4118	0.3182	0.1892	w_n^m
		0.0221	0.0422	0.0547	0.0606	0.058	0.041	$\tilde{w}_n^m$
0.8		0.7059	0.6667	0.6154	0.5454	0.4444	0.2857	w_n^m
		0.0312	0.0512	0.0637	0.0695	0.067	0.0488	$\tilde{w}_n^m$
0.9	0.863	0.8438	0.8182	0.7826	0.7297	0.6429	0.4737	w_n^m
	0.0103	0.0411	0.0606	0.0728	0.0785	0.076	0.0571	$\tilde{w}_n^m$

ment effort in order to induce a lower tax on its emissions (or even to obtain an emission subsidy). This strategic effect is absent when the government can precommit to a specific emission tax before the monopolist chooses its abatement effort. Thus, the monopolist invests more in abatement when the government policy is non-credible.

Finally, we compare the monopolist's profits and the total welfare under non-credible and precommitment environmental policies. We again use numerical simulations to compare TW^* and $\widetilde{TW}^*$. TW^* is given in (7.20), while to obtain $\widetilde{TW}^*$ we substitute t_n^* into (7.25). Normalize TW_n^* = TW^*/A^2 and $\widetilde{TW}_n^* = \widetilde{TW}^*/A^2$. Then TW_n^* and $\widetilde{TW}_n^*$ depend only on the parameters r/s and s. Using a similar procedure we can compare the monopolist's profits in the two cases: π^m is given by (7.19) and $\tilde{\pi}^m$ is obtained by substituting t_n^* into (7.24). The results for the normalized total welfare are reported in Table 7.2.[9] The following summarizes the results:

Result 2 Total welfare is always lower, and monopolist's profits always higher, when the government cannot precommit to a specific emission tax.

Since the monopolist overinvests in abatement to obtain a lower tax on its emissions, the environmental innovation expenditures are excessive for the society. On the other hand, a lower emission tax (or an emission subsidy) leads to a higher level of output, and thus an increase in consumer surplus. In addition, it often leads to higher aggregate emissions, and thus increases the environmental damages. The negative effect dominates the positive effect, hence total welfare is lower when the government is unable to precommit to an emission tax. In fact, total welfare can even be negative under optimal non-credible policies. This could happen when both s and r/s take rather high values (see Table 7.2: for example, for $s = 0.8$ and $r = 0.8$, $TW^* = -0.043A^2$). On the other hand, the monopolist has the first-mover advantage when the government is unable to precommit to a policy. The monopolist is then able to increase its net profits by appropriately choosing its abatement effort to manipulate the government's choice of emission tax.

7.4   CONCLUSIONS

The question addressed in this chapter is whether a government's precommitment to an environmental policy promotes environmental innovation. We show that the government's ability to precommit to an emission tax leads the monopolist to lower its abatement effort relative to the case

Table 7.2 *Total welfare*

$\frac{r}{s}$	0.3	0.4	0.5	0.6	0.7	0.8	0.9	
0.1			0.1246	0.080	0.0447	0.0199	0.0050	TW_n^*
			0.1252	0.0813	0.0463	0.0208	0.0052	$\widetilde{TW}_n^*$
0.2			0.1235	0.0785	0.0438	0.0193	0.0048	TW_n^*
			0.1258	0.0827	0.0476	0.0216	0.0055	$\widetilde{TW}_n^*$
0.3			0.1211	0.0761	0.0418	0.0180	0.0043	TW_n^*
			0.1266	0.0841	0.0490	0.0225	0.0058	$\widetilde{TW}_n^*$
0.4			0.1172	0.072	0.0382	0.0156	0.0034	TW_n^*
			0.1275	0.0855	0.0504	0.0234	0.0061	$\widetilde{TW}_n^*$
0.5		0.1688	0.1111	0.0653	0.032	0.0111	0.0017	TW_n^*
		0.1751	0.1284	0.087	0.0518	0.0244	0.0064	$\widetilde{TW}_n^*$
0.6		0.1621	0.102	0.0547	0.0214	0.0030	–0.002	TW_n^*
		0.1755	0.1295	0.0884	0.0533	0.0254	0.0068	$\widetilde{TW}_n^*$
0.7		0.1528	0.0888	0.0381	0.0035	–0.012	–0.010	TW_n^*
		0.176	0.1307	0.090	0.0548	0.0265	0.0072	$\widetilde{TW}_n^*$
0.8		0.1401	0.0694	0.0118	–0.028	–0.043	0.028	TW_n^*
		0.1766	0.1319	0.0915	0.0563	0.0277	0.0077	$\widetilde{TW}_n^*$
0.9	0.2115	0.123	0.0413	–0.030	–0.085	–0.112	–0.086	TW_n^*
	0.2251	0.1773	0.1331	0.093	0.0579	0.0289	0.0082	$\widetilde{TW}_n^*$

where the environmental policy is at the government's discretion. However, under precommitment, total welfare is always higher than under non-credible policies.[10] The monopolist overinvests in abatement effort to induce the government to decrease the tax on its emissions, or even receive an emissions subsidy. As a result, the optimal time consistent emission tax is always lower than the optimal tax under precommitment.

In this chapter we have restricted attention to the monopoly case. It is worth exploring whether the same results apply when there are more firms in the industry. For instance, oligopolists would have the same strategic incentive to increase their environmental efforts in order to induce the government to decrease the tax on their emissions. However, as this tax decrease will benefit not only the firm under consideration, but also all its rivals, the firm will have less incentive to overinvest in abatement effort. The latter effect will not be present if all firms in the industry participate in an Environmental Research Joint Venture to reduce their unitary emissions. In the latter case, our conjecture is that all the above results will apply. It is also worth exploring the international dimension of our problem. An emissions tax weakens the competitiveness of the domestic firms in the international arena and governments are thus reluctant to adopt such a policy. Our analysis suggests that a government, by not precommitting to a policy, not only induces domestic firms to increase their abatement efforts, but also harms their international competitiveness less as the tax on their emissions is lower in this case.

NOTES

1. See, for example, the survey by Persson and Tabellini (1997).
2. See, for example, Maskin and Newbery (1990); Leahy and Neary (1995, 1996, 1997); Koujianou Goldberg (1995); Herguera *et al.* (1997).
3. Output and abatement can be chosen sequentially, first abatement then output, or simultaneously without any change in the results.
4. This is a rather restrictive assumption which most probably drives out our strong welfare result. As we shall see, welfare is *always* lower if the government is unable to precommit to a specific policy. If the damage function were convex, then the beneficial effect of the more environmentally friendly technology could outweigh the excessive investment made by the monopolist, leading thus to an increase in welfare under time consistent emission taxes. We thank Massimo Motta for pointing this out to us.
5. Of course, if the government can precommit to an emission tax, then the outcome will be the same regardless of whether the monopolist chooses its abatement effort and output simultaneously or sequentially. If, however, the government cannot credibly commit to an emission tax, then these outcomes are different, and the sequential choice is the right way to model the situation. Note that in the presentation of the general model, output and abatement are chosen simultaneously in the precommitment case.
6. That is, v and d are sufficiently high (relative to the market size) to justify a tax on emissions, at least for the case where the government can precommit to an emission tax. We shall see this in the next subsection.
7. All calculations were performed using Mathematica.
8. Of course, if $s = 0.3$, then r/s can only take the value of 0.9; and if $s = 0.4$, $r/s = 0.5$, 0.6, ..., 0.9.
9. The numerical results for the monopolist's profits are available from the authors upon request.
10. This result is in line with the literature. See, for example, Leahy and Neary (1996); Herguera *et al.* (1997).

REFERENCES

Barnett, A.H. (1980), 'The Pigouvian tax rule under monopoly', *American Economic Review*, **70**, 1037–41.

Herguera, I., P. Kujal and E. Petrakis (1997), 'Non-credible policies and leapfrogging in vertically differentiated industries', Universidad Carlos III Working Paper 97-73.

Koujianou Goldberg, P. (1995), 'Strategic export promotion in the absence of government precommitment', *International Economic Review*, **36** (2), 407–26.

Leahy, D. and J.P. Neary (1995), 'Learning by doing, precommitment and infant-industry protection', Centre for Economic Performance Discussion Paper no. 251, London: London School of Economics; forthcoming, in *Review of Economic Studies*.

Leahy, D., and J.P. Neary (1996), 'International R&D rivalry and industrial strategy without government commitment', *Review of International Economics*, **4**(3), 322–38.

Leahy, D. and J.P. Neary (1997), 'Public policy towards R&D in oligopolistic industries', *American Economic Review*, **87**(4), 642–62.

Maskin, E. and D. Newbery (1990), 'Disadvantageous oil tariffs and dynamic consistency', *American Economic Review*, **80**, 143–56.

Persson, T. and G. Tabellini (1997), 'Political economics and macroeconomic policy', CEPR Discussion Paper no. 1759.

8. Diffusion of abatement technologies in a differentiated industry

Emmanuel Petrakis

8.1 INTRODUCTION

The threat of climate change due to the accumulation of carbon dioxide, as well as other greenhouse gases (GHGs), in the atmosphere has recently become a major economic and political issue. There is by now a general consensus that the socioeconomic consequences of global warming could be very harmful to our planet and could even be disastrous for some geographic areas or countries. This attitude was reflected in the Convention for Climate Change organized by the United Nations in Kyoto (Japan) in December 1997, in which as many as 160 countries participated. The main issue at stake for the participants was to control their GHGs emissions in order to achieve the stabilization of global GHGs emissions by 2010 to their 1990 level. This stabilization can only be achieved if the most-industrialized countries can commit to a substantial decrease in their pollutants. The agreement reached in Kyoto, a 5.2 per cent emission reduction on average for the 39 most-developed countries, is a satisfactory first step towards the stabilization of global GHG emissions. In particular, the European Union (EU) has committed to a reduction of its emissions by 8 per cent (which, however, will not be distributed evenly among its country members). The EU's common posture is that an 8 per cent reduction of its emissions level by 2010, with respect to their 1990 level, can be achieved exclusively through a wide diffusion of the best available technologies (BATs) in their most-polluting sectors (such as transportation, industrial sector, energy production, and so on). Therefore, the investigation of the economic forces that facilitate, or hinder, the diffusion of existing 'clean' technologies becomes all the more important. Yet the literature on the diffusion of green technologies is rather scarce.

Recently, a number of empirical studies have investigated the private incentives for adoption of the best available technology in the absence of environmental policies, as well as how these incentives are influenced by policies such as emission taxes and innovation subsidies.[1] Boetti and

Botteon (1996) report that a widespread adoption of some energy-saving technologies is likely to lead to a reduction in carbon dioxide (CO_2) emissions of approximately 10 per cent compared to 1990 levels. However, in the absence of any environmental policy, this reduction could end up being only of the order of 2.5 per cent. In this light, the design of environmental policies influences firms' incentives to adopt an abatement technology and hence plays a crucial role in their effectiveness in reducing emissions.

On the other hand, to my knowledge there is hardly any theoretical literature addressing the issue of diffusion of green technologies. The exception is Carraro and Soubeyran (1996), in which the incentives of a firm to adopt a clean technology under different environmental policies are analysed. However, this paper assumes away any strategic considerations.[2] For instance, when firms compete in the market and also face emissions taxes, a firm may have an incentive to adopt the clean technology earlier in order to reduce the tax burden on its emissions and thus gain market share from its rivals.

This chapter analyses firms' incentives to adopt an existing abatement technology (for instance, the BAT) in a differentiated industry where two firms compete on prices, or quantities, in the product market. Pollution is a byproduct of their production process, and firms' emissions are taxed at a rate τ. The firms choose their dates of adoption of a green technology which becomes available in the market at time 0. A firm, by adopting the green technology, can reduce its per unit of output emissions, and thus decrease its emission tax burden. The costs of purchasing and implementing the green technology decreases, at a decreasing rate, over time. These costs may decline substantially as the development horizon becomes longer due to either learning-by-doing or adoption process innovations.

We analyse both the precommitment and the pre-emptive equilibria of the adoption game. If there are long information lags or if it is prohibitively costly for a firm to alter its adoption plans, firm i can *precommit* at date 0 to an implementation date T_i. If, on the contrary, there are no information lags and, moreover, altering adoption plans has no cost for a firm, each firm adopts *pre-emptively* to prevent, or delay, adoption by its opponent. As a result, firms' profits are equal in the pre-emptive equilibrium. We are thus able to investigate the extent to which diffusion rates depend on how much flexibility a firm has in altering its plans to implement the green technology. Further, by studying a differentiated industry with symmetric demands, we are able to explore the impact of product differentiation on the rate of diffusion of the clean technology.

It is shown that, as the tax rate on emissions increases, firms adopt the abatement technology earlier in both the pre-emptive and the precommitment equilibria. The diffusion pattern of the green technology depends on the type of market competition, the degree of product differentiation, the ability of firms to precommit, or not, to a specific adoption date, as well as the size of the market and the degree to which the innovation reduces firms' unitary emissions. In particular, in both the precommitment and the pre-emptive equilibria, the Cournot follower always adopts earlier than the Bertrand follower. Also, in a precommitment equilibrium the Bertrand leader adopts earlier than the Cournot leader, but only if the goods are sufficiently close substitutes. The opposite is true for lower values of substitutability. However, in a pre-emptive equilibrium the Bertrand leader *always* adopts earlier than the Cournot leader.

Our findings suggest that the dynamic inefficiencies introduced by market imperfections cannot be corrected through a uniform tax on emissions. For each firm there exists an emissions tax rate which induces the firm to adopt the clean technology at the socially optimal date, but these tax rates differ among firms. Therefore, subsidization of the implementation costs of the green technology, coupled with a uniform tax on emissions, is necessary for the socially optimum diffusion pattern to be restored. Further, the right mix of policy tools is sensitive to all the factors mentioned above.

The chapter is organized as follows. Section 8.2 presents the model and outlines the basic assumptions. It also analyses the per-period product market competition under cost asymmetries. In section 8.3 the adoption patterns in a precommitment equilibrium are derived and compared when firms are competing *à la* Cournot, or *à la* Bertrand, in the product market. Section 8.4 derives and compares those adoption patterns observed in a pre-emptive equilibrium. Finally, section 8.5 concludes.

8.2   THE MODEL

We consider an economy with an oligopolistic sector, consisting of two firms which produce differentiated goods, and a competitive numeraire sector. The firms possess identical constant returns to scale technologies and compete on quantities, or on prices, in the product market. The marginal cost of production equals c_0. Pollution of the environment is a byproduct of the firms' production process. In particular, one unit of output produced with the current technology generates λ units of emissions. Firms face an exogenously given per-unit emission tax, τ. We assume that τ has been chosen by the government in the past and that the government has the ability to commit to a specific policy.[3] Then a firm, due to its emissions, has an additional cost, $\lambda\tau$, per unit of output. Therefore, $c = c_0 + \tau\lambda$ is the *effective marginal cost* of a firm producing with its current technology.

At date $t = 0$ an abatement technology that reduces emissions is available in the market. A firm can acquire the green technology at any date $t \geq 0$ and reduce thereafter its unitary emissions to $\lambda - \delta$, $0 < \delta < \lambda$. Thus, the green technology reduces the firm's 'effective' marginal cost by $\tau\delta$. Let $k(t)$ be the *present value* of the costs of purchasing and implementing the green technology by date t. As is standard in this literature, we assume that the current cost, $k(t)e^{rt}$, is decreasing over time, at a decreasing rate; that is, $(k(t)e^{rt})' < 0$ and $(k(t)e^{rt})'' > 0$, where r is the interest rate, $0 < r < 1$ (see, for example, Fudenberg and Tirole 1985). Due to either economies of learning or new results from basic research facilitating the adoption process, adoption costs typically decline as the development horizon becomes longer. To avoid corner solutions, we further assume that (a) $\lim_{t \to 0} k(t) = -\lim_{t \to 0} k'(t) = \infty$, a sufficient condition for immediate adoption to be prohibitively costly; and (b) $\lim_{t \to \infty} k'(t)e^{rt} = 0$, a condition guaranteeing that all adoptions occur in finite time. Finally, we assume that no further green innovations are anticipated in the industry.

The market operates on every date $t \geq 0$. Market demands are stationary over time. Following Dixit (1979), the representative consumer's utility over the differentiated goods (x_1, x_2) and the numeraire good m is:

$$U(x_1, x_2) = a(x_1 + x_2) - (x_1^2 + 2\gamma x_1 x_2 + x_2^2)/2 + m \qquad (8.1)$$

where $a > c_0 + \tau\lambda$ and $0 < \gamma < 1$. The assumption that utility is linear in the numeraire good eliminates income effects and allows us to perform partial equilibrium analysis. This specification of U(.) generates a linear symmetric demand system:

$$p_1 = a - x_1 - \gamma x_2 \quad p_2 = a - x_2 - \gamma x_1 \qquad (8.2)$$

which permits us to study how the adoption timing of the green technology depends upon the substitutability of the two goods. The latter is measured by the parameter γ. As γ increases the goods become better substitutes, and for $\gamma = 1$ they are perfect substitutes. As γ goes to zero, each firm becomes virtually a monopolist for its product. For tractability reasons, define $\rho = \tau/(a - c_0)$. As $(a - c_0)$ is a measure of the market size, ρ represents the emission tax rate per unit of market size.

8.2.1 Cournot Competition

We first analyse Cournot competition. Given the demand system (8.2), firm i chooses x_i to maximize profits, $[p_i - c_i]x_i$, where c_i is its *effective* marginal cost which, of course, depends on how green the firm's technology is. Then the equilibrium per-period quantities are $i, j = 1, 2$:

$$x_i^C(c_i, c_j) = [2(a - c_i) - \gamma(a - c_j)]/(4 - \gamma^2) \tag{8.3}$$

and the equilibrium per-period profits are, $\pi_i^C(c_i, c_j) = [x_i^C(c_i, c_j)]^2$. Firm i's adoption of the abatement technology decreases its effective marginal cost, and thus increases its market share, x_i^C, and decreases the market share of its rival, x_j^C. This latter effect is strategically advantageous for firm i, since from (8.2) its own price is negatively related to firm j's quantity; thus, the adoption of the cleaner technology indirectly increases firm i's profits. Therefore, under emission taxes, quantity competition creates a *positive strategic effect*[4] for green innovations. To avoid corner solutions, we restrict attention to the range of the substitutability parameter where both firms are always active in the market. From (8.3), this is the case if and only if

$$\gamma < \gamma C(\rho, \lambda, \delta), \text{ where } \gamma C \equiv \min[1, 2(1 + \rho\lambda)/(1 + \rho\lambda - \rho\delta)].$$

8.2.2 Bertrand Competition

We now analyse Bertrand competition. By inverting (8.2) we obtain the demand functions

$$x_1 = [(a - p_1) - \gamma(a - p_2)]/(1 - \gamma^2); \quad x_2 = [(a - p_2) - \gamma(a - p_1)]/(1 - \gamma^2) \tag{8.4}$$

Firm i chooses p_i to maximize its profits $[p_i - c_i]x_i$. Then the equilibrium prices are $i,j = 1,2$:

$$p_i^B(c_i, c_j) = [(2 + \gamma)(1 - \gamma)a + 2c_i + \gamma c_j]/(4 - \gamma^2) \tag{8.5}$$

and the equilibrium per-period profits are $\pi_i^B(c_i, c_j) = [p_i^B(c_i, c_j) - c_i]2/(1 - \gamma^2)$. When firm i adopts the green technology, its effective marginal cost decreases, and thus both p_i^B and p_j^B decrease. The latter is disadvantageous for firm i, because its output is positively related to p_j, and thus the adoption of the cleaner technology indirectly decreases firm i's profits. Contrary to Cournot, Bertrand competition creates a *negative strategic effect*. Now, does this imply that firms competing on prices always adopt the abatement technology later than if they were competing on quantities? As we shall see, the answer is no. As in Bester and Petrakis (1993) there is an additional effect, *the market share effect*, which plays an important role. Whenever the green technology leads to a substantial increase in its market share, the firm has a stronger incentive to adopt the innovation earlier since the reduction of its effective marginal cost applies to a higher volume of production. As previously, we restrict ourselves to parameter values for which both firms operate in the market. This happens if and only if $p_i^B(c_i, c_j) > c_i$. From (8.5) this holds if $\gamma < \gamma B(\rho, \lambda, \delta)$, where γB is implicitly defined by $\gamma B \equiv \gamma C[2 - \gamma B^2]/2$. Thus, $\gamma B < \gamma C$.

8.3   ADOPTION PATTERNS UNDER PRECOMMITMENT

In this section we assume that firms can precommit to a specific adoption date. At date 0, firm i chooses its adoption date T_i. Firms then compete on the product market each date $t \geq 0$. Adoption date refers to the date by which the green technology can be implemented. In general, implementation of a new technology requires long-term plans that can be altered later, but only at some cost. Precommitment at date 0 is then a time-consistent behaviour for the firm only if the costs of altering the adoption plans are prohibitively high. In this case, the threat of altering one firm's adoption date as a response to its rival's past actions is not credible.

Let π_0^m, π_2^m be the per-period profits when none or both firms have adopted the green technology. Also, let π_l^m, π_f^m be the per-period profits of the leader (the firm that has already adopted), and the follower (the firm that has not yet adopted), $m = C, B$. Then $\pi_0^m = \pi^m(c_0 + \tau\lambda, c_0 + \tau\lambda)$, $\pi_2^m = \pi^m(c_0 + \tau\lambda - \tau\delta, c_0 + \tau\lambda - \tau\delta)$, $\pi_l^m = \pi_1^m(c_0 + \tau\lambda - \tau\delta, c_0 + \tau\lambda)$ and $\pi_f^m = \pi_2^m(c_0 + \tau\lambda - \tau\delta, c_0 + \tau\lambda)$. At date 0 firm i, $i = 1, 2$ chooses T_i^m to maximize its discounted sum of profits:

$$\Pi_1^m(T_1, T_2) = \int_0^{T_1} \pi_0^m e^{-rt}\, dt + \int_{T_1}^{T_2} \pi_l^m e^{-rt}\, dt + \int_{T_2}^{\infty} \pi_2^m e^{-rt}\, dt - k(T_1)$$
$$\Pi_2^m(T_1, T_2) = \int_0^{T_1} \pi_0^m e^{-rt}\, dt + \int_{T_1}^{T_2} \pi_f^m e^{-rt}\, dt + \int_{T_2}^{\infty} \pi_2^m e^{-rt}\, dt - k(T_1) \quad (8.6)$$

The first-order conditions of (8.6) are:

$$\pi_l^m - \pi_0^m = -k'(T_1^m)e^{rT_1^m}$$
$$\pi_2^m - \pi_f^m = -k'(T_2^m)e^{rT_2^m} \quad (8.7)$$

Let $I_1^m = \pi_l^m - \pi_0^m$, and $I_2^m = \pi_2^m - \pi_f^m$. I_i^m is then firm i's incremental benefit from the adoption of the green technology in market m. Then from (8.3) we obtain the incremental benefits of the leader and the follower in the Cournot market:

$$I_1^C = 4(a - c_0)^2 \rho\delta[(2 - \gamma)(1 + \rho\lambda) + \rho\delta]/(4 - \gamma^2)^2 \quad (8.8)$$

$$I_2^C = 4(a - c_0)^2 \rho\delta[(1 + \rho\lambda)(2 - \gamma) + \rho\delta(1 - \gamma)]/(4 - \gamma^2)^2 \quad (8.9)$$

Also, from (8.5) we get the corresponding expressions for the Bertrand market:

$$I_1^B = (a - c_0)^2 \, \rho\delta \, (2 - \gamma^2)[2(1 + \rho\lambda)(1 - \gamma)(2 + \gamma) + \rho\delta \, (2 - \gamma^2)]/ \\ (1 - \gamma^2)(4 - \gamma^2)^2 \qquad (8.10)$$

$$I_2^B = (a - c_0)^2 \, \rho\delta \, (2 - \gamma^2)[2(1 + \rho\lambda)(1 - \gamma)(2 + \gamma) + \rho\delta \, (2 - \gamma^2 - 2\gamma)]/ \\ (1 - \gamma^2)(4 - \gamma^2)^2 \qquad (8.11)$$

Thus $I_i^m > 0$ and $I_1^m > I_2^m$ for all λ, ρ, $\delta > 0$ and $0 < \gamma < 1$ in both markets. Moreover, I_i^m is increasing in ρ, δ, λ and $(a - c_0)$. Both the leader's and the follower's incremental benefit from adopting the green technology increases with the emission tax rate, as firms save more on tax bills. These incremental benefits also increase with the effectiveness of the green technology in reducing a firm's per-unit emissions. Finally, the higher a firm's emissions with the current technology or the larger the size of the market, the higher are the firm's incremental benefits from adoption.

Now, given (8.7), T_i^m depends only on I_i^m and by our assumption on $k(.)$, we get $T_1^m > T_2^m$ for $m = B, C$. As Quirmbach (1986) noted, the diffusion of new technologies in the market is not due to strategic behaviour, but rather to a pattern of decreasing incremental benefits. Therefore, in order to compare adoption timing patterns under different market structures, we need only compare their respective incremental benefits. Note further that T_i^m is decreasing in ρ, λ, δ and $(a - c_0)$. The following proposition summarizes the results:

Proposition 1 In a precommitment equilibrium, all the adoptions of the green technology occur earlier when (a) the tax rate on emissions is higher, (b) the effectiveness of the green technology in reducing emissions is higher, (c) the initial emissions-output rate is higher and (d) the market size is larger.

We turn now to the comparison of the adoption timing patterns of Cournot and Bertrand markets. Let $g(\rho, \delta) \equiv 2(1 + \rho\lambda)/[2(1 + \rho\lambda) + \rho\delta]$. It can easily be checked that $g < \gamma B$ for all (ρ, δ). Proposition 2 summarizes the results:

Proposition 2 Let $\gamma < \gamma B$. Then in a precommitment equilibrium:
(*i*) For each (ρ, δ) there is a $g(\rho, \delta)$ such that $T_1^C < T_1^B$ for $\gamma < g$ and $T_1^C > T_1^B$ for $\gamma > g$. Moreover, $g(.)$ is decreasing in both ρ and δ.
(*ii*) $T_2^C < T_2^B$ for all γ.

Proof: From (8.8) and (8.10), $I_1^C > I_1^B$ if and only if $[(2 - \gamma)(1 + \rho\lambda) - \gamma(1 + \rho\lambda - \rho\delta)]\gamma^3\rho\delta/(1 - \gamma^2)(4 - \gamma^2)^2 > 0$, or equivalently if $(1 + \rho\lambda)/(1 + \rho\lambda - \rho\delta) > \gamma/(2 - \gamma)$, which is true if $\gamma < g$. Also from (8.9) and (8.11), $I_2^C > I_2^B$ if and only if $[2(1 - \gamma)(1 + \rho\lambda) + (2 - \gamma)\rho\delta]\gamma^3\rho\delta/(1 - \gamma^2)(4 - \gamma^2)^2 > 0$, which is always true. Then by (8.7) we obtain the results. QED

The intuition for part (i) is that for low values of γ the difference in the strategic effect under Cournot and Bertrand competition is dominant, while as γ increases the *market share effect* (Bester and Petrakis 1993) becomes more important. In fact when the two commodities are poor substitutes their demands are hardly related, so a firm's output hardly differs in the two types of market. Thus the reduction of the total effective costs due to adoption is of the same magnitude in both Bertrand and Cournot markets. However, for low values of γ the innovation is more profitable for a Cournot leader because it decreases its rival's output, whereas for a Bertrand leader it decreases its competitor's price. Therefore, a Bertrand leader will adopt at a later point in time when the implementation costs of the green technology become lower.

On the other hand, when the goods are very close substitutes, an innovation that reduces the effective marginal cost of a firm has a significant impact on its market share. Especially, if γ is close enough to γB, the adoption of green technology by the leader reduces its rival's market share almost to zero. In Cournot competition, the rival's reduction of market share is less drastic, because $\gamma B < \gamma C$ implies that the follower retains a 'decent' market share even after the leader's adoption. Therefore, for high values of γ the Bertrand market creates a stronger incentive for the leader to adopt the green technology than the Cournot market. The market share effect dominates and the leader adopts earlier in price competition.

Part (ii) of Proposition 2 tells us that a Cournot follower always adopts earlier than the Bertrand follower. The strategic effect dominates the market share effect for all substitutability values. For low values of γ the intuition is given above. But for high γ it is the strength of price competition that matters: post-adoption profits do not increase much, even if the market share of the follower increases substantially. This is due to the fierce competition between firms which are producing very similar goods. The post-innovation competition is much weaker for a Cournot follower, thus its profits increase sufficiently despite the fact that its market share increases much less than the Bertrand follower's.

8.4 ADOPTION PATTERNS IN THE PRE-EMPTIVE EQUILIBRIUM

If adoption is perfectly observable and instantaneous, and if the costs of altering adoption plans are rather insignificant (Fudenberg and Tirole 1985; Riordan 1992), a firm cannot credibly commit to maintaining its date of implementation of the green technology regardless of what happened in the past. In a precommitment equilibrium the leader makes higher profits than the follower. However, if pre-emption is possible this cannot happen. The follower would have an incentive to adopt the new technology just before the leader does in order to increase its profits. The leader then, facing pre-emption, will innovate at an earlier point in time such that the follower is indifferent between adopting just before that point in time and adopting much later. Thus, in a pre-emptive equilibrium the *rent-equalization principle* holds.

The specification of the game is the same except that history now matters. As a result we need to look for time-consistent innovative behaviour. Once the leader has adopted the new technology, the follower's adoption is a one-player decision problem. It chooses τ_2^m to maximize its profits $\pi_2^m(T_1, T_2)$ (given in (8.6)) with the only restriction that $\tau_2^m \geq \tau_1^m$. The first-order condition of this problem is the same as in the precommitment equilibrium, and is given by (8.7) with τ_2^m replacing T_2^m. Therefore, in both the pre-emptive and the precommitment equilibria the follower adopts at the same date, that is, $\tau_2^m = T_2^m$ for $m = C, B$.

Further, from the rent equalization principle, τ_1^m is determined by equating the discounted sum of profits, that is, $\pi_1^m(\tau_1^m, \tau_2^m)$. From (8.7) and after some manipulations we get:

$$\pi_l^m - \pi_f^m = r\frac{k(\tau_1^m) - k(\tau_2^m)}{e^{-r\tau_1^m} - e^{-r\tau_2^m}} \tag{8.12}$$

with π_l^m and π_f^m, the leader's and follower's flow of profits respectively, in market m, $m = C, B$. Note, given $\tau_2^m = T_2^m$ the leader's optimal adoption date depends only on the differential of the per-period profits of being the leader and being the follower. This is the *pre-emptive incentive* (see, for example, Katz and Shapiro 1987). A comparison of the pre-emptive incentives created by Bertrand and Cournot markets is given in the following proposition:

Proposition 3 For all $\gamma < \gamma B$, the pre-emptive incentives in Bertrand and Cournot markets are **equal**, that is, $\pi_l^C - \pi_f^C = \pi_l^B - \pi_f^B$. Moreover, the pre-emptive incentive increases with ρ, δ, λ and $(a - c_0)$.

Proof: Using (8.3) and (8.5), we have $\pi_l^C - \pi_f^C = (a - c_0)^2[2(1 + \rho\lambda) + \rho\delta]$ $\rho\delta/(4 - \gamma^2) = \pi_l^B - \pi_f^B$. QED

This result is rather specific to the linear demand structure. Nevertheless, it suggests that the pre-emptive incentives in Cournot and Bertrand competition are often of similar magnitude in a broader class of demand conditions. The intuition is that for fixed γ the Bertrand market is more competitive than the Cournot market. This suggests a larger profit differential between the low-cost leader and the high-cost follower in the Bertrand market. However, the leader's adoption generates positive externalities for the follower in the Bertrand market, but negative externalities in the Cournot market. The latter counterbalances the competitiveness effect.

As we saw above, the follower adopts at the same time in both the pre-commitment and the pre-emptive equilibria. Further, the higher the emission tax is, or the higher the effectiveness of the technology in reducing emissions, the earlier the follower adopts the green technology. The following proposition summarizes the results:

Proposition 4 In a pre-emptive equilibrium, $\tau 1^B < \tau 1^C$, and $\tau 2^B > \tau 2^C$ for all γ and (ρ, δ). Moreover, all the adoptions of the green technology occur earlier when (a) the tax rate on emissions is higher, (b) the effectiveness of the green technology in reducing emissions is higher, (c) the initial emissions-output rate is higher and (d) the market size is larger.

Proof: To compare the leader's optimal adoption date in a price-setting and a quantity-setting game, define

$$f(t_1, t_2) = \frac{k(t_1) - k(t_2)}{e^{-rt_1} - e^{-rt_2}} \tag{8.13}$$

Let $C(t) = k(t)e^{rt}$. By assumption $C(t)$ is strictly decreasing and strictly convex. Differentiating (8.13) we have:

$$\frac{\partial f(t_1, t_2)}{\partial t_1} = \frac{e^{-r(t_1 + t_2)} [C'(t_1)(e^{r(t_2-t_1)} - 1) + r(C(t_1) - C(t_2))]}{(e^{-rt_1} - e^{-rt_2})^2} \tag{8.14}$$

By strict convexity of $\exp(x)$ we have $\exp[r(t_2 - t_1)] - 1 > r(t_2 - t_1)$. As $C(t)$ is decreasing and strictly convex, the right-hand term of (8.14) in square brackets $[..] < r\{C'(t_1)(t_2 - t_1) + (C(t_1) - C(t_2))\} < 0$. Thus, $f(t_1, t_2)$ is decreasing in t_1 and in t_2 by the symmetry of (8.13). Hence, $\tau_2^B > \tau_2^C$ implies $f(t_1, \tau_2^B) < f(t_1, \tau_2^C)$. Then from (8.12) and Proposition 3 we have $\tau_1^B < \tau_1^C$. Finally, the second part of Proposition 4 is a direct consequence of Propositions 1 and 3. QED

The leader in a Bertrand market always adopts the green technology earlier from the Cournot leader. In fact, the leader under price competition enjoys the leadership longer than under quantity competition. Given that the pre-emptive incentives per period are the same in both markets, the leader has a stronger overall incentive to pre-empt in a Bertrand than in a Cournot market.

8.5 CONCLUSIONS

In recent years, there has been a growing interest among scientists and politicians about a number of environmental issues, such as the global warming associated with the greenhouse effect, the depletion of the ozone layer, acid rain, and so on. The climate change due to global warming has received much attention as it is expected to cause major economic or natural damage to many countries or areas. Currently, there is a widespread conviction that the concentration of GHGs could be stabilized by 2010 at its 1990 level, and thus global warming could be reduced to a major extent, if the best available technologies (BATs) were to be implemented by the majority of the countries. Consequently, the design of government policies that provide the right incentives for the private sector to adopt the existing clean technologies becomes all the more important.

This chapter contributes to this line of research by studying firms' incentives to adopt an abatement technology in a differentiated oligopolistic industry where firms compete on prices or on quantities. Firms, when faced with a tax on their emissions, have an incentive to adopt the green technology not only in order to reduce their tax burden, but also to steal business from their rivals. The higher the emission tax chosen by the government, the sooner the firms adopt the abatement technology. The diffusion pattern depends on a number of market and technological parameters, such as the type of competition (Cournot or Bertrand), the substitutability between the goods, the ability, or not, of firms to precommit to a specific adoption date, the size of the market, and how drastically the emissions are reduced by the clean technology.

The analysis also provides some insights into the design of environmental policies aimed at correcting the inefficiencies of *laissez-faire*. Of course, the design of optimal policies requires an estimation of the damage function for the country (or for all countries of the globe, as is the case with GHGs). Our findings suggest that the socially optimal diffusion pattern cannot be implemented through the use of a uniform emission tax, but rather that it requires an appropriate mix of emission taxes and subsidies on green technologies adoption costs. This task needs further research using a model where the damage function and the social planner's problem are explicitly specified. Another important issue that is not treated in this chapter is the credibility of government policies. If the government cannot commit to a level of emission tax, then firms will decide on their adoption dates as if the policy were chosen after their own adoption decision.

NOTES

1. Velthuijsen (1993) discusses factors hindering the diffusion of energy-saving technologies. For a discussion of some issues concerning the payback time of a green technology, see Krause *et al.* (1993).
2. Note, however, that there is extensive strategic-theoretical literature on the related subject of the diffusion of cost-reducing innovations. Reinganum (1981a, b, 1983a, b); Fudenberg and Tirole (1985); and Quirmbach (1986) analyse a homogeneous industry, while Petrakis (1994) studies a differentiated industry. Reinganum (1981a, b, 1983a) investigates the diffusion of new technologies in an oligopoly where each firm can commit to a specific adoption date, while Fudenberg and Tirole (1985) consider the opposite case, where firms can pre-empt their rivals. Quirmbach (1986) compares the diffusion rates under alternative innovation market structures and shows that, in a precommitment equilibrium, the rate of diffusion is faster in market structure A than in B if and only if all the incremental benefits of adopting the new technology are larger in A than in B. Petrakis (1994) extends the above analyses in the case of a differentiated product market where firms compete on prices or quantities.
3. Since the tax rate is applied on the firm's emissions only during the production stage, the government often has the incentive to alter its emissions tax level after a firm has adopted the green technology. A firm will then decide on its adoption date, taking into account that the government's policy will change according to the number of firms that have already adopted the green technology. In this chapter we abstract from issues of time consistency of the government policy. We shall assume throughout that the government is able to commit credibly to a specific policy.
4. See Bester and Petrakis (1993).

REFERENCES

Bester, H. and E. Petrakis (1993), 'The incentives for cost reduction in a differentiated industry', *International Journal of Industrial Organization*, **11**, 519–34.
Boetti, M. and M. Botteon (1996), 'Environmental policy and the choice of the best available technology: an empirical assessment', in A. Xepapadeas (ed.), *Economic Policy for the Environment and Natural Resources*, Cheltenham, UK: Edward Elgar.
Carraro, C. and A. Soubeyran (1996), 'Environmental policy and the choice of production technology', in C. Carraro, Y. Katsoulacos and A. Xepapadeas (eds), *Environmental Policy and Market Structure*, Amsterdam: Kluwer.
Dasgupta, P. and J. Stiglitz (1980), 'Uncertainty, industrial structure and speed of R&D', *Bell Journal of Economics*, **90**, 1–28.
Dixit, A. (1979), 'A model of duopoly suggesting a theory of entry barriers', *Bell Journal of Economics*, **10**, 20–32.

Fudenberg, D. and J. Tirole (1985), 'Preemption and rent equalization in the adoption of new technology', *Review of Economic Studies*, **52**, 383–401.

Katz, M. and C. Shapiro (1987), 'R&D rivalry with licensing or imitation', *American Economic Review*, **77**, 402–20.

Krause, F., E. Haites, R. Howarth and J. Koomey (1993), *Cutting Carbon Emissions: Burden or Benefit? The Economics of Energy-Tax and Non-price Policies*, vol. II, part 1, El Cerrito, Cal.: International Project for Sustainable Energy Paths.

Petrakis, E. (1994), 'Technology diffusion in a differentiated oligopoly', Universidad Carlos III Working Paper 94–33.

Quirmbach, H. (1986), 'The diffusion of new technology and the market for an innovation', *Rand Journal of Economics*, **17**, 33–47.

Reinganum, J. (1981a), 'On the diffusion of new technology: a game theoretic approach', *Review of Economic Studies*, **48**, 395–405.

Reinganum, J. (1981b), 'Market structure and the diffusion of new technology', *Bell Journal of Economics*, **12**, 618–24.

Reinganum, J. (1983a), 'Technology adoption under imperfect information', *Bell Journal of Economics*, **14**, 57–69.

Reinganum, J. (1983b), 'Uncertain innovation and the persistence of monopoly', *American Economic Review*, **73**, 741–8.

Reinganum, J. (1989), 'The timing of innovation: research, development and diffusion', in R. Schmalensee and R. Willig (eds), *Handbook of Industrial Organization*, vol. 1, Amsterdam: North-Holland.

Riordan, M. (1992), 'Regulation and preemptive technology adoption', *Rand Journal of Economics*, **23**, 334–49.

Velthuijsen, J.W. (1993), 'Incentives for investment in energy efficiency: an econometric evaluation and policy implications', *Environmental and Resource Economics*, **3**, 153–69.

9. Pollution, Pigouvian taxes and asymmetric international oligopoly

Ngo Van Long and Antoine Soubeyran

9.1 INTRODUCTION

The ongoing efforts of governments to achieve multilateral trade liberalization have not been universally welcome. Environmentalists often express the fear that an increased volume of trade will lead to more pollution and further degradation of natural resources such as forests and waterways. Industrialists in advanced economies worry that, with the reduction in tariffs, there will be increased competition from firms operating in less-developed countries, where lax environmental standards imply that these firms incur relatively lower costs. Powerful pressure groups in advanced economies often ask their governments to penalize imports of goods originating from countries which have laxer environmental or labour standards. Less-developed countries have also been accused of not enforcing environmental and labour standards in order to enable its domestic firms to achieve a 'comparative advantage' in the global market and also to attract foreign capital. Some authors have expressed the concern that there is a 'race to the bottom', which would in the end harm everyone. On the other hand, as put by Anderson (1995): 'developing countries perceive the entwining of these social issues with trade policy as a threat to both their sovereignty and their economies'.

In this chapter we consider a model of oligopolistic trade when governments adopt policies that affect both trade and the environment. An important feature of our model is the assumption that firms are not identical and that governments can adopt discriminatory (that is, firm-specific) taxes or standards. While firm-specific taxes on outputs or on quantities exported (or imported) are not popular and not often encountered in practice (partly because of international agreements or conventions, such as the 'most favoured nation' principle), firm-specific taxes on emissions seem to be gaining acceptance, because they are seen as measures to internalize environmental externalities which, by their nature, are specific to a production environment.

Optimal Pigouvian taxes under oligopoly have been studied by Katsoulacos and Xepapadeas (1995) under the assumption that firms are identical. They show that if the number of firms is exogenous, then the optimal emission tax falls short of the marginal damage cost (because, in the absence of externality, oligopoly output is below the socially efficient level). This result is an extension of the monopoly case.[1] On the other hand, if the number of firms is endogenous and if there are fixed costs, they obtain the conclusion that the optimal Pigouvian tax could exceed the marginal damage cost. In their model, effluent fees serve to 'correct' outputs (and emissions) when there are two sources of market failure: market power and environmental damages.

Matters become more complicated when the polluting oligopoly consists of domestic firms producing in the home country and foreign rivals producing in the foreign countries. From the publications by Ulph (1992), Barrett (1994), Conrad (1996a, b) and Rauscher (1994, 1997), four factors have been identified that affect deviations of optimal emission taxes from marginal damage costs.[2] First, there is the rent-shifting argument: taxes can shift rents from foreign firms to domestic firms. Second, one should not neglect the need to mitigate transboundary pollution from foreign producers. Third, output of an oligopoly tends to be too low relative to consumer benefits. Fourth, when there are several domestic firms, oligopolistic behaviour does not minimize the production cost of a given volume of domestic output. In the literature, specific models have developed models to address some of these issues, but not all four issues simultaneously. Ulph (1996a) has a model with the first three factors present but where there is one one firm in each country, though these firms can have different costs. Barrett (1994) and Kennedy (1994) allow for many firms in each country, but these firms are identical. A main contribution of our chapter is that it integrates all the factors within a model where firms are not identical. We consider the case where firms are *heterogeneous* both in production costs and in emission per unit of output. We allow governments to use firm-specific emission taxes.

In section 9.3, we consider the case where two governments set emission taxes non-cooperatively. We show that at the Nash equilibrium in the game between the two governments, the firm-specific emission tax rates on larger firms are smaller than average. If domestic firms are identical and there is no pollution spillover, then the domestic emission tax is greater (respectively, smaller) than the marginal environmental damage, provided that the number of domestic firms is sufficiently great (respectively, small) relative to the number of foreign firms. However, if foreign pollution has spillover effects on the home country, then domestic emission tax may be smaller than the marginal environmental damage even when the number of domestic firms is great.

In section 9.4 we turn to the analysis of the effect of trade liberalization on emission taxes. We assume that the foreign country imposes no emission or trade taxes, while the home country initially imposes both emission taxes and import tariffs. We examine whether a reduction in import tariffs (trade liberalization) leads to lower emission·taxes and higher domestic emissions. We show that if the weight given to consumers' surplus is zero, then under certain conditions, a partial trade liberalization will lead to a countervailing reduction in emission taxes that leaves total emission in the home country unchanged. However, if the weight given to consumers' surplus is sufficiently great, then a partial trade liberalization will lead to significant reductions in domestic emission taxes and more domestic emission.

9.2 A MODEL OF ASYMMETRIC OLIGOPOLY

Consider an international Cournot oligopoly consisting of n non-identical firms, of which m_H are in the home country (country H), and m_F are in the foreign country (country F). The firms produce a homogeneous good. Firms differ from each other in two respects: (a) production cost, and (b) emission per unit of output. In each country, the government sets emission tax rates that can be firm-specific.

Let x_i denote firm i's output. The cost of producing x_i is $\alpha_i c(x_i)$ where $\alpha_i > 0$ is a parameter and $c(.)$ is a convex and increasing function, with $c(0) = 0$. Its emission of pollutant is $e_i = \varepsilon_i x_i$, where $\varepsilon_i > 0$ is a firm-specific constant. Firm i faces a firm-specific tax t_i per unit of emission, or, equivalently:

$$\tau_i = \varepsilon_i t_i \tag{9.1}$$

per unit of output. Here we assume that in each country the government can charge discriminatory emission taxes.

The firms sell their output in the same market. (This market can be an integrated world market, or the home country's market, or the foreign country's market, or a market in a third country.) Let $H = \{1, 2, ..., m_H\}$ and $F = \{m_H + 1, ..., n\}$. The demand function is represented by $P = P(X)$ where $X = X_H + X_F$ and

$$X_H \equiv \sum_{h \in H} x_h, \quad X_F \equiv \sum_{f \in F} x_f$$

We assume that $P'(X) < 0$, $P(0) > 0$, and that there exists $\bar{X}$ such that $P(\bar{X}) = 0$. In addition, we need the assumption that:

$$(n + 1)P'(X) + XP''(X) < 0 \qquad (9.2)$$

This condition is 3 satisfied if the marginal revenue curve for the industry has a negative slope.[3]

The home country's welfare is the sum of the home consumers' surplus, home producers' surplus, and government's tax revenue, less pollution damages.

We first ask the following question: suppose that country F has set the emission tax rates $(t_{mH+1}, \ldots, t_n)$, what is country H's best responses in terms of its own firm-specific emission taxes? To answer this question, it is convenient to show that choosing home emission tax rates is equivalent to choosing directly home firms' outputs, subject to the constraints that firms' outputs are consistent with a Cournot equilibrium. To see this, let us begin with the first-order condition for firm k:

$$P'(\hat{X})\hat{x}_k + P(\hat{X}) = \alpha_k c'(\hat{x}_k) + \tau_k \qquad (9.3)$$

This equation determines a relationship:

$$\hat{x}_k = \phi_k(\hat{X}, \tau_k) \equiv \phi_k(\hat{X}_F + \hat{X}_H, \tau_k) \qquad (9.4)$$

that must hold between the industry's *equilibrium* output $\hat{X}$ and firm k's *equilibrium* output $\hat{x}_k$. Note that $\phi_{kX} \equiv \partial\phi_k(\hat{X}, \tau_k)/\partial\hat{X} < 0$ under the assumption that $P''(\hat{X})\hat{x}_k + P'(\hat{X}) < 0$, and $\phi_{k\tau} \equiv \partial\phi_k(\hat{X}, \tau_k)/\partial\tau_k < 0$.

Thus the equilibrium output produced in country F is:

$$\hat{X}_F = \sum_{f \in F} \phi_f(\hat{X}_F + \hat{X}_H, \tau_f) \qquad (9.5)$$

This yields:

$$\hat{X}_F = \hat{X}_F(\hat{X}_H, \tau_F) \qquad (9.6)$$

where by definition $\tau_F \equiv (\tau_{m_{H+1}}, \ldots, \tau_n)$, and where

$$\frac{\partial\hat{X}_F}{\partial\hat{X}_H} = \frac{\sum_{f \in F} \phi_{fX}}{1 - \sum_{f \in F} \phi_{fX}} < 0 \qquad (9.7)$$

Equation (9.6) means that, given τ_F, if the home country can control the aggregate output of the home oligopolists, then the aggregate output of the foreign oligopolists is uniquely determined.

Since, in equilibrium, $\hat{X}_H + \hat{X}_F = \hat{X}$, it follows that:

$$\hat{X} = \hat{X}_H + \hat{X}_F(\hat{X}_H, \tau_F) = \hat{X}(\hat{X}_H, \tau_F) \tag{9.8}$$

and

$$\frac{\partial \hat{X}}{\partial \hat{X}_H} = \frac{1}{1 - \sum_{f \in F} \phi_{fX}} > 0$$

To illustrate, consider the special case with a linear demand $P(Q) = A - BQ$, and quadratic costs $\alpha_k c(x_k) = (\alpha_k/2)x_k^2$. Then in equilibrium

$$\hat{x}_f = \gamma_f [(A - \tau_f) - B\hat{X}_H - B\hat{X}_F] \tag{9.9}$$

where $\gamma_f \equiv 1/(B + \alpha_f)$. Let

$$\gamma_F \equiv \frac{1}{m_F} \sum_{f \in F} \gamma_f \tag{9.10}$$

Then:

$$\hat{X}_F(\hat{X}_H, \tau_F) = \frac{A m_{F\gamma F}}{1 + B m_{F\gamma F}} - \frac{\sum_{f \in F} \tau_f \gamma_f}{1 + B m_{F\gamma F}} - \frac{B m_{F\gamma F}}{1 + B m_{F\gamma F}} \hat{X}_H \tag{9.11}$$

and:

$$\hat{X}_F(\hat{X}_H, \tau_F) = \frac{1}{1 + B m_{F\gamma F}} \left[A m_{F\gamma F} - \sum_{f \in F} \tau_f \gamma_f + \hat{X}_H \right] \tag{9.12}$$

Thus, for a given τ_F, the home government can choose $\hat{X}_H$ and the $\hat{x}_h$, $h \in H$, and generate a Cournot equilibrium, supporting it by a suitably chosen vector τ_H so that (9.3) is satisfied.

We now derive an expression for the welfare of the home country. The aggregate emission by firms in country H is $E_H = \sum_{h \in H} \varepsilon_h x_h = \sum_{h \in H} e_h$. Similarly, the aggregate emission by foreign firms is $E_F = \sum_{f \in F} \varepsilon_f x_f$. Assume that the home country's valuation of total damage is $D(E_H + \sigma_F E_F)$ where σ_F is the spillover coefficient from foreign pollution to the home country, $1 \geq \sigma_F \geq 0$. Let $\hat{X}$ denote the Cournot equilibrium output. Define consumers' surplus as:

$$S(\hat{X}) = \int_0^{\hat{X}} P(X)dX - \hat{X}P(\hat{X})$$

Social welfare in the home country is defined as a weighted sum of consumers' surplus, home firms' profit, and government's revenue from emission taxes, less pollution damage (for the moment, we assume there are no tariffs for simplicity):

$$\hat{W}_H = \beta_H S(\hat{X}) + \sum_{h \in H} \hat{\pi}_h + \sum_{h \in H} t_h e_h - D_H (E_H + \sigma_F E_F) \qquad (9.13)$$

where $\hat{\pi}_h$ is firm h's equilibrium profit, and where $\beta_H \geq 0$ is the weight given to consumers' surplus ($\beta_H = 0$ if the good is not sold in the home market).

In what follows, we assume that $D(.)$ is a linear function, with $D'_H = \delta_H > 0$. Using the definition (9.1) and (9.3), we can express $\hat{W}_H$ (9.13) in a Cournot equilibrium as:

$$\hat{W}_H = \beta_H \hat{S} + \hat{X}_H \hat{P} - \sum_{h \in H} \psi_h (\hat{x}_h) - \delta_H \sigma_F E_F \qquad (9.14)$$

where:

$$\psi_h(\hat{x}_h) \equiv \delta_H \varepsilon_h \hat{x}_h + \alpha_h c(\hat{x}_h)$$

where $\hat{x}_h$ is firm h's *equilibrium* output, $\hat{X}$ is *equilibrium* industry output, $\hat{S} = S(\hat{X})$, and $\hat{P}$ is the *equilibrium* price.

9.3 NON-COOPERATIVE PIGOUVIAN TAXES

In this section, we seek answers to the following questions: (a) given a set of emission taxes imposed by a foreign country, what are the home country's optimal emission taxes, under the assumption that the home country cannot vary its trade taxes? and (b) if both countries try to optimize (non-cooperatively) by setting firm-specific emission taxes, what is the resulting Nash equilibrium?

We assume that the cost function $c(x)$ is *strictly convex*. The following proposition characterizes the optimal emission taxes in the home country, for a *given* vector of emission taxes in the foreign country:

Proposition 3.1 (Optimal firm-specific Pigouvian taxes) Given the foreign choice of τ_F, the optimal firm-specific Pigouvian tax per unit of emission by firm h is given by:

$$t_h = \delta_H + \frac{1}{\varepsilon_h}[-\hat{P}']\hat{X}_H\left[\left(A_H - \frac{\beta_H\hat{X}}{\hat{X}_H}\right)\left(\frac{\partial\hat{X}}{\partial\hat{X}_H}\right) - \frac{\hat{x}_h}{\hat{X}_H}\right], \text{ for all } h \in H \quad (9.15)$$

where $\hat{X}_H$ is the home industry output, and

$$A_H \equiv 1 + \frac{\delta_H\sigma_F}{[-P']\hat{X}_H}\sum_{f\in F}\varepsilon_f\frac{\partial\hat{x}_f}{\partial\hat{X}} \quad (9.16)$$

Thus (a) t_h is greater, the greater is the damage cost δ_H; (b) t_h is negatively related to the weight β_H attached to consumers' surplus; and (c) in equilibrium, among all firms that have the same ε_h, smaller firms pay higher tax rates per unit of emission. (This is because small firms are those which have high α_h, they are less efficient, and the optimal policy seeks to reduce their outputs.)

Proof: See the appendix.

Remark 3.1: Consider first the case where $\beta_H = 0$, that is, the good is not sold in the home market. Proposition 3.1 indicates that emission tax t_h is equal to marginal environmental damage (δ_H) plus an adjustment factor. This factor is zero if the export price of the good, P, is exogenous. In the case of an oligopoly, P is not exogenous. If there is no spillover from foreign pollution (that is, if $\sigma_F = 0$) then $A_H = 1$ and the tax formula (9.15) becomes:

$$t_h = \delta_H + \frac{1}{\varepsilon_h}[-\hat{P}']\hat{X}_H\left[\frac{\partial\hat{X}}{\partial\hat{X}_H} - \hat{s}_h\right]$$

where $\hat{s}_h = \hat{x}_h/\hat{X}_H$. Then t_h is smaller than the damage cost δ_H if and only if $\hat{s}_h > \partial\hat{X}/\partial\hat{X}_H$. If, in addition, all domestic firms are identical (implying $\hat{s}_h = 1/m_H$) then t_h is smaller than the marginal damage cost δ_H if and only if the number of domestic firms is sufficiently small:

$$\frac{\partial \hat{X}}{\partial \hat{X}_H} < \frac{1}{m_H} \tag{9.17}$$

In this case the shortfall of t_h over δ_H reflects the desire of the home government to expand domestic output so as to capture a bigger market share. If $\sigma_F = 0$ and $\partial \hat{X}/\partial \hat{X}_H = 1/m_H$, then $t_h = \delta_H$. Condition (9.17) can also be expressed in terms of the slopes of foreign firms' reaction functions.

However, if spillover is present (that is, $\sigma_F > 0$), and $\partial \hat{x}_f/\partial \hat{X} < 0$ (see equation (9.9) above) then $A_H < 1$ and hence it is possible that $t_h < \delta_H$ even if $\partial \hat{X}/\partial \hat{X}_H > 1/m_H$ (that is, even if the home firms are numerous). The reason for this is as follows: by reducing emission tax rates below the marginal environmental damage δ_H, the home country's output $\hat{X}_H$ will expand, and this will reduce foreign output and hence foreign emission (which is harmful to the home country).

Remark 3.2 If $\beta_H > 0$ (the good is sold in the home country) and if $\sigma_F = 0$ (no spillover from foreign pollution) then (9.15) reduces to:

$$t_h = \delta_H + \frac{1}{\varepsilon_h} [-\hat{P}'] \hat{X}_H \left[\{1 - [\beta_H \hat{X}/\hat{X}_H] \} \partial \hat{X}/\partial \hat{X}_H - \hat{s}_h \right]$$

In particular, if there axe no foreign firms, then firm h will be taxed at a rate below the marginal damage δ_H if and only if its output share is greater than $1 - \beta_H$.

We now turn to the task of characterizing a Nash equilibrium emission taxes when both countries try to maximize national welfare.

Proposition 3.2 (Nash equilibrium firm-specific Pigouvian taxes) If both countries set firm-specific Pigouvian taxes in response to each other, then the Nash equilibrium taxes in the game between the two countries are given by:

$$t_h = \delta_H + \frac{1}{\varepsilon_h} [-P'] \hat{X}_H \left[\left(A_H - \frac{\beta_H \hat{X}}{\hat{X}_H} \right) \frac{\partial X}{\partial X_H} - \frac{\hat{x}_h}{\hat{X}_H} \right] \text{ for all } h \in H \tag{9.18}$$

and:

$$t_f = \delta_F + \frac{1}{\varepsilon_f} \, [-\hat{P}']\hat{X}_F \left[\left(A_F - \frac{\beta_F \hat{X}}{\hat{X}_F} \right) \frac{\partial X}{\partial X_H} - \frac{\hat{x}_f}{\hat{X}_F} \right] \text{ for all } f \in F \qquad (9.19)$$

where A_H is given by (9.16) and A_F is defined in a similar way.

Example 3.1   With linear demand $P = 1 - X$ and quadratic cost $c(x) = (1/2)x^2$, conditions (9.18) and (9.19) give:

$$\tau_h = a_h + b_h \, \hat{X} + \frac{1}{1-\gamma_h} \sum_{f \in F} \eta_f \tau_f, \; h \in H \qquad (9.20)$$

$$\tau_f = a_f + b_f \, \hat{X} + \frac{1}{1-\gamma_f} \sum_{h \in H} \eta_h \tau_h, \; f \in H \qquad (9.21)$$

where:

$$a_h \equiv \frac{1}{1-\gamma_h} \left[(\varepsilon_h \delta_H - \gamma_h) - \frac{1}{1 + m_{F\gamma F}} \sum_{f \in F} \gamma_f (1 + \sigma_F \delta_H \varepsilon_f) \right], \; h \in H$$

$$a_f \equiv \frac{1}{1-\gamma_f} \left[(\varepsilon_f \delta_F - \gamma_f) - \frac{1}{1 + m_{H\gamma H}} \sum_{h \in H} \gamma_h (1 + \sigma_H \delta_F \varepsilon_h) \right], \; f \in F$$

$$b_h \equiv \frac{1}{1-\gamma_h} \left(\gamma_h + \frac{1 - \beta_H + m_{F\gamma F}}{1 + m_{F\gamma F}} \right), \; h \in H$$

$$b_f \equiv \frac{1}{1-\gamma_f} \left(\gamma_f + \frac{1 - \beta_F + m_{H\gamma H}}{1 + m_{H\gamma H}} \right), \; f \in F$$

$$\eta_h \equiv \frac{\gamma_h}{1 + m_{F\gamma F}}, \; h \in H$$

$$\eta_f \equiv \frac{\gamma_f}{1 + m_{H\gamma H}}, \; f \in F$$

Furthermore, recall that from (9.11):

$$\hat{X}_F = \sum_{f \in F} \gamma_f (1 - \tau_f) - m_{F\gamma F} \hat{X}$$

and similarly:

$$\hat{X}_H = \sum_{h \in H} \gamma_h (1 - \tau_h) - m_{H\gamma H} \hat{X}$$

Hence the equilibrium output is:

$$\hat{X} = \frac{1}{1 + m_{F\gamma F} + m_{H\gamma H}} \left[\sum_{f \in F} \gamma_f (1 - \tau_f) + \sum_{h \in H} \gamma_h (1 - \tau_h) \right] \qquad (9.22)$$

Substituting (9.22) into (9.20) and (9.21) we obtain n linear equations in τ_h and τ_f, and the Nash equilibrium taxes are uniquely determined.

9.4   EFFECTS OF TRADE LIBERALIZATION ON THE ENVIRONMENT

In this section, we examine the effects of trade liberalization on the quality of the environment under the assumptions that the polluting industry is an international oligopoly and that the home government can adjust emission taxes in response to a required reduction in tariff rates (demanded by an international body, such as the World Trade Organization).

We use the model developed in the preceding section, and consider the case where the goods are sold only in the home market. We assume that the foreign government does not impose any tax (or subsidy) on output (or on emissions). The home country already has in place a set of import tariffs on the good produced by the foreign oligopolists. We assume that these tariff rates are exogenously set[4] (for example, they might be controlled by international bodies such as the World Trade Organization). Given these tariff rates, the home government has as policy instruments firm-specific emission taxes on home firms. These instruments are optimally set to maximize home welfare. We seek the answers to the following questions: suppose that due to a new international agreement, all import tariffs must be cut by a given amount, how would the home government adjust its emission taxes? Would the adjustment result in a lower quality of the environment?

The home welfare function is the sum of W_H, defined in the preceding section, and tariff revenue:

$$W_H^0 = W_H + \sum_{f \in F} T_f x_f$$

where T_f is the import tariff on foreign firm f's good. (Here, we allow a firm-specific tariff, but the special case where all T_f are required to be identical is admitted.)

The relationship between the Cournot equilibrium industry output $\hat{X}$ and firm f's equilibrium output is $\hat{x}_f = \hat{x}_f(X, T_f)$, where T_f now takes the place of τ_f. It is convenient to define $\bar{\varepsilon}_f(T_f)$ as follows:

$$\sigma_F \delta_H \, \bar{\varepsilon}_f(T_f) = \sigma_F \delta_H \, \varepsilon_f - T_f \tag{9.23}$$

Then we obtain:

$$W_H^0 = X_H \hat{P} + \beta_H \hat{S} - \sum_{h \in H} \psi_h(\hat{x}_h) - \sigma_F \delta_H \sum_{f \in F} \bar{\varepsilon}_f \, \hat{x}_f$$

and we can apply the analysis of the problem of maximizing W_H in the previous section to the problem of maximizing W_H^0 of this section. We thus obtain the following optimal emission tax formulas, for exogenously given tariff rates T_f:

$$t_h = \delta_H + \frac{1}{\varepsilon_h} \, [-\hat{P}'] \hat{X}_H \left[\left(\bar{A}_H - \frac{\beta_H \hat{X}}{\hat{X}_H} \right) \left(\frac{\partial \hat{X}}{\partial \hat{X}_H} \right) - \frac{\hat{x}_h}{\hat{X}_H} \right] \tag{9.24}$$

where:

$$\bar{A}_H \equiv 1 + \frac{\sigma_F \delta_H}{[-\hat{P}'] \hat{X}_H} \sum_{f \in F} \bar{\varepsilon}_f \frac{\partial \hat{x}_f}{\partial \hat{X}}$$

We are now ready to determine whether an exogenous reduction in the import tariff rates (that is, a marginal trade liberalization) would lead to a reduction in emission taxes. To simplify computation, we specialize in the case where the demand function is linear and the cost function $c(x)$ is quadratic. Then we obtain the following proposition:

Proposition 4.1
(i) If the weight given to consumers' surplus is zero ($\beta_H = 0$), then, with linear demand and quadratic cost, a partial trade liberalization (that is, a reduction, but not necessarily elimination, of all tariffs) would lead to a reduction in emission taxes in the home country. However, the output (and hence emission) of each home firm will remain *unchanged*. As a result, foreign output and pollution will rise.

(ii) If the weight given to consumers' surplus is positive ($\beta_H > 0$), then, with linear demand and quadratic cost, a partial trade liberalization would lead to (a) a reduction in emission taxes in the home country, and (b) an *increase* in the output (and emission) of each domestic firm.

Proof: See the appendix.

Part (i) of Proposition 4.1 shows that the claim made by some environmentalists that trade liberalization would lead to more pollution in the home country is not always correct. This result is rather special, and one may suspect that it depends on the assumption that pollution is directly proportional to output. If there is scope for abatement activities, the equivalence between an emission tax and an output tax is broken, and thus when emission taxes are reduced to offset the impact on domestic output of a lowering of import tariffs, the level of domestic emission may rise.

9.5   CONCLUDING REMARKS

In this chapter, we studied the properties of equilibrium Pigouvian taxes when these have impacts on international trade. The firm-specific optimal emission taxes were derived. These taxes were shown to exceed or fall short of the marginal environmental damages, depending on the numbers of home and foreign firms, and on their cost characteristics. We also showed that trade liberalization need not always result in a more polluted environment.

One aspect of pollution reduction that we did not deal with here is the relocation of plants. This is the subject matter of a companion paper (Long and Soubeyran 1999). We have also assumed that pollution is a flow rather than a stock which evolves over time. Designing emission taxes for polluting oligopolists in a model with accumulation of the pollution stock has been studied by Benchekroun and Long (1998) in the context of a closed economy. It would seem worthwhile to extend their model to the case of an international oligopoly.

APPENDIX

Proof of Proposition 3.1

$\hat{W}_H$ can be expressed as:

$$\bar{W}_H = \beta_H S(\hat{X}) + \hat{X}_H \hat{P} - \sum_{h \in H} \psi_h(\hat{x}_h) - \sigma_F \delta_H \sum_{f \in F} \varepsilon_f \hat{x}_f \qquad (9.25)$$

Since $\hat{x}_f = \phi_f(\hat{X}, \tau_f)$ for all foreign firms, and country H seeks to maximize (9.25) by choosing firm-specific emission tax $t_h = \tau_h/\varepsilon_h$ ($h = 1, ..., m_H$), given the foreign vector τ_F. In view of (9.3), (9.6), and (9.8), this maximization problem is equivalent to maximizing (9.25) by choosing *directly* both the home industry output $\hat{X}_H$, and the vector $(\hat{x}_1, ..., \hat{x}_{m_H})$ of outputs of the home firms, subject to the constraint:

$$\sum_{h \in H} \hat{x}_h = \hat{X}_H \qquad (9.26)$$

(Afterwards, we can infer the emission taxes from (9.3).) It is convenient to solve this problem in two steps. In the first step, we take $\hat{X}_H$ as given (and hence $\hat{X}$ and $\hat{P}$ as given), and maximize with respect to $(\hat{x}_1, ..., \hat{x}_{m_H})$ subject to (9.26). In the second step, we choose $\hat{X}_H$.

The first step
For a given $\hat{X}_H$, maximization of (9.25) subject to (9.26) involves setting up the Lagrangian

$$L_H = G(\hat{X}_H, \lambda_H) + \sum_{h \in H} [\lambda_H \hat{x}_h - \psi_h(\hat{x}_h)] \qquad (9.27)$$

where:

$$G(\hat{X}_H, \lambda_H) \equiv \beta_H S(\hat{X}) + \{\hat{P} - \lambda_H\}\hat{X}_H - \sigma_F \delta_H \sum_{f \in F} \varepsilon_f \hat{x}_f(\hat{X}, \tau_f) \qquad (9.28)$$

Differentiating with respect to $\hat{x}_h$, we obtain the first-order conditions which say that the full marginal cost of output (production cost plus environmental damage) must be equalized across all home firms:

$$\delta_H \varepsilon_h + \alpha_h c'(\hat{x}_h) = \lambda_H \qquad (9.29)$$

or:

$$\hat{x}_h = c^{t-1}\left(\frac{\lambda_H - \delta_H \varepsilon_h}{\alpha_h}\right) \qquad (9.30)$$

This implies that among firms with identical ε_h, firms with high α_i produce less. From (9.30) we get:

$$\hat{x}_h = \hat{x}_h(\lambda_H) \qquad (9.31)$$

Summing (9.31) over all all $h \in$ H, we get:

$$\sum_{h \in H} \hat{x}_h(\lambda_H) = \hat{X}_H \qquad (9.32)$$

Since $\hat{x}_h(\lambda_H)$ is strictly increasing in λ_H, equation (9.32) uniquely determines the optimal λ_H, for given $\hat{X}_H : \lambda_H = \lambda_H(\hat{X}_H)$.
    To illustrate our approach, consider the following example:

Example   With linear demand P = 1 – Q and quadratic cost $\alpha_i c(x_i) = (\alpha_i / 2)x_i^2$ we get:

$$\hat{x}_h(\lambda_H) = \frac{[\lambda_H - \delta_H \varepsilon_h]}{\alpha_h}$$

and hence (9.32) gives:

$$\hat{\lambda}_H = \upsilon_H \rho_H + \upsilon_H \hat{X}_H$$

where $\rho_H \equiv \delta_H \sum_{h \in H}[\varepsilon_h/\alpha_h]$ and $\upsilon_H \equiv 1/\sum_{h \in H}[1/\alpha_h]$.

The second step
We now determine the optimal $\hat{X}_H$. We follow the duality methods used in Rockafellar (1970).[5] Following Rockafellar, we define the conjugate functions

$$\psi_h^*(\lambda_H) \equiv \max_{x_h}\{\lambda_H \hat{x}_h - \psi_h(\hat{x}_h)\}$$

then, for a given $\hat{X}_H$, the value of the Lagrangian $\hat{L}$ (optimized with respect to the $\hat{x}_h$s) is:

$$\hat{L} = \beta_H S(\hat{X}) + \hat{X}_H\{P(\hat{X}) - \hat{\lambda}_H(\hat{X}_H)\} +$$

$$\sum_{h \in H} \psi_h^*(\hat{\lambda}_H(\hat{X}_H)) - \sigma_F \delta_H \sum_{f \in F} \varepsilon_f \hat{x}_f(\hat{X}, \tau_f) \qquad (9.33)$$

Here, $\hat{L}$ depends only on $\hat{X}_H$ (to be chosen in the second step) and on the foreign tax vector τ_F chosen by the foreign government.

We now differentiate (9.33) with respect to $\hat{X}_H$ and equate it to zero:

$$[\hat{P}']\{\hat{X}_H - \beta_H\hat{X}\}\frac{\partial\hat{X}}{\partial\hat{X}_H} + \hat{P} - \hat{\lambda}_H(\hat{X}_H) - \sigma_F\delta_H\sum_{f \in F}\varepsilon_f\frac{\partial\hat{x}_f}{\partial\hat{X}}\frac{\partial\hat{X}}{\partial\hat{X}_H} = 0 \qquad (9.34)$$

(In deriving this equation, we have used the facts that $d\psi_h^*/d\lambda_H = \hat{x}_h$). If $\hat{L}(\hat{X}_H)$ is concave and the solution is interior, then equation (9.34) determines country H's unique optimal choice of $\hat{X}_H$ for given τ_F.

From the equilibrium condition for firm h (see (9.3) and (9.1)), we have $\varepsilon_h t_h = \hat{x}_h\hat{P}' + \hat{P} - \alpha_h c'(\hat{x}_h)$, and using (9.29), we get $\varepsilon_h t_h = \hat{x}_h\hat{P}' + \delta_H\varepsilon_h + [\hat{P} - \lambda_H]$. Use (9.34) to substitute for $[\hat{P} - \lambda_H]$.

Proof of Proposition 4.1

We make use of (9.9)–(9.12), with $A = B = 1$ for simplicity, where τ_f is now replaced by the tariff T_f imposed by country H on goods imported from country F. We have:

$$\hat{x}_f = \gamma_f[(1 - T_f) - \hat{X}]$$

$$\hat{X}_F = -m_{F\gamma F}\hat{X} + \sum_{f \in F}\gamma_f(1 - T_f) \equiv \hat{X}_F(\hat{X}, T_F)$$

where $\gamma_F \equiv (1/m_F)\sum_{f \in F}\gamma_f$, and, since in equilibrium $\hat{X}_H = \hat{X} - \hat{X}_F(\hat{X}, T_F)$, we must have:

$$\hat{X}_H = (1 + m_{F\gamma F})\hat{X} - \sum_{f \in F}\gamma_f(1 - T_f) \equiv J\hat{X} - K \qquad (9.35)$$

where:

$$J = 1 + m_{F\gamma F}$$

and:

$$K = \sum_{f \in F} \gamma_f (1 - T_f). \tag{9.36}$$

Hence:

$$\frac{\partial \hat{X}_H}{\partial \hat{X}} = 1 + m_{F\gamma F} \equiv J$$

Recall that the first-order condition of the maximization of L with respect to x_h, where $h \in H$, is

$$\hat{x}_h = \frac{\lambda_H - \delta_H \varepsilon_h}{\alpha_h} \tag{9.37}$$

or

$$\hat{x}_h = [a_h \lambda_H - \delta_H b_h], \, h \in H \tag{9.38}$$

where $a_h \equiv 1/\alpha_h$ and $b_h \equiv \varepsilon_h/\alpha_h$. Summing over all $h \in H$ yields:

$$\hat{X}_H = m_H a_H \lambda_H - m_H b_h \delta_H \tag{9.39}$$

where $a_H \equiv (1/m_H) \sum_{h \in H} a_h$ and $b_H (1/m_H) \sum_{h \in H} b_h$. Finally, from (9.34):

$$P(X) - \lambda_H = \frac{\hat{X}_H - \beta_H \hat{X} - \delta_F \sum_{f \in F} \bar{\varepsilon}_f \gamma_f}{J} \tag{9.40}$$

The three equations (9.35), (9.39) and (9.40) determine λ_H, $\hat{X}$ and $\hat{X}_H$. Solving for λ_H:

$$\lambda_H = \frac{J^2 - KJ + 2Jm_H b_H + \beta_H K + \sigma_F \delta_H \sum_{f \in F} \bar{\varepsilon}_f \gamma_f}{[2J - \beta_H]m_H \alpha_H + J^2} \tag{9.41}$$

Now let trade liberalization be represented by a small reduction in all T_f. Write $T_f = T_f^0 - u$. Then, from (9.41), and recalling, from (9.23) and (9.36), that $\check{K}$ and $\bar{\epsilon}_f$ are functions of the T_fs, the effect of a marginal trade liberalization on λ_H is:

$$\frac{\partial \lambda_H}{\partial u} = \frac{\beta_{H\gamma F} m_F}{[2J - \beta_H] m_H a_H + J^2} \geq 0 \tag{9.42}$$

(where we assume $2 \geq \beta_H$) and hence, using (9.38):

$$\frac{\partial \hat{x}_h}{\partial u} = \frac{a_h \beta_{H\gamma F} m_F}{[2J - \beta_H] m_H a_H + J^2} \geq 0 \tag{9.43}$$

and thus the total domestic emission increases:

$$\frac{\partial E_H}{\partial u} = \frac{\beta_{H\gamma F} m_F}{[2J - \beta_H] m_H a_H + J^2} \sum_{h \in H} \epsilon_h a_h$$

Also,

$$\frac{\partial \hat{X}_H}{\partial u} = \frac{m_F a_H \beta_{H\gamma F}}{[2J - \beta_H] m_H a_H J + J^2} \geq 0$$

From (9.35), $\hat{X} = (K + \hat{X}_H)/J$, hence:

$$\frac{\partial \hat{X}}{\partial u} = \frac{1}{J}\left(\gamma_F m_F + \frac{m_F a_F \beta_{H\gamma F}}{[2J - \beta_H] m_F a_F + J^2}\right) > 0$$

Now, the equilibrium condition for home firms is:

$$\epsilon_h t_h = \hat{x}_h P' + P(\hat{X}) - \alpha_h c'(\hat{x}_h)$$

therefore

$$\epsilon_h \frac{\partial t_h}{\partial u} = -\frac{\partial \hat{x}_h}{\partial u} \frac{\partial \hat{X}}{\partial u} - (\alpha_h) \frac{\partial \hat{x}_h}{\partial u} < 0$$

Optimal Tariffs and Optimal Emission Taxes

In Section 9.4, it was assumed that the tariff rates are exogenously set. We now modify the model by allowing for the choice of tariff rates. We wish to find out whether the optimal emission taxes still deviate from marginal damage cost when tariffs are optimally chosen. Maximizing W_H^0 with respect to the tariff rates $T_f, f \in F$, and bearing in mind (9.23), we obtain m_F equations that determine the optimal firm-specific tariff rates, for a given $\hat{X}_H$:

$$[\hat{P}']\{\hat{X}_H - \beta_H \hat{X}\}\frac{\partial \hat{X}}{\partial T_f} + \hat{x}_f - \sigma_F \delta_H \sum_{j \in F} \bar{\varepsilon}_j \frac{\partial \hat{x}_j}{\partial \hat{X}} \frac{\partial \hat{X}}{\partial T_f} = 0, f \in F \qquad (9.44)$$

The optimal choice of $\hat{X}_H$ must satisfy a condition similar to (9.34):

$$[\hat{P}']\{\hat{X}_H - \beta_H \hat{X}\} \frac{\partial \hat{X}}{\partial \hat{X}_H} + \hat{P} - \hat{\lambda}_H(\hat{X}_H) - \sigma_F \delta_H \sum_{fj \in F} \varepsilon_j \frac{\partial \hat{x}_j}{\partial \hat{X}} \frac{\partial \hat{X}}{\partial \hat{X}_H} = 0 \qquad (9.45)$$

To illustrate, consider the special, case where there is only one foreign firm, and the inverse demand function is $P = 1 - X$, and the cost function is $\alpha_f c(x_f) = (\alpha_f/2)x_f^2$, with $\alpha_f = 1$, so that γ_f 1/2. Assume $\beta_H = 1$. Then (9.44) gives:

$$T_f = \sigma_F \delta_H \varepsilon_f = \frac{1}{\gamma_f}\hat{x}_f = \frac{1}{1+\gamma_f}[1 - T_f - \hat{X}_H] \qquad (9.46)$$

Hence:

$$T_f = \frac{\gamma_f}{2+\gamma_f}\left[\sigma_F \delta_H + \left(\frac{\gamma_f}{1+\gamma_f}\right)\left(1 - \hat{X}_H\right)\right] \qquad (9.47)$$

which is positive since $\hat{X}_H \le X \le 1$ given that $P = 1 - X \ge 0$. Finally, substituting (9.47) into (9.24), we obtain the optimal emission taxes:

$$t_h = \delta_H \frac{\hat{x}_h}{\varepsilon_h} < \delta_H$$

This shows that under linear demand and quadratic costs, when the tariff rates are optimally chosen, the optimal emission taxes will fall short of the marginal damage cost.

NOTES

We should like to thank Alistair Ulph, Olivier Cadot and Huilan Tian for very helpful comments.

1. For Pigouvian tax under monopoly, see Buchanan (1969) and Barnett (1980), among others.
2. See also the survey chapters by Ulph in Folmer and Tietenberg (1997–8).
3. For a complete set of assumptions which guarantee the existence and uniqueness of Cournot equilibrium, see Gaudet and Salant (1991). We shall take it that they hold in our model.
4. The case where the tariff rates are not exogenously set is considered briefly in the appendix. There, we show that even if tariff rates are optimally set, the optimal emission taxes still deviate from the marginal damage cost. This is because, of the four factors mentioned in the introduction, tariffs deal only with the first two.
5. See Rockafellar (1970: 284–5, theorem 28.4 and corollary 28.4.1); see also Luenberger (1969:224, theorem 1).

REFERENCES

Anderson, Kym (1995), 'The entwining of trade policy with environmental and labour standards', Working Paper 39–95, Foundation Eni Enrico Mattei.

Barnett, A. (1980), 'The Pigouvian tax rule under monopoly', *American Economic Review*, **70**, 1037–41.

Barrett, Scott (1994), 'Strategic environmental policy and international trade', *Journal of Public Economics*, **54**(3), 325–38.

Baumol, W.J. and W.E. Oates (1988), *The Theory of Environmental Policy*, Cambridge: Cambridge University Press.

Benchekroun, Hassan and Ngo Van Long (1998), 'Efficiency-inducing taxation for polluting oligopolists', *Journal of Public Economics*, **70**, 325–42.

Buchanan, James M. (1969), 'External diseconomies, corrective taxes, and market structure, *American Economic Review*, **59**(1), 174–7.

Conrad, Klaus (1996a), 'Optimal environmental policy for oligopolistic industries under intra-industry trade, in C. Carraro, Y. Katsoulacos and A. Xepapadeas (eds), *Environmental Policy and Market Structure*, Fondazione Eni Enrico Mattei Series on Economics, Energy and Environment, vol. 4, Dordrecht, Boston and London: Kluwer Academic, 65–83.

Conrad, Klaus, (1996b), 'Choosing emission taxes under international price competition', in C. Carraro, Y. Katsoulacos and A. Xepapadeas (eds), *Environmental Policy and Market Structure*, Fondazione Eni Enrico Mattei Series on Economics, Energy and Environment, vol. 4, Dordrecht, Boston and London: Kluwer Academic, 85–98.

Folmer, Henk and Tom Tietenberg (1997–8), *The International Yearbook of Environmental and Resource Economics: 1997/8: A Survey of Current Issues*, New Horizons in Environmental Economics Series, Cheltenham, UK and Lyme, US: Edward Elgar.

Gaudet, Gérard, and Stephen Salant (1991), 'Uniqueness of Cournot equilibrium: new results from old methods', *Review of Economic Studies*, **58**, 399–404.

Katsoulacos, Y. and A. Xepapadeas (1995), 'Environmental policy under oligopoly with endogenous market structure', *Scandinavian Journal of Economics*, **97**, 411–22.

Kennedy, Peter W. (1994), 'Equilibrium pollution taxes in open economy with imperfect competition', *Journal of Environmental Economics and Management*, **27**, 49–63.

Long, Ngo Van and Antoine Soubeyran (1997a), 'Cost manipulation in oligopoly: a duality approach', SEEDS Discussion Paper 174, Southern European Economics Discussion Series, Université d'Aix-Marseille II.

Long, Ngo Van and Antoine Soubeyran (1997b), 'Cost manipulation in an asymmetric oligopoly: the taxation problem', SEEDS Discussion Paper 173, Southern European Economics Discussion Series, Université d'Aix-Marseille II.

Long, Ngo Van and Antoine Soubeyran (1999), 'Environmental policies and delocalisation', typescript, McGill University.

Luenberger. D. (1969), *Optimization by Vector Space Methods*, New York: John Wiley.

Rauscher, Michael (1994), 'Environmental regulation and the location of polluting industries', Discussion Paper 639, Institute of World Economics, Kiel.

Rauscher, Michael (1997), *International Trade, Factor Movements, and the Environment*, Oxford and New York: Clarendon Press.

Rockafellar, R. Tyrell (1970), *Convex Analysis*, Princeton, N.J.: Princeton University Press.

Ulph, Alistair (1992), 'The choice of environmental policy instruments and strategic international trade', in R. Pethig (ed.), *Conflicts and Cooperation in Managing Environmental Resources*, Berlin: Springer Verlag.

Ulph, Alistair (1996a), 'Environmental policy and international trade when governments and producers act strategically', *Journal of Environmental Economics and Management*, **30**(3), 265–81.

Ulph, Alistair (1996b), 'Environmental policy instruments and imperfectly competitive international trade', *Environmental and Resource Economics*, **7**(4), 333–55.

10. R&D cooperation, innovation spillovers and firm location in a model of environmental policy

Carlo Carraro and Antoine Soubeyran

10.1 INTRODUCTION

One of the arguments raised against environmental taxation concerns its effects on the competitiveness of firms located in those countries which decide to introduce an emission tax. For example, it is often argued that a tax on carbon dioxide (CO_2) emissions would induce energy-intensive firms to relocate their plants in countries adopting a less stringent environmental policy.

The economic literature has recently faced this issue[1] by focusing on the tradeoff between fixed and variable (transport) costs of relocation and the burden of the environmental tax. The results seem to show that relocation may occur, but that this may be a desirable option from a social welfare point of view in the case of local pollution if the environmental benefit is larger than the economic loss caused by the move of domestic production activities in a foreign country. In this latter case, the tax is an incentive to relocate abroad polluting plants (the so-called NIMBY – not in my back yard – strategy).

By contrast, in the case of global pollutants, the domestic environmental damage is not reduced by the relocation of firms. It is therefore preferable to prevent polluting (for example, energy-intensive) firms from relocating their plants. This explains why several proposals on the introduction of a carbon tax, such as the one proposed in 1992 by the Commission of the European Communities (CEC), contain tax exemptions for energy-intensive industries.

This chapter attempts to provide a further look at this problem by emphasizing the role of innovation and R&D cooperation in the decision process that may lead firms to relocate their plants as a reaction to the introduction of an emission tax. The well-known argument[2] is that a tax can stimulate R&D and innovation, thus leading firms to become more efficient. This increased competitiveness may offset the negative effects on firms' costs produced by the tax. Moreover, firms developing environmentally friendly technologies may have the possibility to sell the new production processes (or the licences), thus making profits in this new market.

There are therefore two economic forces that guide a firm's decision process. On the one hand, environmental policy increases costs, providing an incentive to relocate plants abroad. On the other hand, inducing more R&D and innovation reduces costs, thus preventing firms from relocating their plants in countries with less-stringent environmental policies. As we shall show, these two forces are a function of the number of firms in the country. As the number of firms which innovate increases, the positive external effects of R&D also increase, making innovation more profitable. At the same, domestic production and pollution expand, increasing the environmental costs paid by firms and making relocation more profitable. This chapter analyses the interaction of these two forces and their role in determining the optimal response of firms to environmental policy.

The questions to be answered are the following: What is a firm's reaction to environmental taxation? Will a firm decide to relocate its plants abroad? Or will it choose to innovate? If so, is the R&D strategy going to be decided jointly with the other firms in the industry (R&D cooperation)?

In order to provide an analytical framework to answer the above questions, this chapter considers a domestic industry in which an emission tax is introduced and in which the tax is such as to induce firms to move their plants to another country – where no tax is levied – unless firms decide to change their production technology. However, the new environmentally friendly technology is not yet available. Therefore, when firms do not relocate, either they develop the new technology or they imitate the technology developed by other firms. The development of new technologies is assumed to be the outcome of some cooperative R&D efforts among firms (the number of cooperating firms will be endogenously determined). Imitation takes place when some firms prefer to buy the licence to use the new technology from the firms which have decided to carry out R&D. Obviously, no imitation can take place without R&D.

The goal of the chapter is twofold: (a) to determine whether some firms decide to carry out R&D and to innovate, while others stay in the country and buy the licence to use the new technology, whereas a third group of firms move to the foreign country; and (b) to single out the crucial parameters which explain the choice of each firm, and to propose some policy strategies that can provide incentives for polluting firms not to exit the country when this is a desirable option.

The structure of the chapter is as follows: the next section presents the model, clarifies its main assumptions and sets the rules of the game; it also determines the optimal production choices of the three groups of firms. Section 10.3 focuses on limitating firms and determines the demand for licences to use the environmentally friendly technology and its price. Section 10.4 analyses the formation of the R&D coalition and discusses under which conditions the three groups of firms are going to emerge. The last section is devoted to analysing the policy implications of the model.

10.2 INNOVATION STRATEGIES AND RELOCATION: THE ANALYTICAL MODEL

Consider an *n* firm, perfectly competitive domestic industry. The production process used by these firms is polluting. This induces the government to introduce a tax to control emissions. Pollution is a local as well as a global problem. Emissions depend on the production level chosen by each firm. The emission rate is affected by the innovation activity carried out by the firms, which in turn also depends on the incentive policies introduced by the government.

Let $k(q_h)$ be the cost function which represents firm h's technology, $k' > 0$, $k'' \geq 0$, and $E_h(q_h) = e(.)q_h$ be its linear emission function, where q_h, $h = 1, 2, ..., n$ is the production level and $e(.)$ is the emission rate, to be specified below.

Firms may decide to locate their plants either at home or abroad, where it is assumed that the foreign government does not levy emission charges (alternatively, taxes are lower in the foreign country). Following Xepapadeas (1997: ch. 2), it can be shown that a government which maximizes consumers' utility sets the optimal tax rate equal to the social marginal damage from emissions, where this marginal damage is a growing function of total domestic emissions. Therefore, let $t(E)$ be the emission tax rate, where E are total emissions in the domestic country. Moreover, let $E_h = E_h(q_h) = e(.)q_h$, $h = 1, 2, ..., n$ be firm h's emissions.

Assume the tax level to be high enough to induce firms to move their plants abroad unless a new technology, characterized by a sufficiently lower emission–output ratio, is adopted.[3] Firms have therefore two main options: either they relocate their plants or they innovate. In this latter case they can choose whether to join the group of firms which cooperate on R&D, or they can decide to imitate the cooperating firms. In the latter case, imitating firms buy licences from the cooperating ones – we assume that property rights on the environmental innovation can be established. The price of the licence is denoted by p_x and is set by the R&D cooperating firms.

There may therefore be three groups of firms. Let n_c denote the number of cooperating firms, n_i the number of those which imitate, and n_d the number of firms which relocate their plants abroad, $n_c + n_i + n_d = n$ and $0 \leq n_h \leq n$, $h = c, i, d$. Moreover, let us denote by C, I and D the three groups of firms respectively, where $C \cup I \cup D = N$ and N $\{1, 2, \ldots, n\}$. The profit functions are as follows:

$$\Pi_c = [pq_c - k(q_c) - t(E)e(.)q_c] + (p_x n_i - F_c)/n_c \qquad c \in C \qquad (10.1a)$$

for R&D cooperation firms, where p is the market price, $p_x n_i$ is the total revenue from the licensing activity, and F_c is the fixed cost of R&D. The R&D profit $(p_x n_i - F_c)$ is shared equally among the n_c firms in the R&D coalition:

$$\Pi_i = [pq_i - k(q_i) - t(E)e(.)q_i] - p_x \qquad i \in I \qquad (10.1b)$$

for the imitating firms (zero innovation spillovers are assumed), and:

$$\Pi_d = [pq_d - k(q_d) - t_d q_d] - F_d \qquad d \in D \qquad (10.1c)$$

for the relocating firms, where t_d are unit transport costs, F_d is the fixed cost of relocation, and $t(E) = 0$ in the foreign country.

The emission rate $e(.)$ is a function of the technology which is used by firms. Firms in the domestic country share the same technology, either because they develop it or because they buy it. Hence, they are characterized by the same emission rate, which implies the same cost structure $k(.)$ + $t(E)e(.)q$ and, as a consequence, the same production level $q \equiv q_i = q_c$. R&D activities modify the available technology because they focus on the development of environmentally friendly production processes. We assume that R&D increasingly reduces the negative impact on the environment of production activities as the number of R&D cooperating firms increases. Therefore, the emission rate is $e(.) = e(n_c)$, $e' \leq 0$.

The consequence of the above remarks is that E – total emissions in the domestic country – can be defined as:

$$E = n_c e(.)q_c + n_i e(.)q_i = (n_c + n_i)e(.)q. \qquad (10.2)$$

The government has two policy instruments: an incentive policy to foster the development of environmentally friendly technologies and a tax policy to internalize damages from polluting emissions. The tax policy leads the government to introduce a tax rate equal to $t(E)$. The tax is obviously paid only by firms which remain in the country. The incentive policy may be directed either to reduce F_c – the fixed cost of R&D – or to reduce $e(n_c)$ – the emission rate – by providing firms with some free basic research, thus increasing the effectiveness of R&D cooperation among the n_c firms in the R&D coalition.

An important assumption on the (exogenously given) tax rate has to be introduced. We already assumed that the tax rate is high enough to induce all domestic firms to relocate their plants in the foreign country if no environmental innovation is developed and adopted. We also assume that it is such as to induce at least one domestic firm to move its plants abroad, even if all domestic firms adopt the innovation and remain in the country.

The first part of the assumption on the tax rate makes clearer the role of innovation in preventing firms from relocating. Indeed, without innovation, all firms would relocate. With innovation, they may not do so. The second part emphasizes the role of negative environmental externalities. If all firms remain in the country, pollution is high enough to imply a tax rate whose level is such as to induce at least one firm to move its plants abroad.

Let us assume the following functional forms: $k(q) = \frac{1}{2}q^2$, $t(E) = tE$, and $e(n_c) = n_c^{-\varepsilon}$, $\varepsilon > 0$, where $\varepsilon = -e'(n_c)n_c/e(n_c)$ is the elasticity of the emission rate to the number of R&D cooperating firms. Then domestic firms' profit maximization leads to:

$$V(b) = \max_{qc} \Pi_c = \max_{qi} \Pi_i = \frac{1}{2}(p-b)^2 \qquad c \in C, \, i \in I \qquad (10.3)$$

where $b = t(E)e(n_c)$ is the cost per unit of production of emissions, $\partial V/\partial b < 0$, and the optimal production level is $q^*(b) = p - b$. An explicit solution can be obtained by solving the system:

$$b = tEe(n_c) \qquad (10.4a)$$

$$E = (n_c + n_i) \, e(n_c) \, q^*(b) \qquad (10.4b)$$

The emission tax rate is:

$$b^*(n_c, n_i) = [p(n_c + n_i)te(n_c)^2]/[\,1 + (n_c + n_i)te(n_c)^2] \qquad (10.5a)$$

whereas total domestic emissions are:

$$E^*(n_c, n_i) = [p(n_c + n_i)e(n_c)]/[1 + (n_c + n_i)te(n_c)^2] \qquad (10.5b)$$

from which:

$$q^*(n_c, n_i) = p/[1 + (n_c + n_i)te(n_c)^2] \tag{10.5c}$$

$$V^*(n_c, n_i) = \tfrac{1}{2}p^2/[1 + (n_c + n_i)te(n_c)^2]^2 \tag{10.5d}$$

What is the relationship between the unit environmental tax burden $b^*(n_c, n_i)$ and the number of imitating and cooperating firms? Taking first derivatives, we obtain $\partial b^*/\partial n_i > 0$ and $\partial b^*/\partial n_c \propto te(n_c)^2[1 - 2\varepsilon/\theta]$ for $n_c \geq 1$, where $\theta = n_c/(n_c + n_i)$. This latter derivative is therefore non-negative when $\theta \geq 2\varepsilon$. Notice that θ belongs to the unit interval. Hence, $\partial b^*/\partial n_c$, is always negative if $\varepsilon > \tfrac{1}{2}$. This implies that an increase in the number of R&D cooperating firms always decreases the unit costs of emissions (this is what we called the strongly convex case). If instead $\varepsilon < \tfrac{1}{2}$, $\partial b^*/\partial n_c$, may be first negative, when θ is very small because a few firms cooperate on R&D, and then positive, as the number of firms in the R&D coalition increases. In this latter (weakly convex) case, an increase of n_c reduces the unit costs of emissions because it increases the environmental efficiency of the new technology. At the same time, a larger number of firms in the domestic country increases the tax burden and therefore the cost of emissions. When n_c is small, the first effect prevails, but when n_c increases, given the decreasing returns of R&D cooperation, the second effect prevails and the unit costs of emissions increase with the number of R&D cooperating firms.[4]

Notice that the dynamics of b^* determines the level of profits for domestic firms. Indeed, we can write the value of profits at the optimal production level as:

$$\pi_c(n_c, n_i) = V(b^*(n_c, n_i)) + (p_x n_i - F_c)/n_c \quad c \in C \tag{10.6a}$$

$$\pi_i(n_c, n_i) = V(b^*(n_c, n_i)) - p_x \quad i \in I \tag{10.6b}$$

Therefore, given p_x and n_i, an increase of b^* reduces domestic firms' profits. This implies that, in the weakly convex case, an increase in the number of firms which join the R&D coalition and remain in the country may be counterproductive, that is, the effect on profits may be negative.

Let us finally consider the value of profits for relocating firms. We have:

$$V_d(t_d) = \max_{q_d} \Pi_d = \tfrac{1}{2}(p - t_d)^2 \quad d \in D \tag{10.7}$$

from which:

$$\pi_d = V_d(t_d) - F_d \quad d \in D \tag{10.8}$$

Notice that this value of profits does not depend on n_c and n_i, and therefore it does not depend on $n_d = n - n_c - n_i$. As a consequence, in the sequel, when the analysis will focus on the determination of n_c and n_i, that is, of the size of the three groups of firms, π_d will be considered as given.

Let us conclude this section by specifying the rules of the game underlying the decision process in the industry. In the first stage, firms choose the group, that is, one of the three strategies – R&D cooperation, purchase of the licence, relocation – which identifies the group. In the second stage, the optimal production level is determined. The first stage is divided into two sub-stages: in the first one, the R&D coalition is formed which sets the price of the licence, taking into account the implications of this choice on the number of imitating firms (and consequently on the number of firms which relocate). In the second sub-stage, given the price of the licence and the number of firms in the R&D coalition, the number of imitating firms and the number of firms which relocate their plants are determined. This sequence is motivated by the following remark. Entry to the R&D coalition cannot be open, because open membership might reduce profits of firms in the coalition. Hence, the first decision to be taken is the optimal size of the group of firms which cooperatively carry out R&D. The remaining firms will then decide whether or not to stay in the country (by buying the licence) or to relocate.

10.3   IMITATION

The second stage of the game – the production stage – was already solved in the previous section (see equations (10.5)). We can thus move to the first stage. Going backwards, let us first determine the size of the group of firms which decide to imitate. These firms, given the available technologies, choose between relocating their plants abroad and buying the less- polluting technology developed by the R&D cooperating firms. In this latter case their profit is π_i. Otherwise, they obtain π_d. At the equilibrium, no firm in group I finds it profitable to join group D, that is to relocate, and no firm in group D prefers to be in I. Therefore, the equilibrium condition is $\pi_i(n_c, n_i) = \pi_d$, or:

$$\tfrac{1}{2} p^2 / [1 + (n_c + n_i) t e(n_c)^2]^2 = p_x + \pi_d \tag{10.9}$$

from which we can solve with respect to n_i. This yields:

$$n_i(p_x, n_c, \varepsilon, t, \pi_d) = (1/t)(n_c)^{2\varepsilon} [2^{-\frac{1}{2}} p(p_x + \pi_d)^{-\frac{1}{2}} - 1] - n_c$$

which describes the demand for licences (each firm is assumed to buy one licence only) as a function of their price p_x, of the 'quality' of the environmental innovation, here captured by the number of firms in the R&D coalition and by the elasticity parameter ε, and of the strength of the environmental policy (the tax rate t). Notice that $\partial n_i/\partial t < 0$, $\partial n_i/\partial p_x < 0$, $\partial n_i/\partial \pi_d < 0$.

Notice also that the demand for licences must satisfy $0 \le n_i \le n - n_c$, which implies:

$$p_x \le p_M(n_c) = (p^2/2)[1 + tn_c^{(1-2\varepsilon)}]^{-2} - \pi d \qquad (10.11a)$$

where $p_M(n_c)$ is the maximum licence price above which the demand for licences is no longer positive, and:

$$p_x > p_m(n_c) = (p^2/2)[1 + tn_c^{-2\varepsilon}n]^{-2} - \pi_d \qquad (10.11b)$$

where $p_m(n_c)$ is the minimum licence price at which no firm wants to relocate its plants abroad. Notice that the assumption on the tax rate implies that (10.11b) must hold as a strict inequality. The two prices $p_M(n_c)$ and $p_m(n_c)$ are non-negative only if:

$$\pi_d \le (p^2/2)[1 + tn_c^{(1-2\varepsilon)}]^{-2} \qquad (10.12)$$

Hence, profits abroad cannot be too large, otherwise all firms would like to relocate.

If (10.11a) also holds as a strict inequality, the demand for licences is strictly positive. This implies that set I is not empty whenever C is non-empty. The number of firms in the R&D coalition – the size of C – will be determined in the next section.

The optimal price for the licence to use the less-polluting technology developed by the R&D cooperating: firms can be computed by maximizing the profit function of the firms belonging to C with respect to p_x, given the demand function defined by (10.10). The profit function is:

$$\pi_c = p_x + \pi_d + \{(1/t)(n_c)^{2\varepsilon}[2^{-\frac{1}{2}} p(p_x + \pi_d)^{-\frac{1}{2}} - 1] - n_c\}p_x/n_c - F_c/n_c \qquad (10.13)$$

whose differentiation with respect to p_x yields:

$$(p_x/A)(\partial A/\partial p_x) = -1 \qquad (10.14a)$$

where $A = (1/t)[2^{-\frac{1}{2}}p(p_x + \pi_d)^{-\frac{1}{2}} - 1]$. This first-order condition can be written as a third-order equation by defining $y \equiv (p_x + \pi_d)^{-\frac{1}{2}}$. Then

(10.14a) becomes:

$$y + \pi_d y^3 = 2\sqrt{2}/p \qquad (10.14b)$$

whose solution uniquely determines y^* and therefore p_x^*. First, $\partial^2 \pi_c / \partial p_x^2 <$ 0 for all $p_x \geq 0$ can easily be computed. Second, the left-hand side of (10.14b) is an increasing function of y which equals zero when $y = 0$, whereas the right-hand side is constant and strictly positive (see Figure 10.1, where the function $y + \pi_d y^3$ and the equilibrium value y^* are shown). Notice that the optimal price for the licence is independent of n_c – the number of R&D cooperating firms.[5]

From Figure 10.1, the effect of a change of p and π_d on the price of licences can be assessed. An increase of p lowers the line $2\sqrt{2}/p$ and therefore y^*. As a consequence p_x^* – the price of licences – is also lowered. An increase of π_d rotates the function $y + \pi_d y^3$ to the left, thus reducing y^*

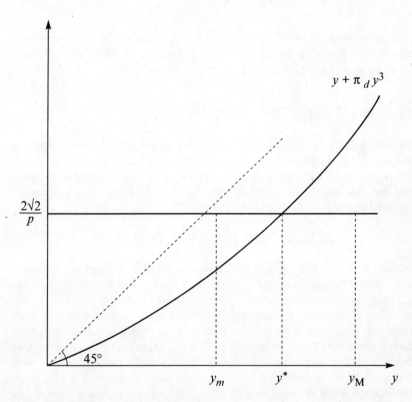

Figure 10.1 Effects on the price of licences

and, p_x^*. The equilibrium price of licences is thus defined by the following function:

$$p_x^* = p_x^*(\pi_d, p)$$

where $\partial p_x/\partial \pi_d < 0$, $\partial p_x/\partial p < 0$. These results are quite intuitive. A reduction of market price or an increase of profits in the foreign market reduces the relative profitability of the domestic market. Hence, R&D cooperating firms need to set a lower price for their licence if they want to induce the other domestic firms to buy the new technology rather than move into the foreign country.

Finally, let us verify if the equilibrium price p_x^* satisfies the constraint (10.11a) and (10.11b). These can be rewritten as:

$$y \geq \sqrt{2}[1 + tn_c^{(1-2\varepsilon)}]/p \equiv y_m \qquad (10.15a)$$

$$y \leq \sqrt{2}[1 + tn_c^{-2\varepsilon}n]/p \equiv y_M \qquad (10.15b)$$

Notice that $\sqrt{2}[1 + tn_c^{(1-2\varepsilon)}]/p \leq \sqrt{2}[1 + tn_c^{-2\varepsilon}n]/p$ because $n_c \leq n$. There exist therefore values of p and π_d such that y^* belongs to the interval defined by equations (10.15a) and (10.15b).

10.4 R&D COOPERATION

Before analysing firms' decision to cooperate on R&D, thus endogenizing the number of firms in the R&D coalition, let us summarize the results so far obtained on the structure of the industry. As we said above, firms in the industry may be divided into three groups, C, I, D. The partitions of the set N including all firms are as follows:

$$\{(C), (I), (D), (C, D), (C, I), (I, D), (C, I, D)\}$$

Notice, however, that (I) and (I, D) are not feasible. Indeed, no imitation can occur if C is empty, that is, if no innovation is developed; (C) and (C, I) are also not feasible because of the assumption on the tax rate; finally, (C, D) is excluded by the assumption on the price of the licences. We are therefore left with two possibilities: either C is empty and all firms prefer to relocate their plants abroad; or C is not empty and three groups of firms (C, I, D) form at the equilibrium. Let us analyse the size of C; then, the size of I – the imitating firms – will be determined by (10.10), given the licence price defined by (10.14b). The remaining $n - n_c - n_i$ firms decide to move their plants abroad.

The number of firms which decide to join the R&D coalition can be determined as follows. After replacing the demand for licences and their optimal price, the profit function for the cooperating firms becomes:

$$\pi^{o}(n_{c}) = y^{*} + (1/n_{c})[n_{c}^{2\varepsilon}A^{*}p_{x}^{*} - F_{c}]$$

where A^{*} can also be written as $A^{*} = (1/t) [py^{*}/\sqrt{2} - 1]$ and y^{*} was previously shown to be independent of n_{c}.

In the case of R&D cooperation, it cannot reasonably be assumed that entry to the coalition is open to all firms. A concept of exclusive membership should rather be used. Indeed, there is no reason to assume that R&D cooperating firms let other firms join the coalition if this is going to reduce their profits. As a consequence, the number of firms which cooperate to develop the environmentally friendly technology is determined by maximizing $\pi^{o}(n_{c})$ with respect to n_{c}. The first-order condition is:

$$(1/n_{c}^{2})[F_{c} - p_{x}^{*}A^{*}(1 - 2\varepsilon)nc^{2\varepsilon}] = 0 \qquad (10.17a)$$

from which:

$$n_{c}^{*} = \{F_{c}/[p_{x}^{*}A^{*}(1 - 2\varepsilon)]\}^{\frac{1}{2\varepsilon}} \qquad (10.17b)$$

Moreover, $d^{2}\pi^{o}(n_{c})/dn_{c}^{2} < 0$ if $1 - 2\varepsilon > 0$ (the weakly convex case). Notice that this condition is also necessary for $n_{c}^{*} < n$. Were $1 - 2\varepsilon < 0$, $d\pi^{o}(n_{c})/dn_{c}$ would be positive for all positive n_{c}. In this (strongly convex) case all firms would find it optimal to join the R&D coalition without excluding any potential member. The reason is the strong impact on cost reduction of additional R&D cooperators whenever $\varepsilon > \frac{1}{2}$.

Notice that the optimal number of R&D cooperators defined by (10.17b) is an increasing function of the fixed cost F_{c}, whereas it decreases with the price of licences p_{x}^{*}. Again the intuition is quite simple, even if not obvious. An increase of F_{c} makes it optimal to have a larger number of cooperators in order to share a larger fixed cost. An increase of p_{x}^{*}, increases the benefits from the market for licences and therefore reduces the optimal number of cooperators because they can make profits even with a small reduction of costs (that is, a small size n_{c}). If n_{c} were larger, profits would have to be shared between a larger number of cooperators, hence receiving an increasingly small benefit from their cooperation. An increase of A^{*}, that is, of π_{d}, also reduces the number of R&D cooperating firms because it increases the incentive for all firms to relocate their plants in the foreign country. Notice that π_{d} can be increased by lower trade barriers, lower transport costs and labour costs, and so on.

Finally, the determination of the optimal coalition size n_c^*, and price of licences p_x^*, imply the determination of $n_i^*(n_c^*, p_x^*, \varepsilon, \pi_d, t)$ – the number of firms which prefer to imitate. As a residual, we obtain the number of firms which decide to relocate their plants abroad, that is, $n_d^* = n - n_c^* - n_i^*$.

10.5 CONCLUSIONS

The implications of the previous analysis can be summarized as follows. In a competitive industry with identical firms, the introduction of environmental taxation induces different replies. Some firms decide to develop a new, environmentally friendly technology, which helps them to reduce the tax burden; other firms prefer (or are forced) to buy the new technology rather than developing it; whereas a third group of firms decide to relocate their plants in a foreign country. This result is obviously conditional on the assumptions discussed in the previous sections. In particular, the restrictions on the tax rate, on the effects of R&D on the emission rate (the weakly convex case), and on the level of profits in the foreign country are crucial to obtain the above conclusion. If, for example, profits in the foreign country are excessively high – inequality (10.12) is not satisfied – all firms would move their plants abroad. If, by contrast, $\varepsilon > \frac{1}{2}$, then all firms would find it optimal to join the R&D coalition and to accept the cooperation of all firms. Hence, no relocation would occur.

The size of the three groups of firms depends on the parameters of the model. We have seen how an increase of the fixed cost of R&D, an increase of transport costs or of trade barriers – which reduces profits in the foreign country, and a decrease in the price of a licence, all increase the number of countries in the R&D coalition. The same result can be achieved by a governmental policy designed to increase the effectiveness of firms' R&D, for example by stimulating R&D efforts, cooperation and spillovers within coalition members.[6]

Notice that the two industrial policy instruments mentioned in section 10.2, that is, a subsidy on R&D fixed costs and an incentive policy to increase R&D effectiveness, have opposite effects. Only this second policy instrument, for example, a larger amount of free basic research available to firms, can increase the number of firms in the R&D coalition, thus reducing the number of firms which decide to relocate their plants abroad.

These results are confirmed by the numerical simulations performed in Boetti *et al.* (1997) using a more complex numerical model based on the theoretical model developed in this chapter. The impact of an incentive policy which increases the effectiveness of R&D cooperation on the emission rate is shown in Figure 10.2, which is drawn from Boetti *et al.* (1998).

As expected, the number of domestic firms increases, whereas the number of those which decide to relocate their plants abroad sharply decreases.

The impact of a subsidy on R&D fixed costs on the size of the three groups of firms is shown in Figure 10.3. As predicted by the theoretical model, this type of subsidy is counterproductive if the goal is to prevent firms relocating their plants in the foreign country.

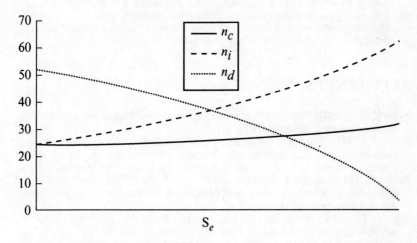

Figure 10.2 Optimal firm distribution as the R&D effectiveness S_e increases

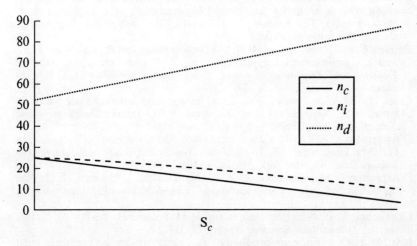

Figure 10.3 Optimal firm distribution as the subsidy on R&D fixed cost S_c increases

NOTES

1. Among the works recently devoted to the issue of firm relocation are Markusen *et al.* (1993, 1995); Rauscher (1995); Hoel (1994); Motta and Thisse (1994); Venables (1996).
2. See Porter (1991).
3. An interesting extension of this chapter would be the endogenization of the tax rate. This would require that the game between the governments of the two countries be modelled and solved.
4. Formally, when $n_c = 0$ the derivative is negative, whereas when $n_c = n$ the derivative is positive if $\varepsilon < \frac{1}{2}$. Therefore, there exists a value n^o such that $\partial b^*/\partial n_c = 0$.
5. This result is always true for any constant elasticity taxation function.
6. Obviously spillovers which favour firms outside the R&D coalition would create a free-riding problem that may undermine the coalition stability.

REFERENCES

Barrett, S. (1994), 'Self-enforcing international environmental agreements', *Oxford Economic Papers*, **46**, 878–94.

Bloch, F. (1997), 'Noncooperative models of coalition formation in games with spillovers', in C. Carraro and D. Siniscalco (eds), *New Directions in the Economic Theory of the Environment*, Cambridge: Cambridge University Press.

Boetti, M., M. Botteon, C. Carraro and A. Soubeyran (1998), 'On the effects of industrial, trade and environmental policies on the location choices of firms', *Revue d'économie industrielle*, **83**, 63–80.

Carraro, C. and D. Siniscalco (1993), 'Strategies for the international protection of the environment', *Journal of Public Economics*, **52**, 309–28.

Carraro, C. and D. Siniscalco (1994), 'Environmental policy reconsidered: the role of technological innovation', *European Economic Review*, **38**, 545–54.

Carraro, C. and D. Siniscalco (1995), 'Policy coordination for sustainability: commitments, transfers, and linked negotiations', in I. Goldin and A. Winters (eds), *The Economics of Sustainable Development*, Cambridge: Cambridge University Press.

Carraro, C. and D. Siniscalco (1997), 'R&D cooperation and the stability of international environmental agreements', in C. Carraro (ed.), *International Environmental Agreements: Strategic Policy Issues*, Cheltenham, UK: Edward Elgar.

Cesar, H. and A. de Zeeuw (1994), 'Issue linkage in global environmental problems', in A. Xepapadeas (ed.), *Economic Policy for the Environment and Natural Resources*, Cheltenham, UK: Edward Elgar.

D'Aspremont, C.A. and J.J. Gabszewicz (1986), 'On the stability of collusion', in G.F. Matthewson and J.E. Stiglitz (eds), *New Developments in the Analysis of Market Structure*, New York: Macmillan Press, 243–64.

D'Aspremont, C.A., A. Jacquemin, J.J. Gabszewicz and J. Weymark (1983), 'On the stability of collusive price leadership', *Canadian Journal of Economics*, **16**, 17–25.

Donsimoni, M.P., N.S. Economides and H.M. Polemarchakis (1986), 'Stable cartels', *International Economic Review*, **27**, 317–27.

Hoel, M. (1994), 'Environmental policy as a game between governments when plant locations are endogenous', paper presented at the 21st EARIE Conference, Crete, 4–6 September.

Markusen, J.R., E.R. Morey and N. Olewiler (1993), 'Environmental policy when market structure and plant locations are endogenous', *Journal of Environmental Economics and Management*, **24**, 69–86.

Markusen, J.R., E.R. Morey and N. Olewiler (1995), 'Competition in regional environmental policies with endogenous plant location decisions', *Journal of Public Economics*, **56**, 55–77.

Motta, M. and J. Thisse (1994), 'Does environmental dumping lead to de-location?', *European Economic Review*, **38**, 563–76.

Porter, M. (1991), 'America's green strategy', *Scientific American*, **264(4)**, 96.

Rauscher, M. (1995), 'Environmental regulation and the location of polluting industries' *International Tax and Public Finance*, **2**, 229–44.

Venables, A. (1996), 'Equilibrium locations of vertically linked industries', *International Economic Review*, **37**, 341–59.

Xepapadeas, A. (1997), *Advanced Principles in Environmental Policy*, Cheltenham, UK: Edward Elgar.

Yi, S. (1997), 'Stable coalition structures with externalities', *Games and Economic Behavior*, **20(2)**, 201–37.

11. Relative standards as strategic instruments in open economies

Udo Ebert[1]

11.1 INTRODUCTION

There is a familiar rule in allocation theory which says that at least as many (appropriate) instruments are required for a correction of inefficiencies as there are distortions in the economy. In economic policy, particularly in environmental policy, the number of instruments available is often assumed to be smaller. In this case an instrument has to take on several roles: it has to correct more than one distortion at the same time; then the goals cannot be attained fully, in general. Therefore, the optimal level of the instrument is typically a compromise between competing objectives. A first-best allocation cannot be achieved, but a second- or third-best allocation can. The outcome depends on the details and the framework chosen, as a considerable body of literature on the choice of instruments in environmental economics demonstrates.

The present chapter contributes to this literature. It investigates environmental policy in open economies with imperfectly competitive markets. Production and consumption externalities are considered. While most articles dealing with these problems examine environmental taxes, this chapter analyses the use of relative standards. They restrict the level of emissions per unit of the commodity produced or consumed. This instrument has recently been treated in Ebert (1998) in a closed-economy context. It turned out that it is an inefficient instrument, not able to achieve a first-best allocation. Nevertheless, it proved to be attractive for politicians: many process standards and product standards can be interpreted as relative standards. Though they are inefficient, they possess advantages in comparison to environmental taxes since their implementation and monitoring is much simpler. This type of standard is also relevant to open economies. In a situation in which there are no tariffs or subsidies, governments have incentives to distort the relative standard away from the first-best and second-best optimum in order to attain welfare gains. These strategic distortions of optimal standards will be identified and interpreted. In general, governments prefer to weaken their relative standards, that is, the standard and the marginal abatement cost are lower than they should be in a closed economy. In this respect the results are similar to those derived elsewhere for environmental taxes, but of course the details depend on the model treated.

There are several papers in the literature dealing with the relationship between strategic environmental policy and international trade. They differ with respect to their approach and focus. Nevertheless, four key aspects may be used for a classification. First, the structure of the model considered and the market structure play a major role. Krutilla (1991) examines environmental regulation by a large trading country, assuming that the behaviour of the rest of the world is specified by an excess demand function. Copeland (1994) investigates reforms in a small open economy. Barrett (1994) supposes that the industries of two countries sell their output in a third market. Kennedy (1994) and Hung (1994) assume imperfect competition among the producers of two countries. Ludema and Wooton (1994) consider a model in which a production externality in the foreign country hurts the importing country. Second, most papers do not admit abatement. Ludema and Wooton introduce an abatement technology explicitly into their model. Third, in general it is assumed that countries behave non-cooperatively. Then two different methodologies can be employed. Either the Nash equilibrium between welfare-maximizing governments is investigated (for example, Barrett 1994; Hung 1994) or the conditions for welfare-improving policies or reforms are derived (Copeland 1994). Fourth, some authors restrict themselves to an examination of one instrument (for example, Kennedy 1994); others discuss the choice of instruments (Ulph 1992) or, like Copeland (1994), deal with taxes and quotas (or absolute standards) at the same time.

The approach of this chapter is similar to that of Hung (1994). It considers an international duopoly. In a two-country model each country's industry sells its product in the domestic and foreign markets. Both markets are assumed to be segmented; that is, there are no transportation costs for the firms under consideration. But it is assumed that such costs are prohibitive for anybody else (cf. Brander 1981; Dixit 1984). Competition is imperfect. Abatement is admitted. Only one instrument – a relative standard – is investigated. Both countries maximize welfare. Therefore the properties of optimal standards will be derived. The chapter is organized as follows. Section 11.2 introduces the notation and presents the basic model. Section 11.3 is devoted to an analysis of the non-cooperative game between the governments of both countries. The outcome is compared to first- and second-best solutions. Finally, section 11.4 concludes the chapter.

11.2 BASIC MODEL

The analysis is confined to two countries. In order to simplify matters we assume that there is one firm in each country. The firm in the home country produces y units of a homogeneous commodity. Its technology is represented by a linear cost function $C(y) = F + cy$ where F denotes a fixed cost and $MC = c$, a marginal cost. The firm is active in the home and the foreign markets, which are assumed to be segmented. It sells x at home and exports z units to the other country. The foreign country and foreign firm are described analogously. The corresponding variables and functions will be indicated by an asterisk. $q = x + z^*$ and $q^* = x^* + z$ denote the respective consumption of the commodity considered.

Two types of emission will be investigated: one is associated with the production activity, the other with the consumption activity. It is assumed that there is a fixed relation between gross emissions v and output y and consumption q, respectively. Without loss of generality we identify v either with y or q. The firm is able to reduce its own emissions or the emissions generated by consumption by means of abatement. The abatement technology is implicitly given by the cost function[2] $AC(w) = ew$, where w denotes the number of units of v which are abated. $MAC = e$ denotes marginal abatement cost. As the referee remarked, the specification of a linear abatement cost technology abstracts from the stylized fact that marginal abatement costs tend to rise as the ratio of abatement to output approaches unity. A linear technology has to be interpreted as a local approximation to a more general technology. Taking into account abatement we have to distinguish between gross emissions v and net emissions $s = v - w$. The latter pollute only the environment of the home country; that is, pollution is local and not transboundary. Pollution (the negative externality) immediately generates damages in the period under investigation. They are reflected by a social damage function $D(s)$. It evaluates damages in monetary units. Marginal damage $MD(s)$ is positive and non-decreasing.

The government introduces a relative standard α for the firm(s). In case of a production externality the amount of emissions which has to be abated is given by αy. Then pollution is restricted relative to output since the firm has to obey the restriction:

$$\frac{s}{y} = \frac{v - w}{y} = \frac{y - \alpha y}{y} \leq (1 - \alpha).$$

We consider the case where the restriction is binding. Thus net emissions are given by $s = (1 - \alpha)y$. It is obvious that the firm reduces pollution only to meet the standard. There is no incentive to increase abatements above the level required because the firm behaves as a profit-maximizer and therefore is a cost-minimizer. In the case of a consumption externality the level of emissions depends on the way the commodity is produced. Without any treatment, $v = q$ units are emitted when the good is consumed. This level can be reduced by changing the inherent properties of the commodity. The corresponding costs are again given by AC(w) and AC$^*(w^*)$, respectively. The process is also called abatement for simplicity. Then the relative standard α is imposed on production x for the home market and on imports z^*; therefore the firm in the home country has to abate αx and the other one αz^* units. As a consequence, the standard is also satisfied for total consumption q: $\alpha(x + z^*) = \alpha q$ units are abated; net emissions are equal to $s = (1 - \alpha) q$.

While the technology of production and abatement has been assumed to be linear, no restrictions are imposed on the functional structure of the demand functions $p(q)$ and $p^*(q^*)$ at this point. (One has to choose either linear cost functions or linear demand functions in order to guarantee definite results for comparative statics.) They are independent. Demand is strictly concave in q and decreasing in price, $p'(q) < 0$ and $p^{*'}(q^*) < 0$. Furthermore, it is supposed that the Hahn condition is satisfied: the marginal revenue of each firm should decrease as the output of any competitor which is sold in the same market increases:

$$p''(\tilde{q}) \, q + p'(\tilde{q}) < 0 \text{ and } p^{*''}(\tilde{q}^*)q^* + p^{*'}(\tilde{q}^*) < 0 \text{ for all } q, \tilde{q}, q^*, \tilde{q}^*.$$

These conditions will imply stability of the Nash–Cournot equilibrium. Finally, we define the net export $Z = z - z^*$ and the trade surplus $T = p^*(q^*) \, z - p(q) \, z^*$ which can have either sign. Their definition implies that $Z^* = -Z$ and $T^* = -T$.

Now we turn to a discussion of the firms' behaviour and the equilibrium of the model.

11.2.1 Production Externality

We examine the firm in the home country. It maximizes its profit, Π, defined by:

$$\Pi = p(x + z^*) \, x + p^*(x^* + z) \, z - C(x + z) - AC\,(\alpha(x + z))$$

when the government imposes the relative standard α. The firm has to choose its sales x in the domestic market and its exports z:

$$\max_{x,z} \Pi$$

Assuming imperfect competition we obtain the first-order equations:

$$\frac{\partial \Pi}{\partial x} = p'(q)x + p(q) - MC(y) - \alpha\, MAC = 0 \qquad (11.1)$$

$$\frac{\partial \Pi}{\partial z} = p^{*\prime}(q^*)z + p^*(q^*) - MC(y) - \alpha\, MAC = 0 \qquad (11.2)$$

Because of the Hahn condition and the linearity of $C(y)$ and $AC(w)$ the second-order conditions are satisfied as well.

Both firms compete in quantities in the home market and the foreign market. The Cournot–Nash equilibria are determined by the first-order conditions of both firms, given by:

$$p'(x + z^*)\, x + p(x + z^*) - c - e\alpha = 0 \qquad (11.3)$$

$$p^{*\prime}(x^* + z)z + p^*(x^* + z) - c - e\alpha = 0 \qquad (11.4)$$

$$p^{*\prime}(x^* + z)\, x^* + p^*(x^* + z) - c^* - e^*\alpha^* = 0 \qquad (11.5)$$

$$p'(x + z^*)\, z^* + p(x + z^*) - c^* - e^*\alpha^* = 0 \qquad (11.6)$$

That is, we consider an international duopoly. Both markets separate: equations (11.3) and (11.6) describe the equilibrium of the home market, (11.4) and (11.5) that of the foreign market (cf. Dixit 1984). An analogous result is derived in Hung (1994) for environmental taxes under the condition that marginal costs are zero. This case can be subsumed in our model if taxes t and t^* are identified with $e\alpha$ and $e^*\alpha^*$, respectively, and c and c^* are set zero.

It is easy to establish:

Proposition 1 The Cournot–Nash equilibria described by (11.3)–(11.6) exist and are stable.

It follows immediately from the Hahn conditions introduced above (Novshek 1985). Multiple equilibria can occur; they are excluded. Moreover, all endogenous variables depend on both standards α and α^*. This means that environmental regulation in one country influences the actions of both firms and has to be taken into account by the government of the other country. Therefore we observe (strategic) interdependence. The details are given by:

Proposition 2 The qualitative impact of a marginal increase in the exogenous variables α and α^* on the endogenous variables of the model is presented in Table 11.1.

Table 11.1 Implications of an increase in α or α^* on the endogenous variables (i)

	x	z	q	y	Z	T	x/q	z/q^*	$p(q)$
α	−	−	−	−	−	−	−	−	+
α^*	+	+	−	+	+	+	+	+	+

Note: + means an increase, − means a decrease of the corresponding variable.

The proof of Proposition 2 is provided in the appendix. The reactions listed are as expected. We consider a tightening of the relative standard α, at first. It decreases home production, sales at home and exports, and it increases foreign production, the sales of the foreign firm at home and its exports to the home country. On the other hand, consumption in both countries is decreased and prices are raised. Net exports Z and the trade surplus T are diminished as well. The market share of the home country's firm decreases in both markets. Choosing a tighter relative standard α^* yields analogous results.

Referring to the analogy between relative standards and environmental taxes mentioned above, we conclude that the same comparative static properties hold for environmental taxes within this model, which generalizes Hung's (1994) Lemma.

11.2.2 Consumption Externality

Again we consider the home country. The domestic firm has to take into account both relative standards. In order to meet the domestic standard it has to abate αx units and to incur abatement cost $AC(\alpha x)$. This standard is relevant only for sales in the home market. Exports z are regulated by the foreign standard α^*. Therefore the firm abates $\alpha^* z$. The corresponding abatement costs are given by $AC(\alpha^* z)$. Whenever the abatement technologies differ the relative standards α and α^* can also be interpreted as product standards: both countries are able to impose different rules on product design. Summing up, the profit equals:

216 *Environmental regulation and market power*

$$\Pi = p(x + z^*) \, x + p^*(x^* + z)z - C(x + z) - AC(\alpha \, x) - AC^*(\alpha^* z)$$

which is maximized by the firm. This yields the first-order conditions:

$$\frac{\partial \Pi}{\partial x} = p'(q)x + p(q) - MC(y) - \alpha \, MAC = 0 \qquad (11.7)$$

$$\frac{\partial \Pi}{\partial z} = p^{*'}(q^*)z + p^*(q^*) - MC(y) - \alpha^* MAC^* = 0 \qquad (11.8)$$

The second-order conditions are satisfied again.

Both firms compete on quantities. The Cournot–Nash equilibria can be characterized by:

$$p'(x + z^*)x + p(x + z^*) - c - e\alpha = 0 \qquad (11.9)$$

$$p^{*'}(x^* + z)z + p^*(x^* + z) - c - e^*\alpha^* = 0 \qquad (11.10)$$

$$p^{*'}(x^* + z) \, x^* + p^*(x^* + z) - c^* - e^*\alpha^* = 0 \qquad (11.11)$$

$$p'(x + z^*) \, z^* + p(x + z^*) - c^* - e\alpha = 0 \qquad (11.12)$$

Analogous first-order conditions would be implied if both countries chose consumption taxes t and t^* as instruments (replace $e\alpha$ and $e^*\alpha^*$ by t and t^*, respectively). Thus the following results could be interpreted accordingly.

By assumption both markets are also separated for the case of a consumption externality. Furthermore, a relative standard imposes restrictions only on the respective national market. The equilibrium of the domestic (foreign) market is described by equations (11.9) and (11.12) (equations (11.10) and (11.11)). Consumption $q = x + z^*$ depends on the standard α: $x = x \, (\alpha)$ and $z^* = z^* \, (\alpha)$, but it is independent of α^*. We obtain:

Proposition 3 The Cournot–Nash equilibria described by (11.9)–(11.12) exist and are stable.

Multiple equilibria are again excluded. Turning now to comparative statics we are able to prove:

Proposition 4 The standard α has an impact on the endogenous variables x, z^*, y, y^*, q, Z and T. But only the reaction of domestic consumption is qualitatively unique:

$$\frac{dq}{d\alpha} < 0.$$

Unfortunately, it is not possible to derive unambiguous comparative static properties for all variables affected by the relative standard α. Therefore we also examine the result for the special case where the demand curves are linear:

$$p(q) = a - bq, p^*(q^*) = a^* - b^*q^* \text{ for } a, a^*, b, b^* > 0. \qquad (11.13)$$

Imposing linearity, we are able to establish:

Proposition 5 Assume condition (11.13). The qualitative impact of a marginal increase in the exogenous variables α and α^* on the endogenous variables affected is presented in Table 11.2.

Table 11.2   *Implications of an increase in α or α^* on the endogenous variables (ii)*

	x	z	q	y	Z	T	p	$\dfrac{x}{q}$	$\dfrac{z^*}{q}$
α	–	0	–	–	+	?	+	+	
α^*	0	–	0	–	–	?	0	0	

Notes
1. + means an increase, – a decrease, and 0 constancy of the corresponding variable.
2. The impact on the trade surplus is ambiguous.

It is also proved in the appendix. All effects work in the intuitively expected directions. Tightening the domestic standard α reduces pollution and consumption q and increases the market price $p(q)$. Net exports are increased since imports decrease. The distribution of market shares becomes more unequal: if the market share of the home (foreign) firm x/q (z^*/q) exceeds the foreign (domestic) firm's share z^*/q (x/q), it is raised further by an increase in α. This effect can provide an incentive to tighten the standard, an incentive which is missing in the case of a production externality.

11.3   STRATEGIC ENVIRONMENTAL POLICY

It was mentioned above that the model introduced can be interpreted as an international duopoly model describing the impact of relative standards *or* of environmental taxes. This interpretation is appropriate as long as only the implications or the comparative static properties of these instruments are investigated. Also the derivation of the first-best allocation does not depend on the choice of instrument but is influenced only by the type of externality.

In the following we shall turn to a normative and positive analysis of environmental policy in a second-best framework; then the type of instrument employed has to be taken into account from the beginning. It restricts the possibilities which are available to a social planner or the government of a country. In the normative part of the examination we shall characterize a second-best optimum for both countries. It corresponds to a situation in which the welfare of both countries is jointly maximized and represents a reference allocation referred to in the positive analysis. There it is supposed that countries do *not* cooperate: each country chooses its relative standard to maximize national welfare, given the other country's policy. Then we have to expect strategic distortions of environmental policies for trade-related goals. Indeed, neither a first-best nor the second-best optimum is achieved. Environmental and trade effects compete. The optimal standard of a country presents a compromise between both goals. The details depend of course on the type of externality; therefore we separate the analysis into two parts.

11.3.1   Production Externality

First we consider the social welfare (SW) of the home country. It can be decomposed into three components:

SW = consumers' surplus + producer's surplus – damages

The details depend on the framework investigated. In each case, the producer's surplus comprises revenue, production cost and abatement cost. Therefore we obtain:

$$SW = \left[\int_0^{x+z^*} p(\tilde{q}) \, d\tilde{q} - p(q)\,(x + z^*) \right] + \left[p(q)\,x + p^*\,(q^*)\,z - C(x + z) \right.$$
$$\left. - \text{abatement cost} \right] - \text{damages} \tag{11.14}$$

Obviously the terms $p(q)x$ and $-p(q)x$ cancel; $p^*(q^*)z - p(q)z^*$ corresponds to the trade surplus T. Thus trade is reflected at several places:

$$SW = \int_0^{x+z^*} p(\tilde{q}) \, d\tilde{q} + T - C(q) - \text{abatement cost} - \text{damages}$$

Analogously we can represent the social welfare SW^* of the foreign country.

The first-best allocation for both countries together is a good point of departure for further discussions. In this case the details are given by:

$$\text{abatement cost} = AC(w)$$
$$\text{damages} = D(x + z^* - w)$$

where AC and D possess the properties introduced in section 11.2. We have to maximize overall social welfare:

$$\max_{x,\, x^*,\, z,\, z^*,\, w,\, w^*} \int_0^{x+z^*} p(\tilde{q}) \, d\tilde{q} + \int_0^{x^*+z} p^*(\tilde{q}^*) \, d\tilde{q}^* - C(x+z) - C^*(x^*+z^*) -$$
$$AC(w) - AC^*(w^*) - D(x+z-w) - D^*(x^*+z^*-w^*).$$

The surpluses T and T^* are mutually offsetting and drop out. The solution to this optimization problem is as expected:

$$MC + MD = p = p^* = MC^* + MD^* \tag{11.15}$$

$$MAC = MD \text{ and } MAC^* = MD^* \tag{11.16}$$

Prices p and p^* are identical and reflect the social marginal cost. Emissions are abated up to the point where marginal abatement cost and marginal damage coincide. These conditions follow from the first-order conditions of welfare maximization. It is assumed that second-order conditions are satisfied.

A first-best solution abstracts from any institutional details (such as the instrument available) and leaves aside the fact that agents pursue their own goals. In order to get a second-best solution we assume now that a relative standard is used and that firms maximize profits. The firms' behaviour has to be taken into account as a restriction to the optimization problem. If a relative standard is employed we have to define:

$$\text{abatement cost} = AC(\alpha \, y)$$
$$\text{damages} = D((1 - \alpha) \, y).$$

Since profit maximization implies that $q = q(\alpha, \alpha^*)$ and $y = y(\alpha, \alpha^*)$ we obtain social welfare as:

$$W_p(\alpha, \alpha^*) = \int_0^{q(\alpha, \alpha^*)} p(\tilde{q})\, d\tilde{q} + T - C(y(\alpha, \alpha^*)) - AC(\alpha\, y(\alpha, \alpha^*)) - D((1 - \alpha)\, y(\alpha, \alpha^*))$$

and $W_p^*(\alpha^*, \alpha)$ analogously, where the subscript p refers to the production externality.

The second-best allocation is described by the solution of the following problem:

$$\max_{\alpha, \alpha^*} W_p(\alpha, \alpha^*) + W_p^*(\alpha^*, \alpha).$$

We derive the first-order condition for the environmental standard α (the analogue can be obtained for α^*):

$$\frac{\partial(Wp(\alpha, \alpha^*) + W^*p(\alpha^*, \alpha))}{\partial\alpha} = p(q)\frac{dq}{d\alpha} + p^*(q^*)\frac{dq^*}{d\alpha} - MC\frac{dy}{d\alpha} - MC^*\frac{dy^*}{d\alpha}$$

$$- MAC\, y - \alpha\, MAC\frac{dy}{d\alpha} - \alpha^* MAC^*\frac{dy^*}{d\alpha} - MD \cdot \left(-y + (1-\alpha)\frac{dy}{d\alpha}\right)$$

$$- MD^* \cdot (1 - \alpha^*)\frac{dy^*}{d\alpha} = 0$$

Assuming now identical countries ($p \equiv p^*$, $C \equiv C^*$, $AC \equiv AC^*$, $D \equiv D^*$, $\alpha = \alpha^*$), this equation can be rearranged to:

$$[p(q) - MC - \alpha MAC]\left(\frac{dy}{d\alpha} + \frac{dy^*}{d\alpha}\right) - (1-\alpha)\, MD \cdot \left(\frac{dy}{d\alpha} + \frac{dy^*}{d\alpha}\right) + MDy - MAC\, y = 0$$

since

$$\frac{d(q + q^*)}{d\alpha} = \frac{d(y + y^*)}{d\alpha}$$

Profit maximization of the home firm implies (cf. equation (11.1)):

$$p'(q)x + p(q) - MC - \alpha\, MAC = 0$$

Therefore the first bracket in the above equation can be replaced by $-p'(q)x$. Thus we obtain:

$$\text{MD} - \text{MAC} = (1 - \alpha)\,\text{MD}\,\frac{d(y + y^*)}{d\alpha}\frac{1}{y} + p'(q)x\frac{d(y + y^*)}{d\alpha}\frac{1}{y} \quad (11.17)$$

which must be compared to (11.16).
 The term

$$\frac{d(y + y^*)}{d\alpha}\frac{1}{y} \quad \text{equals} \quad \frac{y + y^*}{\alpha\, y}\,\eta_y,$$

where η_y, denotes the elasticity of total production with respect to the relative standard α. It is negative, since total production $y + y^*$ is equal to total consumption $q + q^*$, which decreases as α rises (cf. the comparative static properties listed in Table 11.1). Assuming for a moment that firms are price-takers ($p' \equiv 0$), we recognize that the right-hand side of equation (11.17) is strictly negative for an interior solution $\alpha < 1$; that is, the marginal abatement cost is greater than the marginal damage. The more the world production reacts to a change in α, the more the marginal abatement cost exceeds the marginal damage. This result is not really surprising if it is compared to the optimal relative standard in a closed economy (cf. Ebert 1998). It can be explained easily: there is only one distortion, the negative production externality and one instrument. The standard should provide incentives for the firm to choose the optimal level of production *and* of abatement. But each is not independent. The firm automatically abates αy units of emissions (see the discussion above). For any tightening of the relative standard, the net emissions fall by more than the increase in abatement, due to the output effect. This gives an intuitive explanation of the fact that the marginal abatement cost exceeds the marginal damage of the second-best optimum. Therefore a relative standard is never an appropriate instrument, which yields a first-best allocation; it is *a priori* second best.
 Now let us turn to the second term of the right-hand side: it is positive and well known, and is related to imperfect competition. The firm possesses some room for pricing-up, therefore its supply is lower than it would be under perfect competition. This monopolistic (or duopolistic) output restriction has to be taken into account as well (cf. for example, Barnett 1980; Ebert 1991, 1998). The optimal standard has to internalize the negative externality *and* stimulate production. One objective stands in contradiction to the other, as the signs of both terms of the right-hand side in equation (11.17) indicate. The effects operate in opposite directions. The sign of the right-hand side is indeterminate; in any case the environmental standard is relaxed (compared to perfect competition). This also becomes obvious if condition (11.17) is solved for α:

$$\alpha = 1 - \left(\frac{MAC}{MD} - 1\right) y \left| \frac{d(y + y^*)}{d\alpha} + \frac{p'(q)x}{MD} \right. . \qquad (11.18)$$

The last term reflecting the market structure lowers the relative standard. Thus we obtain:

Proposition 6 In the case of a production externality, marginal abatement cost and marginal damage generally differ in a second-best optimum, which is characterized by conditions (11.17) or (11.18).

This result was derived for two identical countries. It should be clear that inefficiency is retained if countries differ. Now we shall assume that countries behave non-cooperatively. Each country maximizes its own welfare given the other country's policy (relative standard). The outcome is the Nash equilibrium.

Without loss of generality we consider the home country. It maximizes $W_p(\alpha, \alpha^*)$:

$$\max_\alpha W_p(\alpha, \alpha^*), \alpha^* \text{ fixed.}$$

Maximization yields the first-order condition which has also to be satisfied in a Nash equilibrium:

$$\frac{\partial W_p}{\partial \alpha} = p(q)\frac{dq}{d\alpha} + \frac{dT}{d\alpha} - MC\frac{dy}{d\alpha} - MAC\,y - \alpha MAC\frac{dy}{d\alpha} - MD \cdot \left(-y + (1-\alpha)\frac{dy}{d\alpha}\right) = 0.$$

It can be rearranged to:

$$p(q)\frac{dq}{d\alpha} - p(q)\frac{dy}{d\alpha} + [p(q) - MC - \alpha\,MAC]\frac{dy}{d\alpha}$$

$$+ \frac{dT}{d\alpha} - MAC\,y - MD \cdot \left(-y + (1-\alpha)\frac{dy}{d\alpha}\right) = 0$$

Using a first-order condition of profit maximization again allows us to replace the expression in square brackets by $-p'(q)\,x$.

Furthermore we are able to rewrite the first two terms:

$$p(q)\left(\frac{dq}{d\alpha} - \frac{dy}{d\alpha}\right) = p(q)\frac{d(x + z^* - (x + z))}{d\alpha} = p(q)\frac{d(z^* - z)}{d\alpha} = -p(q)\frac{dZ}{d\alpha}$$

Then we arrive at the solution:

$$MD - MAC = [(1 - \alpha) \, MD + p'(q)x] \frac{dy}{d\alpha} \frac{1}{y} + \left[p(q) \frac{dZ}{d\alpha} - \frac{dT}{d\alpha} \right] \frac{1}{y} \quad (11.19)$$

The difference between the marginal damage and the marginal abatement cost is determined by two terms: the first one was essentially derived above and is called the second-best effect. It describes the distortion necessary to obtain a second-best solution and was interpreted above. The second one is related to the trade between both countries and is called the trade effect. This effect represents a strategic distortion of the relative standard. The trade effect comprises two parts: one is connected with the change of net exports Z. For a production externality it is negative. When the environmental regulation is tightened, that is, if α is increased, exports decrease and imports increase. The other one reflects the change in the trade surplus. This term is always positive since the surplus is decreased when the relative standard α is raised. Since each effect operates in opposite directions it is not possible to determine the sign of the trade effect. But probably the change in the surplus T dominates the other one, since the last bracket can be written as:

$$p(q) \frac{dz}{d\alpha} - (p^*(q^*) + p^{*\prime}(q^*)z) \frac{dz}{d\alpha} - p^{*\prime}(q^*)z \frac{dx^*}{d\alpha} + p'(q)z \frac{dq}{d\alpha}$$

where only the first term is negative. Moreover, the external effect is a production externality; that is, the environmental regulation imposes restrictions only on the domestic firm. Its costs are raised and its market shares in the domestic and the foreign market decrease. Furthermore, the foreign firm increases its exports. Therefore the effect on the trade surplus T seems to be predominant. Then the overall trade effect is positive and lowers the optimal standard, which can be seen from:

$$\alpha = 1 + \left[\left(\frac{MAC}{MD} - 1 \right) y \left| \frac{dy}{d\alpha} + \frac{p'(q)x}{MD} \right| + \left[p \frac{dZ}{d\alpha} - \frac{dT}{d\alpha} \right] \right] \bigg/ \left(MD \frac{dy}{d\alpha} \right) \quad (11.20)$$

since $dy/d\alpha$ is negative.

We have established:

Proposition 7 In case of a production externality, the optimal standard in a Nash equilibrium is distorted by a second-best effect and a trade effect (cf. equations (11.19) and (11.20)). The latter probably weakens the environmental standard.

Finally we examine the special case of a closed economy and of perfect competition: then the trade effect and the term reflecting imperfect competition drop out. We obtain:

$$MD - MAC = \frac{(1-\alpha)}{\alpha} MD \frac{dy}{d\alpha} \frac{\alpha}{y} = \frac{(1-\alpha)}{\alpha} MD \, \eta_y$$

This result coincides with the condition for an optimal standard derived in Ebert (1998). In that paper a relative standard β limits the amount of *net* emission βy. Then abatement efforts are given by $(1 - \beta)y$. Therefore $\alpha = 1 - \beta$. Defining $\varepsilon y: = (dy/d\alpha)(\beta/y)$ we obtain:

$$\varepsilon_y = \frac{dy}{d(1-\alpha)} \frac{1-\alpha}{y} = \frac{(1-\alpha)}{\alpha} \frac{dy}{d(-\alpha)} \frac{\alpha}{y} = \frac{(1-\alpha)}{\alpha} \eta_y$$

and $MAC/MD = 1 + \varepsilon_y$, which is identical to equation (11.12) in Ebert (1998).

11.3.2 Consumption Externality

Internalizing a production externality primarily amounts to a regulation of domestic firms. The picture changes when a consumption externality is considered. Then any regulation imposes restrictions on imports and therefore on foreign firms as well. Thus the social welfare of the home country is described by (11.14) where:

$$\text{abatement cost} = AC(w_1) + AC^*(w_2)$$
$$\text{damages} = D(x + z^* - w_1 - w_2^*)$$

Here w_1 and w_2 denote the level of abatement for domestic supply x and exports z, respectively. Accordingly, a social planner has to solve:

$$\max_{x, x^*, z, z^*, w_1, w_1^*, w_2, w_2^*} \int_0^{x+z^*} p(\tilde{q})d\tilde{q} + \int_0^{x^*+z} p^*(\tilde{q}^*)d\tilde{q}^*$$

$$- C(x + z) - C^*(x^* + z^*) - AC(w_1) - AC^*(w_2)$$

$$- AC^*(w_1^*) - AC(w_2^*) - D(x + z - w_1 - w_2^*) - D^*(x^* + z^* - w_1^* - w_2)$$

in order to obtain a first-best optimum. It is characterized by the same conditions as derived above: prices have to be equal and to equal social marginal cost. Marginal abatement costs (in both countries) have to coincide with the respective marginal damage.

Similarly we are able to derive a second-best optimum. Taking into account the relative standard α and α^* we must define:

$$\text{abatement cost} = AC(\alpha\, x) + AC^* (\alpha^* z)$$
$$\text{damages} = D((1 - \alpha)\, (x + z^*)).$$

Profit maximization implies that x and q depend on α, z on a^*, and y on both relative standards. Then social welfare is defined by:

$$W_c(\alpha, \alpha^*) = \int_0^{q(\alpha)} p(\tilde{q})\, d\tilde{q} + T - C(y(\alpha, \alpha^*)) - AC\,(\alpha x\,(\alpha)) - AC^*(\alpha^*\, z(\alpha^*))$$
$$- D((1 - \alpha)\, q(\alpha))$$

and $W_c^*(\alpha^*, \alpha)$ analogously. The subscript c refers to the consumption externality. Then the second-best allocation is characterized by the solution to the following problem:

$$\max_{\alpha, \alpha^*} W_c(\alpha, \alpha^*) + W_c^*(\alpha^*, \alpha).$$

The Nash equilibrium condition for the domestic standard α is given by

$$\frac{\partial(W_c(\alpha, \alpha^*) + W_c^*(\alpha, \alpha^*))}{\partial \alpha} = [p(q) - MC - \alpha\, MAC]\frac{dx}{d\alpha} +$$

$$[p(q) - MC^* - \alpha\, MAC]\frac{dz^*}{d\alpha} - MACq - MD \cdot (-q + (1 - \alpha))\frac{dq}{d\alpha} = 0$$

where the structure of the model has already been employed: We have:

$$\frac{dq^*}{d\alpha} = \frac{dz}{d\alpha} = \frac{dx^*}{d\alpha} = 0$$

and therefore:

$$\frac{dy}{d\alpha} = \frac{dx}{d\alpha} \text{ and } \frac{dy^*}{d\alpha} = \frac{dz^*}{d\alpha} \text{ (cf. Table 11.2)}.$$

Making use of the first-order conditions of profit maximization in order to replace the expressions in square brackets and rearranging we arrive at:

$$\text{MD} - \text{MAC} = (1 - \alpha) \ \text{MD} \frac{dq}{d\alpha} \frac{1}{q} + p'(q) \left(x \frac{dx}{d\alpha} + z^* \frac{dz^*}{d\alpha} \right) \frac{1}{q} \quad (11.21)$$

This result is not surprising. Under perfect competition ($p'(q) = 0$) the marginal abatement cost must exceed the marginal damage; that is, relative standards are again inefficient. The inefficiency is reduced if imperfect competition is taken into account: the second term of the right-hand side is positive and reduces therefore the level of the optimal standard, which is given by:

$$\alpha = 1 + \left(\frac{\text{MAC}}{\text{MD}} - 1 \right) q \left| \frac{dq}{d\alpha} + \frac{p'(q)}{\text{MD}} \left(x \frac{dx}{d\alpha} + z^* \frac{dz^*}{d\alpha} \right) \right| \frac{dq}{d\alpha} \quad (11.22)$$

But for a consumption externality the impact of imports on the domestic price is relevant as well. Thus we have established:

Proposition 8 In the case of a consumption externality, marginal abatement cost and marginal damage generally differ in a second-best optimum which is characterized by condition (11.21) or (11.22).

Finally, we examine the non-cooperative Nash equilibrium. Then the home country maximizes:

$$\max_a \text{W}_c(\alpha, \alpha^*), \alpha^* \text{ fixed.}$$

The necessary first-order condition can be written as:

$$\frac{\partial \text{W}_c(\alpha, \alpha^*)}{\partial \alpha} = [p(q) - \text{MC} - \alpha \, \text{MAC}] \frac{dx}{d\alpha} + p(q) \frac{dz^*}{d\alpha}$$

$$+ \frac{d\text{T}}{d\alpha} - \text{MAC} \, x - \text{MD} \cdot \left(-q + (1 - \alpha) \frac{dq}{d\alpha} \right) = 0$$

Since $dz/d\alpha = 0$ the term $p(q)dz^*/d\alpha$ equals $-p(q)dZ/d\alpha$ and the expression in square brackets $-p'(q)x$. Thus the condition can be rearranged to:

$$\text{MD} - \text{MAC} = \left[(1 - \alpha) \, \text{MD} \frac{dq}{d\alpha} \frac{1}{q} + p'(q)x \frac{dx}{d\alpha} \frac{1}{q} \right] +$$

$$\left[p(q) \frac{dZ}{d\alpha} - \frac{d\text{T}}{d\alpha} \right] \frac{1}{q} - \text{MAC} \frac{z^*}{q} \quad (11.23)$$

The first bracket represents the second-best effect. It essentially corresponds to the distortion necessary for a second-best allocation. There is only one difference: the market power of the foreign firm is ignored. The second and third terms have to be explained by trade. The bracket has already been interpreted above. In this case it is strictly positive: a change in the relative standard increases net exports (since imports are diminished and exports remain unchanged). Thus this term is positive; the other one is indeterminate, but both terms can be reduced to a single expression:

$$p(q) \frac{dZ}{d\alpha} - \frac{dT}{d\alpha} = p(q)\left(\frac{dz}{d\alpha} - \frac{dz^*}{d\alpha}\right)$$

$$-\left(p^{*\prime}(q^*)z \frac{dq^*}{d\alpha} + p^*(q^*) \frac{dz}{d\alpha} - p'(q)z^* \frac{dq}{d\alpha} - p(q)\frac{dz^*}{d\alpha}\right) = p'(q)z^* \frac{dq}{d\alpha} > 0$$

since z and q^* do not depend on α. The remaining expression reflects the additional payment to the foreign country caused by the price increase $p'(q)dq/d\alpha$. It lowers the level of the relative standard. The third term of the right-hand side works in the opposite direction and leads to an increase in α since the share z^*/q of abatement costs is borne by the foreign country. This could be called the cost-shifting effect. Thus the overall impact of trade is generally ambiguous:

$$\alpha = 1 + \left[\left(\frac{\text{MAC}}{\text{MD}} - 1\right)q\Big|\frac{dq}{d\alpha} + \frac{p'(q)x}{\text{MD}}\frac{dx/d\alpha}{dq/d\alpha}\right]$$

$$+ \left[p\frac{dZ}{d\alpha} - \frac{dT}{d\alpha}\right]\Big/\left(\text{MD}\frac{dq}{d\alpha}\right) - \frac{\text{MAC}}{\text{MD}}z^*\Big|\frac{dq}{d\alpha} \tag{11.24}$$

If the implied marginal price change $|p'(q)dq/d\alpha|$ is small compared to the marginal abatement cost MAC, the cost-shifting effect outweighs the trade effect in the narrow sense. Then the country has an incentive to increase the relative standard in order to take advantage of the cost-shifting. We obtain:

Proposition 9 In the case of a consumption externality, the optimal standard in a Nash equilibrium is distorted by a second-best effect, a trade effect and a cost-shifting effect (cf. equations (11.23) and (11.24)). The net effect of trade is indeterminate, but it leads to a tightening of the standard if the cost-shifting effect is predominant.

As above, the case of a closed economy can be examined in this framework. The results are identical to those derived in subsection 11.3.1, since in a closed economy a production and a consumption externality cannot be distinguished in our framework.

11.4   CONCLUSION

The analysis in this chapter demonstrates that relative standards are strategically distorted by trade effects. This has been proved by a comparison of first- and second-best solutions to the Nash equilibrium of competing countries. It is possible to present the respective optimal level of the relative standard explicitly. Unfortunately, the implications of trade are in general ambiguous. The details depend on the type of externality and the model chosen. For a production externality the effect on the trade surplus is probably dominant. It yields a weakening of the standard. The same outcome is always achieved for a consumption externality as far as the impact on net exports and the trade surplus is concerned. On the other hand, each government has an incentive to tighten the standard in this case since the abatement costs are partially shifted to the other country. This effect is correlated to the importing country's market share. The investigation has been restricted to one instrument – a relative standard. It must certainly be modified if further instruments such as tariffs, taxes or subsidies are available.

APPENDIX

Proof of Proposition 2

Equations (11.1)–(11.4) correspond to the first-order conditions of profit maximization. The equilibrium of the home (foreign) market is determined by (11.1) and (11.4) ((11.2) and (11.3)). The markets are separated (cf. Dixit 1984 and also Hung 1994). Therefore it is sufficient to consider the home market. The total differential of (11.1) and (11.4) is given by:

$$(p''(q) \, x + 2p'(q)) \, dx + (p''(q) \, x + p'(q)) \, dz^* = ed\alpha \qquad (11A.1)$$

$$(p''(q) \, z^* + p'(q)) \, dx + (p''(q) \, z^* + 2p'(q)) \, dz^* = e^* d\alpha^* \qquad (11A.2)$$

Defining $\beta := p''(q) \, x + p'(q)$ and $\gamma := p''(q) \, z^* + p'(q)$ we obtain:

$$H \begin{pmatrix} dx \\ dz^* \end{pmatrix} = \begin{pmatrix} ed\alpha \\ e^* d\alpha^* \end{pmatrix}$$

where:

$$H := \begin{pmatrix} \beta + p'(q) & \beta \\ \gamma & \gamma + p'(q) \end{pmatrix}.$$

The determinant of H is positive because of the Hahn condition:

$$\Delta := \det H = (\beta + p')(\gamma + p') - \beta\gamma$$

$$= p'(q)^2 + p'(q)(\beta + \gamma) > 0.$$

Thus H is non-singular. Its inverse H^{-1} can be derived explicitly as:

$$H^{-1} = \frac{1}{\Delta} \begin{pmatrix} \gamma + p'(q) & -\beta \\ -\gamma & \beta + p'(q) \end{pmatrix}.$$

This allows us to solve (11A.1) and (11A.2) for dx and dz^*:

$$\begin{pmatrix} dx \\ dz^* \end{pmatrix} = H^{-1} \begin{pmatrix} ed\alpha \\ e^* d\alpha^* \end{pmatrix} \tag{11A.3}$$

Employing (11A.3), we are able to determine the impact of a change in α and α^* on the endogenous variables and to prove the comparative static properties:

$$dx = \frac{1}{\Delta}((\gamma + p'(q)) ed\alpha - \beta e^* d\alpha^*)$$

$$dz^* = \frac{1}{\Delta}(-\gamma ed\alpha + (\beta + p'(q)) e^* d\alpha^*)$$

$$dy = dx + dz^* = \frac{1}{\Delta}(p'(q) ed\alpha + p'(q) e^* d\alpha^*)$$

$$dy = dx + dz = \frac{1}{\Delta}(\gamma + p'(q)) ed\alpha - \beta e^* d\alpha^*$$

$$+ \frac{1}{\Delta^*}(-\gamma^* e^* d\alpha^* + (\beta^* + p^{*\prime}(q)) ed\alpha)$$

Here the symmetry of the solution is used for dz:

$$dZ = d(z - z^*) = \frac{1}{\Delta^*}(-\gamma^* e^* d\alpha^* + (\beta^* + p^{*'}(q^*))\, ed\alpha)$$

$$- \frac{1}{\Delta}(-\gamma\, ed\alpha + (\beta + p'(q))\, e^* d\alpha^*)$$

$$\frac{dT}{d\alpha} = p^{*'}(q^*)z\left(\frac{dz^*}{d\alpha} + \frac{dz}{d\alpha}\right) + p^{*'}(q^*)\frac{dz}{d\alpha} - p'(q)z^*\left(\frac{dx}{d\alpha} - \frac{dz^*}{d\alpha}\right) - p'(q)\frac{dz^*}{d\alpha}$$

$$= p^{*'}(q^*)z\frac{dx^*}{d\alpha} + (p^{*'}(q^*)z + p^*(q^*))\frac{dz}{d\alpha} - p'(q)z^*\frac{dx}{d\alpha} - (p'(q)z^* + p(q))\frac{dz^*}{d\alpha}$$

$$= (-) \cdot (+) + (+) \cdot (-) - (-) \cdot (-) - (+) \cdot (+) < 0$$

since the marginal revenue $p^{*'}(q^*)z + p^*(q^*)$ and $p'(q)z^* + p(q)$, respectively, is positive.

Finally, we obtain:

$$\frac{d}{d\alpha}\left(\frac{z^*}{q}\right) = \frac{1}{q^2}\left(\frac{dz^*}{d\alpha}\right)q - z^*\frac{dq}{d\alpha} = (+)\,[(+) \cdot (+) - (+) \cdot (-)] > 0.$$

and

$$\frac{d}{d\alpha^*}\left(\frac{x}{q}\right) = \frac{1}{q^2}\left(\frac{dx}{d\alpha^*}\right)q - x\frac{dq}{d\alpha^*} = (+)\,[(+) \cdot (+) - (+) \cdot (-)] > 0 \qquad \square$$

Proof of Propositions 4 and 5

Again markets can be investigated separately. Concentrating on (11.5) and (11.8) we get:

$$\begin{pmatrix} dx \\ dz^* \end{pmatrix} = H^{-1}\begin{pmatrix} ed\alpha \\ ed\alpha \end{pmatrix}, \tag{11A.4}$$

that is, only the right-hand side differs from (11A.3). The solution is given by:

$$dx = \frac{1}{\Delta}(\gamma - \beta + p'(q))\, ed\alpha$$

$$dz^* = \frac{1}{\Delta}(\beta - \gamma + p'(q))\, ed\alpha$$

$$dq = \frac{1}{\Delta} 2p'(q) \, ed\alpha$$

$$dy = \frac{1}{\Delta}(\gamma - \beta + p'(q)) \, ed\alpha + \frac{1}{\Delta^*}(\beta^* - \gamma^* + p^{*\prime}(q^*)) \, e^* d\alpha^*$$

The sign of $\gamma - \beta + p'(q)$ and $\beta - \gamma + p'(q)$ cannot be determined uniquely, since:

$$\gamma - \beta + p'(q) = (p''(q) \, z^* + p'(q)) - (p''(q) \, x + p(q)) + p'(q)$$

$$= p''(q) \, (z^* - x) + p'(q)$$

and $\beta - \gamma + p'(q) = p''(q)(x - z^*) + p'(q)$

The sign of $z^* - x$ is indeterminate. Restricting ourselves to linear demand functions we obtain $p''(q) \equiv 0$ and definite comparative static properties for x, z, q, y and Z:

$$dZ = \frac{1}{\Delta} p'(q) \, ed\alpha - \frac{1}{\Delta^*} p^{*\prime}(q^*) \, e^* d\alpha^*.$$

Though the expression of $d\mathrm{T}/d\alpha$ is much simpler than above, we get:

$$\frac{d\mathrm{T}}{d\alpha} = p'(q)z^* \frac{dx}{d\alpha} - (p'(q)z^* + (p(q))) \frac{dz^*}{d\alpha}$$

$$- (-) \cdot (-) - (+) \cdot (-) \gtreqless 0.$$

Finally, consider the change in market shares:

$$\frac{d}{d\alpha}\left(\frac{z^*}{q}\right) = \frac{1}{q^2}\left(\frac{dz^*}{d\alpha} q - z^* \frac{dq}{d\alpha}\right) = \frac{1}{q^2}\left(\frac{1}{\Delta} p'(q) \, e \, q - z^* \frac{1}{\Delta} 2 \, p'(q) \, e\right)$$

$$= \frac{p'(q) \, e}{q^2 \Delta}(x + z^* - 2z^*) = \frac{p'(q) \, e}{q^2 \Delta}(x - z^*)$$

If $x/q > z^*/q$ the derivative is negative: z^*/q decreases and x/q increases; if $z^*/q > x/q$ the converse holds.

□

NOTES

1. I thank Oskar von dem Hagen and an anonymous referee for helpful comments and suggestions. The usual disclaimer applies.
2. AC denotes total abatement costs; it should be distinguished from 'average cost'.

REFERENCES

Barnett, A.H. (1980), 'The Pigouvian tax rule under monopoly', *American Economic Review*, **70**, 1037–41.
Barrett, S. (1994), 'Strategic environmental policy and international trade', *Journal of Public Economics*, **54**, 325–38.
Brander, J.A. (1981), 'Intra-industry trade in identical commodities', *Journal of International Economics*, **11**, 1–14.
Copeland, B.R. (1994), 'International trade and the environment: policy reform in a polluted small open economy', *Journal of Environmental Economics and Management*, **26**, 44–65.
Dixit, A. (1984), 'International trade policy for oligopolistic industries', *Economic Journal, Supplement* **94**, 1–16.
Ebert, U. (1991), 'Pigouvian tax and market structure', *Finanzarchiv*, **49**, 154–66.
Ebert, U. (1998), 'Relative standards: a positive and normative analysis', *Journal of Economics*, **67**, 17–38.
Hung, N.M. (1994), 'Taxing pollution in an international duopoly context', *Economics Letters*, **44**, 339–43.
Kennedy, R.W. (1994), 'Equilibrium pollution taxes in open economies with imperfect competition', *Journal of Environmental Economics and Management*, **27**, 49–63.
Krutilla, K. (1991), 'Environmental regulation in an open economy', *Journal of Environmental Economics and Management*, **20**, 127–42.
Ludema, R.D. and I.W. Wooton (1994), 'Cross-border externalities and trade liberalization: the strategic control of pollution', *Canadian Journal of Economics*, **27**, 950–66.
Novshek, W. (1985), 'On the existence of Cournot equilibrium', *Review of Economic Studies*, **52**, 85–98.
Ulph, A. (1992), 'The choice of environmental policy instruments and strategic international trade', in R. Pethig (ed.), *Conflicts and Cooperation in Managing Environmental Resources*, Berlin: Springer-Verlag.

12. Ecological dumping: harmonization and minimum standards

Alistair Ulph

12.1 INTRODUCTION

The Maastricht Treaty generated much discussion about the nature of subsidiarity with respect to environmental policy, that is, what should be the roles of the European Commission and national governments in setting environmental policy within the European Union (see, for example, Siebert 1991; Rauscher 1991; CEPR 1993).[1] Two reasons are usually given why it may not be efficient to leave environmental policy to national governments: the problem of transboundary pollution, and the concern that, in order to secure a competitive advantage for their domestic producers in a regime of free trade, national governments may engage in 'environmental dumping'. In both cases, it is believed that national governments acting non-cooperatively would set environmental policies which are too lax compared to the policies that would be set if they acted cooperatively. The role of the Commission, then, is seen as securing a Pareto improvement over the non-cooperative outcome.

In this chapter I shall ignore transboundary pollution and use the example of environmental dumping. There has been considerable debate about whether environmental dumping is a significant problem, both theoretically and empirically (see Ulph 1997a for a recent survey). For the purposes of this chapter I shall work with a model in which environmental dumping is indeed the outcome. The question I shall focus on is how the European Commission should set environmental policy if it believes that national governments are engaging in environmental dumping. Much of the theoretical work on this topic has not progressed beyond simply deriving the cooperative and non-cooperative outcomes and showing that they are different.[2] The implication is that the Commission should just implement the cooperative solution.

But the policy debate on these matters follows rather different lines. It is frequently suggested that any incentives for downward competition in environmental policy should be countered by harmonizing environmental policies across countries. For example, in the agreement between the EU and Poland, Article 80 refers to harmonization of environmental regulations (Rauscher 1994). But it is well known that harmonization may not be desirable if there are significant asymmetries between countries (ibid. and Ulph 1996a). An OECD *Report on Trade and the Environment* (1995) states that:

> Harmonization of non-product related PPM-related requirements may be less desirable or feasible in the case of local environmental problems. Because environmental conditions and preferences differ widely among countries, environmental process-related requirements for local problems may be best tailored to local circumstances.[3]

But they then confuse the issue by saying: 'However, some convergence of these non-product related PPM-related requirements and standards ... might be beneficial'.[4] An alternative suggestion is that, rather than harmonizing environmental policies, the Commission should simply set 'minimum standards' for environmental policies, with the hope that there will be a form of 'ratchet effect', whereby if some countries are forced to raise their environmental standards in order to meet the minimum standard, then all other countries will respond by raising their environmental standards.

However, there has been little formal analysis of policies such as harmonization or minimum standards. In a model where environmental policy (which takes the form of environmental standards) may induce relocation of firms from countries with tough policies to countries with weaker policies, Kanbur *et al.* (1995) have shown that environmental dumping will indeed take place in this model. But they went on to show that if countries are sufficiently different (in terms of size), then harmonization of environmental policies may not secure a Pareto improvement over the non-cooperative outcome, whereas a policy of minimum standards could bring about such an improvement.

This chapter presents a rather different model of imperfect competition in which there is no possibility of relocation by producers. The model will be a simple variant of the Brander–Spencer (1985) model (see Barrett 1994 and Ulph 1996b). Governments may use either emission limits or emission taxes as their policy instruments and countries differ in their environmental damage cost functions. The first result will be a replication of the finding of Kanbur *et al.* (1995), namely, that if countries have sufficiently different damage costs then harmonization will not yield a Pareto improvement over the non-cooperative outcome. However, the second result of this chapter is that whether minimum standards will achieve a Pareto improvement over the non-cooperative outcome depends on the policy instrument used by governments: when governments use emission limits, minimum standards will not secure a Pareto improvement over the non-cooperative outcome either, which is contrary to the finding of Kanbur *et al*. On the other hand, if governments use emission taxes, then setting minimum environmental taxes can secure Pareto improvements, albeit modest ones. The difference in results is due to the slopes of the government reaction functions, that is, whether the policy instruments are strategic complements or strategic substitutes. With emission taxes, an increase in the emission tax by one country to meet the minimum level of emission tax leads to an increase in emission taxes by other countries, so that a ratchet effect occurs; however, with emission limits a toughening of standards by a high-pollution country leads to a relaxation of emission limits by countries with lower emissions.[5]

In the next section the basic model is set out and the cooperative and non-cooperative solutions derived for the cases where governments use emission limits and where they use emission taxes. Section 12.3 analyses harmonization and minimum standards. Conclusions are in section 12.4.

12.2 NON-COOPERATIVE AND COOPERATIVE EQUILIBRIA

12.2.1 The Basic Model

The model is similar to that in Barrett (1994) and Ulph (1996b). There are two identical firms, each located in a separate country, producing a differentiated product with output levels x and y respectively. In what follows the firm and country producing output x (think of it as the home country and the other as the foreign country) will be the primary focus, with the description for the other firm and country following by symmetry. Where it is essential, I shall distinguish the home and foreign countries by superscripts h and f. Total costs of production are denoted by the convex cost function $C(x)$. Output is sold only to a third group of countries, and the total revenue function is denoted $R(x, y)$ with $R_{xx} < 0$, $R_{xy} < 0$. Product market competition is of the Cournot variety. Each unit of output produces a unit of pollution. However, there is a technology for abating pollution so net emissions are $e = x - a$ where a is the level of abatement and costs of abatement are denoted by the strictly convex function $A(a)$. Net emissions of pollution affect only the country in which they are emitted. The only allowed element of asymmetry between the two countries is that they may differ in their damage costs. Thus, if ε denotes the level of net emissions in the foreign country, then damage costs in the home and foreign country are respectively $dD(e)$ and $\delta D(\varepsilon)$ where $D(.)$ is a strictly convex function.

The government in each country can affect the level of pollution by means of either an emission limit (an upper limit on pollution emitted by its domestic firm) or an emission tax. The emission limit and emission tax in the home (foreign) country are denoted by $\bar{e}$ and t respectively ($\bar{\varepsilon}$ and τ). Government welfare is profits plus tax revenue (if any) minus damage costs. The move structure is that of a two-stage game: in the first stage the governments set their policy instruments (these can be set either cooperatively or non-cooperatively); and in the second stage the firms take these policy instruments as given and choose output levels in a Cournot game. In the rest of this section the cooperative and non-cooperative equilibria when the governments use emission limits and emission taxes will be set out.

12.2.2 Emission Limits

Second-stage game
The firm in the home country takes as given the emission limit, $\bar{e}$, and the output of the other firm, y, and chooses x to maximize $\pi(x, y, \bar{e}) \equiv R(x, y) - C(x) - A(x - \bar{e})$. The resulting Nash equilibrium outputs are denoted $X(\bar{e}, \bar{\varepsilon})$ and $Y(\bar{\varepsilon}, \bar{e})$, and it is straightforward to show that $X_{\bar{e}} > 0$, $X_{\bar{\varepsilon}} < 0$, $Y_{\bar{e}} < 0$, $Y_{\bar{\varepsilon}} > 0$, $X_{\bar{e}} + Y_{\bar{e}} > 0$, $X_{\bar{\varepsilon}} + Y_{\bar{\varepsilon}} > 0$, so that an increase in emission limits by one government will increase its firm's output, decrease the rival firm's output, but increase overall industry output. It is now possible to solve for the equilibrium profit function for the home government:

$$\Pi(\bar{e}, \bar{\varepsilon}) \equiv \pi[X(\bar{e}, \bar{\varepsilon}), Y(\bar{\varepsilon}, \bar{e}), \bar{e}]$$

where

$$\Pi_1 = \pi_y Y_{\bar{e}} + A' > 0 \tag{12.1a}$$

$$\Pi_2 = \pi_y Y_{\bar{\varepsilon}} < 0 \tag{12.1b}$$

and it can be shown that

$$\Pi_{11} < \Pi_{12} < 0; \Pi_{22} < 0; \tag{12.1c}$$

so a firm's profits are increasing in its own government's emission limits and decreasing in the other government's emission limits.

First-stage game

Consider again the home country. The home government's welfare function is:

$$V(\bar{e}, \bar{\varepsilon}, d) \equiv \Pi(\bar{e}, \bar{\varepsilon}) - dD(\bar{e}) \tag{12.2}$$

The foreign country has corresponding welfare function $V(\bar{\varepsilon}, \bar{e}, \delta)$. It will be useful to establish the properties of the welfare function. From (12.2) it is readily seen that:

$$V_{11} = \Pi_{11} - dD'' < V_{12} = \Pi_{12} < 0; \qquad V_{13} = -D' < 0;$$

$$V_{21} = V_{12} < 0; \qquad V_{22} = \Pi_{22} < 0; \qquad V_{23} = 0; \tag{12.3}$$

I shall assume that $V_{11} + V_{22} < V_{12} + V_{21} < 0$.

Two ways of determining equilibrium emission standards are considered: a non-cooperative equilibrium and a cooperative equilibrium.

Non-cooperative equilibrium The home country takes as given the emission standard of the foreign country, $\bar{\varepsilon}$ and chooses $\bar{e}$ to maximize (12.2). The first-order condition, using (12.1a) is:

$$V_1 = \Pi_1 - dD' = \pi_y Y_{\bar{e}} + A' - dD' = 0 \tag{12.4}$$

Since the term $\pi_y Y_{\bar{e}}$ is positive, (12.4) shows that each government will set emission limits such that marginal abatement cost is below marginal damage cost, so that emission limits will be set less stringently than would be implied by the simple rule of equating marginal damage and abatement costs. The reason for deviating from this rule is because the term $\pi_y Y_{\bar{e}}$ represents the *strategic trade incentive* for the government to use its environmental policy to encourage its domestic firm to produce more output, since the government calculates that the rival firm will respond by reducing its output, thereby raising the profits of the domestic producer.

Equation (12.4) can be written as the *reaction function* of the home government, $\bar{e} = R^h(\bar{\varepsilon}, d)$. From (12.3) it follows that $-1 < R_1^h = -V_{12}/V_{11} < 0$, and $R_2^h = -V_{13}/V_{11} < 0$. Thus the reaction functions are downward-sloping and stable, and an increase in the damage cost parameter of the home country reduces its emission limit for any given emission limit of the foreign country. Since the slope of the reaction function is important for the results in the next section, it is important to understand why the reaction function slopes down when emission limits are used. The reason is that when the foreign government toughens its emission limit, that will force the foreign firm to cut its output and allow the domestic firm to expand its output. If the domestic government kept its emission limit unaltered, the domestic firm would have to match the increase in output with exactly the same increase in abatement, raising marginal abatement costs but leaving marginal damage costs unaffected. The optimal policy would be to have some of the extra output show up as extra pollution. Thus when governments use emission limits, their policies are *strategic substitutes* (Bulow *et al.* 1985).

It is now possible to solve for the Nash equilibrium in emission limits, which I denote by $\hat{e}\,(d, \delta)$ and $\hat{\varepsilon}\,(\delta, d)$ for the home and foreign governments respectively. It is easily shown that $\hat{e}_d < 0$, $\hat{e}_\delta > 0$, $\hat{\varepsilon}_\delta < 0$, $\hat{\varepsilon}_d > 0$. As already noted, an increase in the home country's damage cost parameter shifts down the home government's reaction function, lowering the equilibrium emission limits set by the home government and raising the emission limits set by the foreign government. We can also define the equilibrium levels of welfare for the home country as:

$$\hat{V}(d, \delta) \equiv V[\hat{e}(d, \delta), \hat{\varepsilon}(\delta, d), d] \text{ where } \hat{V}_d = V_\varepsilon \hat{e}_d + V_d < 0, \ \hat{V}_\delta = V_\varepsilon \hat{e}_d > 0$$

so that welfare decreases with an increase in own damage cost parameter, but rises with an increase in the other country's damage cost parameter.

Cooperative equilibrium In this case, emission limits in the home and foreign country are chosen to maximize $V(\bar{e}, \bar{\varepsilon}, d) + V(\bar{\varepsilon}, \bar{e}, \delta)$. Carrying out the optimization yields the first-order conditions for the cooperative equilibrium emission limits for the home country: $\pi y\,(X_{\bar{e}} + Y_{\bar{e}}) + A' - dD' = 0$. (Similar analysis applies to the foreign country.) Since the term $\pi_y\,(X_{\bar{e}} + Y_{\bar{e}}) < 0$, emission limits in the home country are set such that marginal abatement costs are above marginal damage costs, that is, the environmental policy would be tougher than the simple rule of equating marginal damage and abatement costs. The rationale for deviating from this simple rule is that the governments of the two countries wish to encourage their firms to move closer to the industry maximizing level of profits, and this requires reducing output from the Cournot level. Since we know that the non-cooperative equilibrium involves emission limits which are laxer than the simple rule, it follows that the cooperative equilibrium emission limits are more stringent (lower) than the non-cooperative emission limits, so that environmental dumping does indeed occur.

The cooperative equilibrium emission limits will be denoted by: e^* (d, δ), ε^* (δ, d) where $e_d^* < 0$, $e_\delta^* > 0$, $\varepsilon_\delta^* < 0$ $\varepsilon_d^* > 0$ and where I have established that e^* $(d, \delta) < \hat{e}(d, \delta)$, ε^* $(\delta, d) < \hat{\varepsilon}(\delta, d)$. The cooperative and non-cooperative equilibria in emission limits are shown in Figure 12.1.

12.2.3 Emission Taxes

Second-stage game
The firm in the home country takes as given the emission tax rate, t, and the output of the other firm, y, and chooses its output, x, and its abatement level, a, to maximize $\pi(x, y, a, t) \equiv R(x, y) - C(x) - A(a) - t(x - a)$. An interior solution involves the home firm setting abatement $\hat{a}(t)$ such that $A'(\hat{a}(t)) = t$, that is, marginal abatement cost equals the emission tax; the convexity of the abatement cost function implies that $\hat{a}'(t) > 0$, that is, abatement is an increasing function of the emission tax. The equilibrium levels of output for the home and foreign firms are denoted by $X(t, \tau)$ and $Y(\tau, t)$. It is readily shown that $X_t < 0$, $X_\tau > 0$, $Y_\tau < 0$, $Y_t > 0$, $X_t + Y_t < 0$, $X_\tau + Y_\tau > 0$. Thus, an increase in the home country's emission tax will reduce the domestic firm's output, increase the foreign firm's output, and reduce industry output. As with emission limits, a relaxation of the home country's environmental policy (reduction in emission tax) will increase the home firm's output and decrease the foreign firm's output. Finally, equilibrium profits in the first-stage game for the home and foreign firm are denoted respectively by $\Pi(t, \tau)$ and $\Pi(\tau, t)$, where, for example, for the home firm:

$$\Pi(t, \tau) \equiv \pi[X(t, \tau), Y(\tau, t), \hat{a}(t), t]$$

and

$$\Pi_1 = \pi_y Y_t - [X(t, \tau) - \hat{a}(t)] < 0 \qquad (12.5a)$$

$$\Pi_2 = \pi_y Y_\tau > 0 \qquad (12.5b)$$

and it can be shown that:

$$\Pi_{11} < [-\Pi_{12}] < 0; \Pi_{22} < 0; \qquad (12.5c)$$

so equilibrium first-stage profits are decreasing in own country's emission tax rate and increasing in the other government's emission tax rate.

First-stage game
The home country's welfare function is denoted by $W(t, \tau, d) \equiv \Pi(t, \tau) + t[X(t, \tau) - \hat{a}(t)] - dD[X(t, \tau) - \hat{a}(t)]$. The foreign country will have a

corresponding welfare function $W(\tau, t, \delta)$. Again, it will be useful to establish the properties of the welfare function. It can be shown (Ulph 1997c) that, for most parameter values:

$$W_{11} < [-W_{12}] = [-W_{21}] < 0; W_{22} < 0; \qquad (12.6a)$$

while it is always the case that:

$$W_{13} = -D'[X_t - \hat{a}']; W_{23} = 0; \qquad (12.6b)$$

and I shall assume that:

$$0 < W_{12} + W_{21} < |W_{11} + W_{22}|. \qquad (12.6c)$$

Non-cooperative equilibrium The home country takes as given the emission tax of the foreign country and chooses its emission tax t to maximize welfare, which, using (12.5a), yields the first-order condition:

$$W_1 = \Pi_1 + [X(t, \tau) - \hat{a}(t)] + [t - dD']\{X_t - \hat{a}'\} = \pi_y Y_t + [t - dD']\{X_t - \hat{a}'\} = 0 \qquad (12.7)$$

Since the terms $\pi_y Y_t$ and $\{X_t - \hat{a}'\}$ are both negative, (12.7) says that each country will set its emission tax below marginal damage cost, so that, as with emission limits, environmental policy is set so that marginal abatement cost (equal to emission tax) is below marginal damage cost. The rationale is exactly the same as for emission limits.

Equation (12.7) can be written as the home country government's *reaction function* $t = R^h(\tau, d)$.

From (12.6) it follows that $0 < R_1^h = -W_{12}/W_{11} < 1$ so that the reaction functions are upward sloping and stable, while $0 < R_2^h = -W_{13}/W_{11}$, so that an increase in the home country's damage cost parameter will increase the emission tax it sets for any emission tax set by the foreign country. Again the important result is that the reaction functions are upward sloping; the rationale is that if the foreign government raises its emission tax, that will cut the foreign firm's output and raise the output of the home-country firm. If the home country government keeps its emission tax unaltered, all the extra output will show up in extra pollution, whereas the optimal policy will require some of the extra pollution to be abated. Thus, emission taxes are *strategic complements*.

It is now possible to solve for the Nash equilibrium levels of emission taxes denoted: $\hat{t}(d, \delta)$ and $\hat{\tau}(\delta, d)$ where $\hat{t}_d > 0$, $\hat{t}_\delta > 0$, $\hat{\tau}_d > 0$, $\hat{\tau}_\delta > 0$, and for the Nash equilibrium values of welfare for the home and foreign countries denoted by $\hat{W}(d, \delta)$ and $\hat{W}(\delta, d)$ where, for the home country, $\hat{W}$ $(d, \delta) \equiv W[\hat{t}(d, \delta), \hat{\tau}(\delta, d), d]$. It is readily seen that $\hat{W}_d = W_\tau \hat{t}_d - D$, $\hat{W}_\delta = W_\tau \hat{t}_\delta$ and $W_\tau = \Pi_\tau + (t - dD')X_\tau$. The two terms in W_τ are respectively positive and negative, but I shall assume that overall W_τ is positive. This makes $\hat{W}_\delta$ positive, and the first term in $\hat{W}_d$ also positive, though I shall assume that the second, negative, term dominates, making $\hat{W}_d$ negative. Thus home-country welfare is decreasing in its own damage cost parameter and increasing in the foreign country's damage cost parameter, as was the case with emission limits.

Cooperative equilibrium Emission taxes in the home and foreign country are chosen to maximize $W(t, \tau, d) + W(\tau, t, \delta)$. The first-order conditions can be written as:

$$\pi_y(X_t + Y_t) + (t - dD')[X_t - \hat{a}'(t)] + (\tau - \delta D')Y_t = 0$$
$$\pi_y(X_\tau + Y_\tau) + (\tau - \delta D')[Y_\tau - \hat{a}'(\tau)] + (t - dD')X_\tau = 0$$
(12.8)

Since the first terms in both equations are positive, the terms in square brackets are negative, while the terms X_τ and Y_t are positive and smaller in absolute value than the terms in square brackets, it is clear that in general the solution to (12.8) will require that for both countries emission taxes should be above marginal damage costs. This is the same as for the case of emission limits, and for the same reason. Since the non-cooperative equilibrium involved emission taxes below marginal damage costs, once again the cooperative equilibrium involves more stringent environmental policy than the non-cooperative equilibrium, that is, there is environmental dumping.

The cooperative emission taxes will be denoted $t^*(d, \delta)$ and $\tau^*(\delta, d)$, where I have shown that $t^*(d, \delta) > \hat{t}(d, \delta)$, $\tau^*(d, \delta) > \hat{\tau}(d, \delta)$. It is straightforward to show that, as with the non-cooperative equilibrium, cooperative taxes are increasing functions of the damage cost parameters of both countries.

12.2.4 Summary

This completes the analysis of the non-cooperative and cooperative equilibria. The analysis assumes Cournot competition between the two firms. Nothing of substance would change if Bertrand competition had been assumed. It would still be the case that whatever policy instrument was used, the non-cooperative equilibrium involves both countries setting less stringent environmental policies than they would if they cooperated.

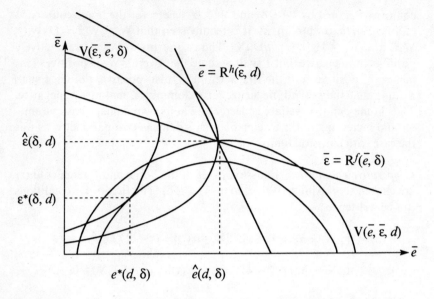

Figure 12.1 Cooperative and non-cooperative equilibria: emission limits

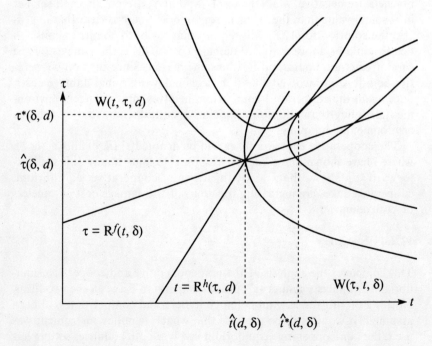

Figure 12.2 Cooperative and non-cooperative equilibria: emission taxes

Moreover, the slopes of the reaction functions and iso-welfare contours for emission standards and taxes would be exactly the same as in Figures 12.1 and 12.2 respectively.[6]

12.3 HARMONIZATION AND MINIMUM STANDARDS

In this section it will be assumed that the European Commission seeks to improve upon the non-cooperative outcomes derived in the last section, but, for reasons not explored here, cannot just impose the cooperative solution on the two parties. Two mechanisms that the Commission may use to improve upon the non-cooperative outcome will be explored: environmental policy harmonization and minimum standards. It will be demonstrated that if countries are sufficiently different in their damage costs, then harmonization cannot effect a Pareto improvement over the non-cooperative outcome, regardless of whether emission taxes or emission limits are used. If emission limits are used, then the use of minimum standards, to the extent that this does not imply harmonization, can never effect a Pareto improvement over the non-cooperative outcome; whereas if emission taxes are used, then minimum standards can effect a small Pareto improvement.

12.3.1 Harmonization

Emission limits
The argument is best understood by reference to Figure 12.3. Fix a particular value of the home-country damage cost parameter, d. Define:

$$E(d) = \arg \max V[E, E, d]; \quad \bar{V}(d) = V[E(d), E(d), d]$$

that is, $\bar{V}(d)$ is the maximum welfare the home country can obtain under a policy of harmonized emission limits, with $E(d)$ the corresponding level of harmonized emission limits. It is clear that the point $[E(d), E(d)]$ is where the home country's iso-welfare contour is tangent to the 45° line. Now define $\bar{\delta}(d)$ by $\hat{V}(d, \bar{\delta}(d)) = \bar{V}(d)$, that is, the value of δ for which the corresponding non-cooperative equilibrium gives the home country the same welfare as the maximum it can achieve under harmonization. Since $\hat{e}[d, \bar{\delta}(d)] > \hat{e}[\bar{\delta}(d), d]$, it must be the case that $\bar{\delta}(d) > d$. Now by the properties of the equilibrium welfare function established in the last section, $\forall \delta > \bar{\delta}(d) \hat{V}(d, \delta) > \hat{V}(d, \bar{\delta}(d)) = \bar{V}(d)$, so that $\bar{\delta}(d)$ is the maximum value by which the foreign country's damage cost parameter can exceed the home

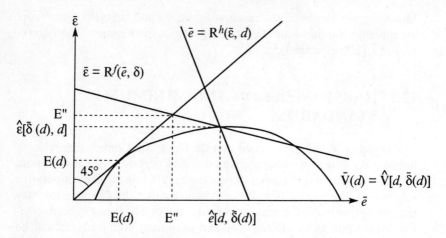

Figure 12.3 Harmonization and minimum standards: emission limits

country's damage cost parameter before harmonization makes the home country worse off than in the non-cooperative equilibrium. The intuition is simple: harmonization is designed to make both countries reduce their emissions; but the country with the lower damage cost parameter has to make a bigger reduction than the other country, so there are also changes in market share as well as overall reductions in emissions, and if the initial difference in countries is large enough, then this effect dominates any gain in reducing aggregate emissions.

Emission taxes
Exactly the same argument can be made in the case of emission taxes, for which the reader is referred to Figure 12.4. Thus, for any d, define:

$$T(d) = \arg\max W(T, T, d); \quad \bar{W}(d) = W[T(d), T(d), d]; \quad \hat{W}[d, \hat{\delta}(d)] = \bar{W}(d)$$

where $\hat{\delta}(d) > d$. Then $\forall \delta > \hat{\delta}(d) \hat{W}(d, \delta) > \hat{W}[d, \hat{\delta}(d)] = \bar{W}(d)$, so that $\hat{\delta}(d)$ is the maximum value of the foreign country's damage cost parameter beyond which harmonization would make the home country worse off than in the non-cooperative equilibrium. The rationale again is that harmonization requires both countries to raise their emission taxes, but the increase will be greater for the country with the lower emission tax rate; and if the difference is large enough, the switching of market shares outweighs the gain from aggregate reduction in emissions.

There is one final point to emphasize. What may make harmonization infeasible is the individual rationality constraints which require that both countries are no worse off than in the non-cooperative equi-

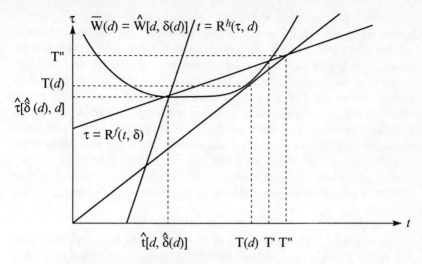

Figure 12.4 Harmonization and minimum standards: emission taxes

librium, together with the assumption that the only instruments available to the Commission are environmental policy instruments. It is straightforward to show that there will always be a cooperative set of environmental policies such that policy instruments are equal in both countries, but what this section has derived is a set of sufficient conditions on the differences in damage costs between countries such that no harmonized policy can make both countries no worse off than in the non-cooperative equilibrium. Clearly, if lump-sum financial transfers were available to the Commission, it would always be possible to implement the cooperative harmonized policy and then satisfy the individual rationality constraints using financial transfers. But it is not clear why such a harmonized cooperative solution should command more support than any other cooperative solution.

12.3.2 Minimum Standards

It is fairly obvious that if the asymmetries between countries are too large, then a policy of harmonizing environmental policies is unlikely to yield a Pareto improvement over the non-cooperative equilibrium. However, it is frequently thought that using minimum standards, that is, minimum levels of strictness of environmental policy, will obviate this problem since only the countries which fall below the minimum standard will be required to tighten their standards, while other countries can choose to set standards above the minimum. The hope is that these latter countries will respond to the raising of standards in the former group of countries by also tightening their environmental standards – a form of ratchet effect. As noted in the introduction, Kanbur *et al.* (1995) provide an example where such a minimum standards policy will work. This section will demonstrate that when governments use emission limits as their policy instrument (the case considered by Kanbur *et al.*), then, to the extent that minimum standards yield an outcome different from harmonization, the use of minimum standards will make the country with lower damage costs (higher emissions) worse off than in the non-cooperative equilibrium, even if countries differ only slightly in their damage costs. Conversely, when emission taxes are the chosen policy instrument, then the use of minimum standards can achieve a Pareto improvement.

Emission limits

Again it will be convenient to refer to Figure 12.3; although the figure shows the home country's iso-welfare contour corresponding to $\hat{V}(d, \delta(d)) = \bar{V}(d)$, for the purposes of this section it is sufficient that the iso-welfare contour is $\hat{V}(d, \delta)$ associated with the Nash equilibrium [$\hat{e}(d, \delta)$, $\hat{\varepsilon}(\delta, d)$] for *any* $\delta > d$, and hence $\hat{e}(d, \delta) > \hat{\varepsilon}(\delta, d)$. Note that there must exist a value E" such that $\hat{e}(d, \delta) > E" = R^f (E", \delta) > \hat{\varepsilon}(\delta, d)$, that is, the foreign country's reaction function crosses the 45° line at a point E" which lies between the Nash equilibrium emission limits of the home and foreign countries.

A policy of minimum standards in this context would require that the home and foreign countries set their emission limits, $\bar{e}$ and $\bar{\varepsilon}$ respectively, below some upper limit $\bar{E}$, say, set by the Commission. There are three cases:

1. If $\bar{E} \geq \hat{e}(d, \delta) > \hat{\varepsilon}(\delta, d)$, then both countries will set their emission standards below the upper limit, and the equilibrium will just be the existing non-cooperative equilibrium.
2. If $\hat{e}(d, \delta) > \bar{E} > E"$ then the home country will be constrained to set $\bar{e} = \bar{E}$ while the foreign country can set $\bar{\varepsilon} = R^f (\bar{E}, \delta)$, that is, the foreign country can make its best response to the emission limit the home country is constrained to set. Clearly $V(\bar{E}, R^f (\bar{E}, \delta) < \hat{V}(d, \delta)$, so the home country is made worse off than in the non-cooperative equilibrium.
3. If $\bar{E} \leq E"$ then both countries are constrained to set their emission limits at the level set by the Commission, and the minimum standards policy is equivalent to harmonization. We already know that harmonization will not make the home country better off than in the non-cooperative equilibrium if $\delta > \bar{\delta}(d)$.

Thus only in case 3 are minimum standards both effective and distinct from harmonization, and in this case the country with the lower damage cost parameter is unambiguously made worse off than in the non-cooperative equilibrium. The reason is simple: minimum standards do *not* generate a ratchet effect in this case: when the country with the higher emission limit is forced to toughen its environmental policy by reducing its emission limits, the other government can respond by relaxing its emission limits. Both these moves make the country with the initially higher emission limits worse off than it was at the non-cooperative equilibrium. The reason why this result contradicts that of Kanbur *et al.* (1995) is that in my model the policy instruments are strategic substitutes, and so the reaction functions slope downwards, while in their model emission limits are strategic complements.

Emission taxes

From the previous remarks and the analysis of the previous section it will come as no surprise that when the governments use emission taxes then a policy of minimum standards can deliver a Pareto improvement over the non-cooperative equilibrium. It will be useful to refer to Figure 12.4, although again all that is necessary for this section is that the foreign country has a higher damage cost parameter than the home country, that is, $\delta > d$, so that in the Nash equilibrium $\hat{t}(d, \delta) < \hat{\tau}(\delta, d)$. Note that there must exist values T' and T" such that $W(T', R^f(T', \delta)) = \hat{W}(d, \delta)$, and T" $= R^f(T'', \delta)$, that is, T' is the value of home-country emission tax at which the foreign country's reaction function crosses the home country's iso-welfare contour corresponding to the non-cooperative Nash equilibrium, while T" is the value of emission tax at which the foreign country's reaction function crosses the 45° line. Note that both T' and T" are greater than the non-cooperative emission tax of the high-cost country. As drawn, T' < T", but the reverse could be true.

In this case, minimum standards imply that each country must set its emission tax above some minimum level $\bar{T}$, say, specified by the Commission. There are the same broad three cases as with emission limits:

1. If $\bar{T} \leq \hat{t}(d, \delta) < \hat{\tau}(\delta, d)$ then both countries will simply set their emission taxes at the level given by the Nash equilibrium, so the Commission's policy does not bite.
2. If $\hat{t}(d, \delta) < \bar{T} < T''$ then the home country is constrained to set $\bar{t} = \bar{T}$ while the foreign country can set $\bar{\tau} = R^f(\bar{T}, \delta) > \bar{T}$. There are then two possibilities: (a) if $\bar{T} \leq T'$, then $V(\bar{T}, R^f(\bar{T}, \delta)) \geq \hat{V}(d, \delta)$, so that the home country is no worse off than at the non-cooperative equilibrium, and since the foreign country is strictly better off there is a

Pareto improvement over the non-cooperative equilibrium; (b) if $T' < \bar{T} < T''$ then $V(\bar{T}, R^f(\bar{T}, \delta)) < \hat{V}(d, \delta)$. Note that this latter possibility may not exist, while the former must always exist.

3. If $\bar{T} \geq T''$, then both countries are constrained to set the minimum emission tax specified by the Commission and the minimum standards policy is equivalent to harmonization.

Thus there is a range of values where a minimum emission tax policy can deliver a Pareto improvement over the non-cooperative equilibrium, and this is so because the minimum standards policy does produce a ratchet effect whereby raising the emission tax of the low-cost country induces the high-cost country also to increase its emission tax. This arises because the policy instruments are strategic complements, so the reaction functions are upward sloping.

To conclude this section, it has been shown that if countries are sufficiently asymmetric in their damage cost functions, then harmonization of environmental standards or taxes cannot yield a Pareto improvement over the non-cooperative outcome. If governments use emission limits as policy instruments, then, for this model, minimum standards, to the extent that they are different from harmonization, make the low damage cost country worse off than the non-cooperative equilibrium and does not achieve any tightening of environmental policy in the high damage cost country. On the other hand, if governments use emission taxes, then setting a minimum level of emission tax can generate an increase in emission taxes in all countries, though the extent of the increase that can be generated without making the low damage cost country worse off is limited.

12.4 CONCLUSIONS

In this chapter I have taken the simplest possible model which generates incentives for nation states acting non-cooperatively to engage in 'environmental dumping', that is, setting weak environmental regulations to try to give domestic producers a competitive advantage. I have analysed two widely discussed policy approaches for trying to overcome environmental dumping: the harmonization of environmental regulations and the use of minimum standards for environmental regulations. I have shown that neither of these policies may be capable of making all countries better off than when they act non-cooperatively, depending on the degree of difference in key characteristics of countries, such as damage costs, and also depending on the policy instruments used by national governments for implementing environmental regulations.

The obvious question is why we should be interested in policies such as harmonization or minimum standards, since there will be cooperative policies which make all the countries engaging in environmental dumping better off than in the non-cooperative equilibrium. One reason why a supranational agency may not be able to implement such a cooperative policy may be that information about key characteristics such as damage costs are known only to national governments. The implications of such an asymmetry of information are explored in Ulph (1997b, c), where it is shown that this cannot provide any rationale for policies such as harmonization. Another feature which may inhibit the imposition of a simple Pareto-improving cooperative solution is that governments at the national and supranational levels may be captured by special interest groups (environmentalists, industrialists), so there may be a wish to narrow the discretion given to both national and supranational governments. Ulph (1998) and Johal and Ulph (1997) show that this may provide a rationale for harmonization of environmental policies.

NOTES

1. While I shall use the example of the European Union for concreteness, the issues addressed here apply to any federal system, or indeed to the role of international organizations such as the World Trade Organization with respect to national governments.
2. The same is broadly true of the closely related literature on fiscal federalism where there is tax competition between countries or between states within a federation: see Mintz and Tulkens 1986; Oates and Schwab 1988; Wildasin 1991, for game theoretic studies of tax competition with full information.
3. PPM stands for production and process methods; setting environmental standards which are too lax compared to the cooperative outcome is only likely when pollution is related to the process of production.
4. Both quotes come from OECD (1995: 30, para. 82).
5. These results were derived in an earlier paper (Ulph 1997b) using special functional forms. The model in this chapter uses general functional forms.
6. Of course, as Barrett (1994) and Ulph (1996c) have noted, there is one important difference between the Cournot and the Bertrand cases. In the Cournot case environmental policy in the non-cooperative case will be more lax than in the non-strategic case where governments use the simple rule of setting emission taxes equal to marginal damage costs. Conversely, in the Bertrand case environmental policy will be tougher in the non-cooperative case than in the non-strategic case. But in this chapter it is the comparisons between the cooperative and non-cooperative outcomes which are of interest rather than the comparison between the strategic and non-strategic outcomes.

REFERENCES

Barrett, S. (1994), 'Strategic environmental policy and international trade', *Journal of Public Economics*, **54**(3), 325–38.
Brander, J. and B. Spencer (1985), 'Export subsidies and international market share rivalry', *Journal of International Economics*, **18**, 83–100.

Bulow, J., J. Geanakoplos and P. Klemperer (1985), 'Multimarket oligopoly: strategic substitutes and complements', *Journal of Political Economy*, **93**, 488–511.

Centre for Economic Policy Research (CEPR) (1993), *Making Sense of Subsidiarity*, Monitoring European Integration Report 4, London: CEPR.

Johal, S. and A. Ulph (1997), 'Tying governments' hands: political economy models of environmental policy in a federal system', University of Southampton, mimeo.

Kanbur, R., M. Keen, and S. van Wijnbergen (1995), 'Industrial competitiveness, environmental regulation and direct foreign investment', in I. Goldin and A. Winters (eds), *The Economics of Sustainable Development*, Paris: OECD, 289–301.

Mintz, J. and H. Tulkens (1986), 'Commodity tax competition between member states of a federation: equilibrium and efficiency', *Journal of Public Economics*, **29**, 133–72.

Oates, W. and R. Schwab (1988), 'Economic competition among jurisdictions: efficiency enhancing or distortion inducing?', *Journal of Public Economics*, **35**, 333–54.

OECD (1995), *Report on Trade and Environment to the OECD Council at Ministerial Level*, Report of the Trade and Environmental Policy Committees, Paris: OECD.

Rauscher, M. (1991), 'National environmental policies and the effects of economic integration', *European Journal of Political Economy*, **7**, 313–29.

Rauscher, M. (1994), 'Trade law and environmental issues in central and east European countries', CEPR Discussion Paper 1045, London: CEPR.

Siebert, H. (1991), 'Europe '92: decentralising environmental policy in the single European market', *Environmental and Resource Economics*, **1**, 271–88.

Ulph, A. (1996a), 'Strategic environmental policy, international trade and the single European market', in J. Braden, H. Folmer and T. Ulen (eds), *Environmental Policy with Economic and Political Integration: The European Community and the United States*, Cheltenham, UK: Edward Elgar, 235–57.

Ulph, A. (1996b), 'Environmental policy instruments and imperfectly competitive international trade', *Environmental and Resource Economics*, **7**(4), 333–55.

Ulph, A. (1996c), 'Strategic environmental policy and international trade: the role of market conduct', in C. Carraro and Y. Katsoulacos (eds), *Environmental Policy and Market Structure*, Dordrecht: Kluwer, 99–130.

Ulph, A. (1997a), 'Environmental policy and international trade: a survey of recent economic analysis', in C. Carraro and D. Siniscalco (eds), *New Directions in Economic Theory and the Environment*, Cambridge: Cambridge University Press, 147–92.

Ulph, A. (1997b), 'International environmental regulation when national governments act strategically,' in J. Braden and S. Proost (eds), *The Economic Theory of Environmental Policy in a Federal System*, Cheltenham, UK: Edward Elgar, 66–96.

Ulph, A. (1997c), 'Harmonisation, minimum standards and optimal international environmental policy under asymmetric information', Discussion Paper in Economic and Econometrics 9701, University of Southampton.

Ulph, A. (1998), 'Political institutions and the design of environmental policy in a federal system with asymmetric information', *European Economic Review*, **42**, 583–92.

Wildasin, D. (1991), 'Some rudimentary "duopolity" theory', *Regional Science and Urban Economics*, **21**, 393–421.

Index

abatement cost functions 118–19, 212–13, 235, 239
see also marginal abatement cost
abatement effort
  allocation of 47–63, 75, 78–9
  government precommitment and *see* government precommitment to emission taxes
abatement measures, types of 119
abatement subsidies 44, 47, 146, 153, 158, 159, 162, 172, 184, 199, 206–7
abatement technology, adoption of
  command-and-control regulation and 96–7
  cost reductions associated with 119–27, 132–3, 142
  diffusion of green technologies in differentiated duopolies xv–xvi
    with Bertrand (price) competition 164, 166–72
    with Cournot (quantity) competition 164–7, 169–72
    and market share 163, 166–7, 169
    model of 164–9
    with precommitment 167–9
    in pre-emptive equilibrium 170–72
    socially optimal diffusion pattern 172–3
  emission taxes and xiv–xvi, 19–20, 116–18, 126–33, 139, 142–3, 162
  government precommitment and *see* government precommitment to emission taxes
  relocation or innovation response to xvii, 186
    analytical model of 197–201
    assumptions on tax rate 199, 204
    incentive policies to increase R&D effectiveness 199, 206–7

R&D cooperation 196–201, 204–7
R&D spillovers 198, 206
relocating firms 198, 200–201, 204, 206–7
technology licensing xvii, 196–8, 201–7
timing of adoption xv–xvi
emissions trading and xiv–xv, 116–18, 133–43
environmental quality improvements and R&D costs xiv, 28, 29, 30, 34, 36, 37
private incentives for, in absence of environmental policies 162–3
subsidies for 44, 47, 146, 153, 158, 159, 162, 172, 184, 199, 206–7
accelerated consumption benefits 110–12
accelerated income 103, 110–12
accelerated product introduction 98, 100–103, 106–12
acid rain 49, 172
additional cost 84
adoption date 167
adoption process innovations 163, 165
Advanced Micro Devices (AMD) 102
air pollution 162
  carbon tax 195
  cars and 27, 28, 30, 162
  Clean Air Act (1990) 81
  Clean Air Act Amendments (CAAA) 64, 101
  European Union and 27, 162
  greenhouse gases 2, 90, 162, 163, 172, 195
  nitrogen oxide (NO_x) emissions 64
  sulphur dioxide (SO_2) emissions 49, 64, 81, 90, 97–8
  see also Intel–XL Air Permit programme
airframes 113

251